# Sacred Space,
# Sacred Sound

*South doorway, Church of St. Mary and St. David, twelfth century,*
*Kilpeck, Herefordshire, England*

# Sacred SPACE, Sacred SOUND

## The ACOUSTIC MYSTERIES of HOLY PLACES

SUSAN ELIZABETH HALE

Foreword by DON CAMPBELL,
author of *The Mozart Effect*®

QUEST

BOOKS

Theosophical Publishing House
Wheaton, Illinois • Chennai, India

Quest Books
Theosophical Publishing House
PO Box 270
Wheaton, IL 60189-0270

www.questbooks.net

Photo credits—Cover image: © Georgemarc Schevené
Page ii: © Aaron Watson
Pages xii, 180: © Cindy A. Pavlinac/www.sacred-land-photography.com
Page xxii: Erich Lessing/Art Resource, NY
Page 8: © Erik Larson/www.soundhealingresources.com
Pages 26, 34, 46, 224: © Georgemarc Schevené
Pages 58, 152, 236: © Susan Elizabeth Hale
Page 72: © Freddy Silva
Page 82: © Chris Dunn
Page 98: © M.A. Center Photo by Beverly Noia
Page 110: © Steve Racicot/www.fireintheheart.net
Page 118: © Gay Block
Page 134: © Kenneth A. Konia
Pages 162, 172: © Christopher Smith, Gloucester
Page 192: © Rosslyn Trust
Page 208: © Jennifer Anderson
Page 216: © Tim Anderson.

Cover design, book design, and typesetting by Kirsten Hansen Pott

LIBRARY OF CONGRESS CATALOGING-IN-PUBLICATION DATA

Hale, Susan Elizabeth.
Sacred space, sacred sound: the acoustic mysteries of holy places / Susan
Elizabeth Hale. —1st Quest Books ed.
    p.    cm.
Includes bibliographical references and index.
ISBN-13: 978-0-8356-0856-5
ISBN-10: 0-8356-0856-5
1. Sacred space.    2. Sound—Religious aspects.    3. Hale, Susan Elizabeth—
Travel.    I. Title.
BL580.H35 2007
203'.7—dc22                                                    2007003273

5    4    3    2    1    *    07    08    09    10    11    12

*To my mother,*

*NORMA LEE HAWKINS,*

*September 23, 1920–April 2, 2007,*

*who sang to me,*

*and to my father,*

*DERRAL WESLEY HAWKINS,*

*April 21, 1920–April 2, 2002,*

*who once said,*

*"Susie, someday you ought to write a book."*

# CONTENTS

# CONTENTS

# FOREWORD

The power and resonance of space is an essential component in the way sound impacts us. The magic of our voices in the dome of our national Capitol or at St. Paul's Cathedral in London becomes astonishing. A calm whisper can be heard over a hundred feet away. In the great outdoor arena at Epidaurus in Greece, thousands of people can easily hear the dramatist without any enhancement. Yet in our hectic, noise-filled lives such experiences are the exception. More typical is the difficulty in having a decent conversation in a crowded restaurant

Three components make up the perfection of music and sound: the sound itself, the resonance of the space, and the ability of the listener to focus and take in the auditory information. How we listen is as important as what we are hearing and where we are hearing it.

Susan Hale is not only a gifted music therapist and an enchanting singer, she is also an exquisite listener, and we are fortunate to benefit from her sensitivity. At long last, in this book a true adventurer in sound and music healing addresses the key issue of how sacred spaces hold the power of sound to give us a sense of the ineffable and the numinous. Susan's previous research and writings explored the voice and its therapeutic value. Along the way, she began to realize the importance of acoustic resonance in the great formula for inspiration and transformation. Her insight and passion for the subject led her to journey to sacred sites throughout the world, where she began to *listen* to them as well as to sing and chant within them. This remarkable book is the result, unique in its exploration of the acoustic mysteries of sacred places.

Today, certain institutions are recognizing the importance of sound in healing body and spirit and are beginning to incorporate such principles into their environments. Marianjoy Rehabilitation Hospital in Wheaton, Illinois, for instance, has devoted a new wing to sacred space and sacred sound. It includes a Chartres labyrinth, where prayerful music is played to enrich the experience of walking and wheelchairing in a healing space. The hospital has also installed an "Enabling Garden" as a place to reduce stress and anxiety. And its new meditation room is a place of profound quiet and inspiration. All these spaces have music and natural sounds that tune the person within the hospital environment. Aesthetic Audio Systems, a company I began three years ago, concentrates in bringing beauty and ambient sounds into healthcare facilities such as Marianjoy. Fortunately, the medical world is beginning to realize what the ancients already knew—that space and sound harmonize the spirit.

This book by Susan Hale makes a significant contribution to reclaiming that understanding. Whether you are an individual pilgrim of the spirit, a lover of sacred architecture, or a person in need of healing, it is my hope that it will awaken your ears, eyes, and sense of space. May it inspire us to experience sound throughout our bodies and to be aware of the power of acoustics to evoke the sacred in our homes, our businesses, and our outdoor environments as well as in our places of worship.

Don Campbell
Author of *The Harmony of Health*
and *The Mozart Effect*®
Boulder, Colorado
February, 2007

# ACKNOWLEDGMENTS

A book is not just the effort an individual writer. It is a composition created from ancestral whispers, bird song, and a chorus of people who have added their own music to the book's harmonic tapestry. Among these are my chief angels Don Campbell, David Hale, John Reid, Sheila Rosen, Nancy Ryan, Georgemarc Schevené, and Eleanor Zimmerman. Much gratitude goes to my Taos writing groups, apprentices, students, family, and friends. Many people lent me books, read early drafts of the manuscript, provided pictures, supported trips to Egypt, England, and France, and believed in my vision. I sing a million songs of thanks to you all.

A special crescendo goes to my Quest editor Sharron Dorr, who worked closely with me into the eleventh hour, honing every thought and every word. Like the flying buttresses supporting a Gothic cathedral, she helped ground the book so that its meaning could soar. Thanks also to my publicist Emily Mullen and to the rest of the staff at Quest for making this book a beautiful reality.

*Pavement-stones labyrinth, nave, Basilica of St. Quentin,*
*1495, Aisne-Picardy, France*

# INTRODUCTION

*Each place has a voice.*
*Sending a voice, a voice responds.*
—Joan Halifax

The search for the sacred has existed in every culture since the dawn of time. The building of holy places is part of what makes us human. But what is it, exactly, that makes a place sacred? One answer would be to say that a sacred space is a natural or created place where spiritual experiences are enhanced and ritual acts of worship are performed. Religions call certain places sacred because of important events that have taken place there. Christians revere Mount Golgotha where Jesus was crucified. Buddhists consider the Bo tree under which Buddha attained enlightenment as holy. Muslims go on pilgrimage to Mecca. But places do not have to be named as holy by the culture in order to be sacred. We may have a private place, special only to us, where it is meaningful to pray or meditate.

A sacred space is a *temenos*, a Greek word meaning an enclosure that makes it possible to enter into a relationship with a greater reality. Entering into sacred space, one crosses a threshold and moves from *chronos*, human time and space, into *kairos*, eternal time.

There are places on the earth, often where ley lines and underground water streams converge, that emanate powerful vibrations. These vibrations alter our sense of ordinary reality and put us in contact with the numinous—with mythic reality and the greater mysteries that cannot be named. Early people the world over revered such places, be they mountains, caves, rocks, or forests. Later, sacred structures were built on these spots, aligned with the stars and constellations to protect, contain, and amplify the mysterious earth energies.

Such sacred places are inherently musical. They are places where we go to attune and be tuned, to be in harmony with holy realms. Early humans sought out natural places for their acoustic properties. They found resonant caves, echo canyons, and other places where sound reverberated in mysterious ways. Later, one might say that "music" was literally built into temples and churches in the form of sacred geometry. They were not only visual masterpieces but acoustic masterpieces as well. From the Taj Mahal to the Great Pyramid of Giza to soaring Gothic Cathedrals, these places sing!

The truth of that phenomenon awes me, for singing has always been as important to me as the air I breathe. My mother said I sang before I talked. I was fed by her lullabies. The feeling of being safely wrapped in a blanket of song was my first experience of sacred space. Held in my mother's embrace, I could hear her voice hum through me. As she sang "Somewhere over the Rainbow," I imagined the rainbow bridge and felt I would go there someday.

Since childhood, I have been sensitive to psychic undercurrents and the intersection among song, dreams, and spirit. I feel these currents as vibrational realities, poetic sound threads that weave the world together. Sometimes I have had big dreams I know I must follow. At one point music became *MUSIC*, an archetype that has led me to my life's path as a music therapist, voice teacher, and healer. For over twenty-five years I have explored music's effects on consciousness, helped people find their voices, and taught university classes in archetypal psychology and the healing power of sound and song. My experience of working in psychiatric hospitals, homeless shelters, recovery programs, senior centers, special education schools, and my own private practice has brought me to one constant: music's ability to move people deeply and open the soul's inner landscape.

Sound is primary in forming consciousness. Iegor Reznikoff, a specialist in early music, antiquity, and the resonance of sacred sites, believes that deep consciousness is mostly structured through sound, as is our first notion of space.[1] Sound is always there, imprinting and inspiring us. Sound matters. As humans we are sound beings, highly sensitive acoustic soundboards. Sound is woven into the marrow of our bones.

It is also woven into the space all around us. When we sing we change the molecules in the atmosphere and set them vibrating. Bernice Johnson Reagon of the a cappella singing group Sweet Honey in the Rock talks about how activists used song in the civil rights movement to claim the air. Whenever a policeman came into a meeting to intimidate those gathered there, someone would start singing. Even the policeman couldn't help tapping his feet along with the beat.

When sound is set into motion, it expands like a balloon. As the balloon gets bigger, the acoustic energy at any point on it diminishes by the square root of its change in size, a principle known as the inverse square law. Accordingly, sound never really dies. An aura of inaudible sound permeates our world. Everything—every word ever spoken, every song ever sung, every prayer ever uttered—is still in the air.

Since the beginning of human experience, we have encircled the earth with painted caves, cathedrals, stupas, oracle chambers, shrines, kivas, megalithic monuments, pyramids, and other buildings to celebrate and give praise to the Divine. We have created these places to hear ourselves and Spirit more clearly, to create relationship with the seen and the unseen worlds.

While we can't really know if the ancients used acoustics intentionally in the design of sacred sites, I believe knowledge of resonance was passed down from the oral cultures of the Paleolithic and the Neolithic and straight to the door of Chartres. From voice to voice, ear to ear, heart to heart, this understanding was transferred from generation to generation, as if in an ancient game of telephone. I believe that early people *noticed* when something vibrated in their landscape and then built their structures to enhance these effects. Singing in caves and canyons, they heard echoes and later built sacred architecture to enshrine the air. I believe that early shamans were sound technicians who knew how to manipulate sound and space to create portals into other dimensions. Can I prove this? No. But even eating breakfast on my back porch talking to my cat I can hear his name reverberate from the portal. There is a moment of awe. "Boogie" has become *Boogie,* not just a name but a word filled with magic.

In 1995 I had a vision that led me on a journey to explore such acoustic mysteries. I saw myself deep in a crypt inside a French cathedral. A medieval knight and lady were entombed, resting side by side. I moved closer to them, holding a glowing torch in my hand. The lady sprang to life. "Follow the Lady of Roses. Follow her music," she said. I heard the words *langue d'oc* before the vision faded.

I knew I must go to France. In 1996 I was finally able to begin my pilgrimage. Before my trip I read that troubadours once sang to the Lady in the *langue d'oc,* a regional language in Southern France. Was this her music? I read fascinating stories about Black Madonnas, Mary Magdalene, the Knights Templar, and the Cathars. When I asked who the Lady of Roses might be, I received many answers. Some said that she was the Virgin Mary and that I would find her at Lourdes. In New Mexico, where I live, friends pointed me to the Virgin of Guadalupe who appeared to a peasant man, Juan Diego, in Mexico in 1534. When the priest doubted his vision, Juan Diego took off his coat, from which—in the dead of winter—live roses cascaded to the floor. Inside his cloak a picture of the Virgin was imprinted.

Others told me that the Lady of Roses was the Black Madonna and that I would find her throughout France and in the crypt of Chartres Cathedral. I knew I had to go there and sing.

Before going to France I attended the Voices of Heaven and Earth Conference in Findhorn, Scotland. There three hundred people sang from all over the world. I sang hallelujahs with Ysaye Barnwell from the group Sweet Honey in the Rock and was immersed in an ocean of sound with Susan Osborn. I sang overtones with Iegor Reznikoff. I listened to Don Campbell's personal healing voyage through toning, chanted Vedic hymns, and sang Taize chants in the moonlight. In the air were Japanese, French, Spanish, British, and German accents. Hearing the lilt of Scottish voices, the wind from the North Sea, the song from the flowers in the garden, I realized that the voice itself is a cathedral. We are all sound chambers resonating with the One Song, heard in different variations, timbres, and rhythms. Each unique, but part of the whole, we make up the chorus of life.

After the conference I visited France. As I stood in the center of the labyrinth at Chartres Cathedral and heard my voice resound from the nave, I knew I needed to write this book. After Chartres I went to Lascaux. There my voice reflected off the cave walls in the Gallery of the Bulls.

Each of these experiences taught me something about space and sound. I experience sacred sites as amplifiers of consciousness. Singing brings a holy place into vibration, as if it were a tuning fork being struck. In these journeys the tuning fork was also my body, set into motion in a new way. I discovered that the ancients built their temples according to ratios of sacred geometry, universal principles that exist in numbers, shapes, and musical intervals and in the proportions that compose our bodies.

When I returned to New Mexico I was assaulted by the sounds of Interstate Highway 40 in Albuquerque, the buzz of bulldozers, the rush of traffic, and the general static of life in the fast lane. In spite of a drought, a community in the East Mountains was putting in a water pipeline to build a golf course. That irony seemed symbolic of values gone awry on many levels. I remembered Iegor Reznikoff asking, "What kind of churches are we building now? Where are the songs? Where is the painted glass?"[2]

During the ten years I have spent writing this book, the terrain of sacred space and sound has taken up residence within me. I read about sacred sites and searched out reverberant spaces to sing, from red rock canyons and crevices in trees to shrine rooms inside New Mexico stupas. I listened to stories of people who sang during their own pilgrimages. As I read I noticed that most books on sacred architecture were visually oriented. Rarely did I find more than a few paragraphs relating to the acoustic properties of sacred space. Yet singing has always been essential to culture and is the earliest form of musical expression, a fundamental human need.

On my quest, I have learned how different religions have created buildings that most suited their message. Cavernous stone cathedrals with their incredible reverberation were perfect for Gregorian chant. In Protestant religions, which emphasize speech over music, small chapels with elevated pulpits were built so the minister's sermon could best be heard. The cloth hangings, silk paintings, and wooden ceilings in Tibetan temples "restrict reverberation and produce a high clear sound."[3] This arrangement is ideal for the sounds of horns, drums, and cymbals that punctuate the chanting of Buddhist monks. Pueblo kivas in New Mexico, built of adobe bricks, create a womb-like space in the earth that enhances the experience of intimacy.

Questions about religion are in my blood. My eleventh great-grandfather was William Brewster, the founder of the Pilgrim Church. Other ancestors of mine also sailed on the Mayflower to escape religious persecution in England. My great-great grandparents were early Mormons who followed Joseph Smith. My great-great grandmother walked alongside a wagon train from Illinois to Utah. Eventually, she and her husband settled a small Arizona town and named it Eden. Later, my father broke from his Mormon tradition when he married my mother and became a Presbyterian. He asked to be excommunicated from the Mormon Church and was happy with his choice.

The group of seekers, rebels, and pioneers from whom I am descended have been ready to cross oceans or walk in the wilderness for their beliefs. While my search has led to different conclusions, this striving to find a new path outside of traditional religions is my legacy. Interfaith services and the mystic undercurrents rippling beneath orthodox religions have always drawn me, for I believe there are many paths, each streaming toward a larger source. I honor the uniqueness of each while searching for the threads that unite us all.

Music is one of those threads, our common language for matters of the spirit. I found sound practices variously within the Jewish,

Islamic, Christian, and Hindu traditions. Some that most impressed me fall outside the mainstream because of my particular interest in the feminine. My search has led me to people, places, and books that have expanded my understanding of the sacred. With the Episcopal priest Matthew Fox, I believe that "there can be no global peace and justice without global spirituality."[4]

This book is in the service of that belief. It is intended as a song journey to explore the sound mysteries at many of the world's holy places. We will also explore the blueprint of human development and how we become music in the womb. And we will discover the miracles of the ear, an organ that never sleeps.

The book moves sequentially through time, from Paleolithic caves to Neolithic passage graves, the first sacred architecture where acoustic conjuring was done. We will follow pilgrimage routes, well worn with the song prayers of pilgrims, both ancient and modern. We'll enter the King's Chamber in the Great Pyramid and go into temples, chapels, and cathedrals to discover how music is integral to the life journey and how each faith consecrates space with sound.

The book continues to our present time where dissonance reigns. The final chapters reflect a return to the temple, where people are seeking resonant places to sing and are building new sacred sites out of breath, song, love, vision, and intention.

Along the way, I share my own experiences in singing at sacred sites in New Mexico and during several trips to the United Kingdom and to Egypt. I recount my talks with singers, sound healers, voice teachers, poets, acoustic engineers, acoustic archaeologists, Egyptologists, rabbis, Native Americans, and seers. My intention has been to weave a web of connections among the feminine, religion, science, dreams, visions, myth, history, music, and my own story. My hope is that I have achieved a harmonic resolution in which the reader may enjoy fresh insight about the human need for sacred proportions in architecture and music. Now, more than ever, people are searching for new ways to pray, to experience the Divine, and to relate to life's highest mysteries. This book explores the acoustics of sacred space as one avenue for understanding. It is about, not just ordinary music, but music that awakens us to new dimensions within ourselves and with our universe. It is about *MUSIC* that is written into us at birth, that is part of our human heritage singing through us with every breath.

*Venus of Laussel, Paleolithic bas-relief sculpture, Musee d'Aquitaine, Bordeaux, France*

~ *Chapter 1* ~

# BLUEPRINT

*The strongest, deepest and oldest consciousness
is sound consciousness.*
—Iegor Reznikoff

In the Museum of Prehistory in Les Eyzies, I stand before a Venus of Laussel. Les Eyzies is a small village in the Dordogne Region of France. Here, by the Vezere River, cliffs protect a green valley, fertile with prehistoric caves and carvings. It is a place of music. The nightingales sing the praises of the scalloped water lapping the river's shores. In April the earth is upturned and brown as cake awaiting the farmer's seeds. Outside the museum a statue of a caveman greets visitors. Inside, the main attraction, carved out of rosy rock, is the twenty-thousand-year-old Venus that holds a hand over her pregnant belly. Like the land of the Dordogne, she is a cornucopia of waiting life. Her vulva and legs form the shape of an "M." She holds an upturned bison's horn with thirteen marks on its moonlike crescent, symbolic of the moon's phases. She seems to say this is where to begin—here in a woman's pregnant body, in the mysteries and miracles of birth. This is where we become music.

Our mother's womb is the first space we know. Heartbeat, breath, mother's voice, father's voice—all filter through and echo the pulse of life and the sounds of the world inside a growing fetus. Cells divide and the blueprint unfolds, recapitulating evolution—fish, mammal, and human. Flesh and bones, spine and skull, a heart that starts to beat at four weeks, lungs, eyes, throat, tongue, and ears

1

all grow within the matrix of our mother. Head, trunk, leg, foot, hand, and arm all follow the proportions of sacred geometry. As we grow we vibrate to the continuous pulsing of our mother's veins and arteries.

The inner ear is complete at four-and-a-half months in utero, 135 days after conception. The ear starts first at the surface of the skin as a small, gill-like slit. Gradually it burrows, spiraling inward deep down in the petrous portion of the temporal bone. According to Dr. Albert Soesman, this is the hardest bone in the body. Humans are the only mammals in which the inner ear is protected so carefully. This fetal ear is comparable to a fully functioning adult ear. We hear our mother's heartbeat as a steady song. It is our food. If being nourished by sound were not a fundamental need, why else would we hear so soon and so well?

In many of the world's mythologies, sound generates life. Perhaps we are encoded with a knowing of the primary importance of sound before birth. In utero, an aural field is created that keeps our growing body in place. Mother's heartbeat and breath entrain us with a steady pulse to lock in our own inherent patterns. Our senses develop out of the matrix of the ear. Touch, taste, smell, and sight all have their foundations in the ear, which, as Dr. Branford Weeks states, "precedes the nervous system."[1] In evolutionary terms, hearing is at least three hundred million years old.

Sound is necessary to feed the brain, to help it create neural pathways. According to Alfred Tomatis, a French physician, psychologist, and educator, "a primary function of the ear is to charge the brain with electric potential."[2] The brain is charged through the cells of Corti in the inner ear, where they transform sound waves into electrical input. It is this process that tones and tunes the nervous system.

Of all the sense organs, the ear comes first to nourish the brain. All the brain cells a person will ever have are in place by the fifth month in utero. After that, neurons grow larger and become insulated, and millions upon millions of connections are made. And all of them begin with the heartbeat, breath, mother's voice, father's voice, heard deep within that first sacred space of the womb.

During birth we receive the imprint of our entire body surface as we pass through the vagina. The skin, the body's largest organ, is an extension of the ear. In the birth canal we "hear" with our skin as well as our ears. Our sound-body is mapped. Our mother's birthing sounds help her cervix to open and vibrate her pelvic bones. We hear these sounds before coming into the world, before air enters our lungs for our first cry. As newborns, we orient to the sound of our parents' voices, which we had heard inside the womb as a steady presence. Now these voices are heard outside the body, through air, rather than inside through liquid. The shift between hearing in one medium and another is so intense that Tomatis calls it a "sonic labor."[3]

At a friend's invitation, I attended the birth of her daughter. As the newborn Connie nursed for the first time, her mother cooed with delight, pouring sounds over her that flowed as easily as the milk did. I was reminded of Tomatis, who believes that the sound issuing from our mother's mouth spreads over our bodies like liquid. Syllables wash over us. He says the "entire body surface marks their progress through the skin's sensitivity, as if controlled by a keyboard that is receptive to acoustic touch."[4] He thinks it is through hearing our mother's sounds, songs, and words that we acquire a body image.

And we move to the sound of her music. Studies by Boston University Professors W. S. Condon and W. Ogston show that as soon as twenty minutes after birth a baby's movements are determined by its mother's speech. One of a baby's first sounds is humming while nursing. This sound is universal to humans and animals alike.

A woman rancher who helps bring calves and sheep into the world gave a poetry reading I attended. She said that the bonding of cows and sheep with their babies is not always immediate. When the mother is ready to bond she bellows an "Mmm" just short of a "Moo." When the newborn calf is ready to bond with her it echoes her. This is true of sheep as well. Newborn lambs echo their mothers with a soft gurgling hum. For babies in Western culture, "Mmm" becomes *Mama*. For babies in Tibet, it becomes *Mo*, in China *Ma*, in India *Amma*, in Albania *Nana*, in Spanish *Madre*, in France *Mere*, in Germany *Mutter*, in Denmark *Mor*, in Arabia *Omi*, in Estonia

*Ema,* in Navajo *Shima.* Mother is also matter. *"Mother, mater, matter, matrix, meter* and *measure* all have the same root."[5]

Our mother defines our sense of place. After we are housed in her womb, we are held within the circle of her arms. As we begin to crawl, and later walk, we are held within the sound of her voice. Her voice measures the space we inhabit.

A woman in one of my classes invited me to sing at her child's birth. She wanted my vocal support during labor. Hearing how her sounds mirrored her body and how they created a space inside for her baby to pass through, I learned more about the voice in those seven hours than in any of my voice lessons. When she was resting I was silent or hummed. She sounded through each contraction and I added my own voice to give her strength. When the baby, Mikaela, was born she was handed to me and I sang a melody that emanated from this warm presence in my arms. Mikaela is five now. She says she remembers when I sang at her birth.

Birth and song belong to an ancient tradition. The Australian Aborigines, whose culture is 150,000 years old, believe that spirit children are deposited on the earth through the chanting of the Dreamtime Ancestors. An Aboriginal woman conceives by stepping on one of these songs. The spirit child on that spot enters into her womb. The woman remembers the exact location and informs the elders. This is the conception site and belongs to the person who will be born; it is where the child's essence resides.

In East Africa there is a tribe that literally sings a child into being. When a woman decides she wants to bear a child with a particular man, she goes out alone in nature and listens for the song of the child she wishes to birth. After receiving the song she goes back to the village and teaches this song to the father. They sing it together as they make love. After conception, the mother sings to her child in the womb. As birth draws near, she teaches the song to the midwives and old women who have come to assist. They welcome the child into the world with its special song. The song is later sung at all the important ceremonies that mark its life—naming, puberty, and marriage. At death the song is sung one last time.[6] Just as the body returns to spirit, the song returns to the air. I believe song creates the template for the soul to enter at birth and to leave at death.

## EARTH

In some cultures the infant is presented to the earth to receive her imprint before being handed to its mother. In Australia the Aboriginal midwife shapes out a hollow depression in the earth. Here the mother squats to give birth. Like the conception site, the place of a child's birth "will shape his identity and his ritual obligation for the rest of his life."[7]

In the Rio Grande Pueblos of New Mexico, a song is sung by the person who first takes the child from its mother, placing the newborn on the earth. The song is a blessing so that the child may have good thoughts of the Earth Mother, "the food giver."[8]

The texture and smell of the earth's touch become part of the child's imprint, part of its knowing. The word *human* comes from *humus*, the earth. Even if our own birth was not welcomed in this way, these rituals are part of our collective memory. Even though we live in a culture that does not honor the earth as Mother, we know it to be true in the deepest strata of our being.

Womb. Mother. Earth. Body. These are sacred places, long denied in modern culture but essential to the roots of our existence. Every millisecond of every day, miracles happen within and around us. We are alive. Our hearts beat. We breathe. The stapedius muscle that moves one of the tiny bones in the middle ear never rests. Our ears never sleep. Outside, birds sing and we are tuned by their particular songs each spring. Here, at my home in Arroyo Seco, the meadow lark wakes me up. Each April frogs return and start singing.

The ear is primary; it registers ten octaves. The eye registers only one, the vibrational wavelengths of the color spectrum. "Almost all cranial nerves lead to the ear.... The ear also has a fascinating tie in to the tenth cranial nerve or the vagus nerve. The vagus nerve is literally responsible for our gut reactions, since it is the link between the automatic functions of the internal organs and the brain."[9]

What we hear stirs us. We are moved to sing. This human impulse starts at the place of listening. When we feel pain, we groan and sing the blues. When we are heartsore, we wail with grief. When we are in awe, we give praise. Sometimes life is so beautiful and mysterious we have no words; only sound and song will express what we feel.

As babies we come into this world with sound. We cry and coo immediately. First we make only vowel sounds. At six months we begin to babble, adding consonants to our repertoire. At one year we begin to speak and sing spontaneously. Around two the larynx drops down into the throat and our vocabulary jumps to over fifty words. Between two and two-and-a-half years of age, we can sing fragments of songs, not always accurately. By three we can converse using more than a thousand words and sing many song fragments with accuracy. Remember some of your earliest songs? Or the songs you now sing to your children or grandchildren? Many, like the nursery rhyme "Rain, Rain, Go Away," start with the descending minor third, which is heard when the first two words are sung. It is the first interval that is learned regardless of culture and so seems encoded into us.

By four we sing song phrases in different keys, but can sing accurate pitches within each phrase. By five-and-a-half we can sing whole songs accurately.

A friend emailed me a story about his four-and-a-half-year-old daughter. As she sat on his lap while he was working at the computer, she began to sing spontaneously. He was so amazed by the song he stopped what he was doing and wrote down the words:

> Everyday goes by and by for eternity.
> Everyday you go past a lazy boy or a lazy girl.
> Love to be sound and love to be not.
> Who wants to be everyday?
> Everyday I will help your love to be true.
> Everyday you go dumpity dump, dumpity dump, dumpity dump.
> Everyday you go past a merry fellow.
> Would you take up your truth?
> Everyday you go past a loving soul.[10]

It is thought that, as early humans, we chanted for perhaps half a million years before we talked. "Researchers have found that about two-thirds of the cilia—the thousands of minute hairs in the inner ear that lie on a flat plane like piano keys and respond to different frequencies of sound—resonate only at the higher 'musical' frequencies (3,000 to 20,000 hertz), indicating that, at one time, human beings probably communicated primarily through song or tone."[11]

We began in the Pleistocene Age, some two hundred thousand years ago. But, in fact, "our genome—the sum of an individual's genetic material...is the product of millions of years of evolution."[12] These are the biological facts of who we are, each the product of a hundred million mysteries.

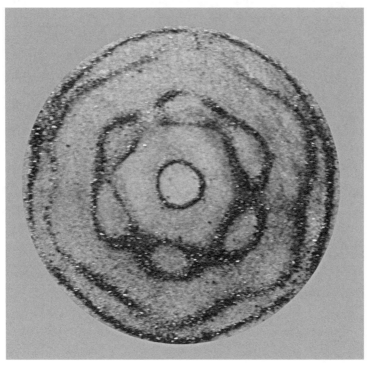

*Cymatic pattern of a male voice producing a sine wave*
*"Ooooh" sound on a CymaScope in sand.*

# ~ *C h a p t e r 2* ~

# FOUNDATION

*The ways of making are indeed wondrous —the child born of its mother,*
*the sun rolling into the sky, the song rising from the lips,*
*the world springing from the word of god.*
—Normandi Ellis

We are filled with daily miracles. The temple of the ear, containing the labyrinth of the semicircular canal, orients us in time and space by measuring angular velocity and charting mathematical ratios. We are set in motion by a world that sounds through us, vibrating our atoms, like Aeolian harps singing with the currents of the wind.

We sing through open spaces in our bodies. These resonate with the bones and cavities in our chest and heads, creating a complex web of frequencies that issue from our mouths and into the air around us. If we could see sound in the air, we would see moving patterns that are constantly changing. Each time we sing or speak, a "sonic bubble" leaves our mouths and expands outward at seven hundred miles per hour. British acoustics engineer John Reid says that the "surface of this bubble is a beautifully delicate, kaleido-scopic tracery ... which repeats itself in its harmonic structure. The precise structure of this pattern is unique to each human being."[1]

In theory, Reid says, "the sonic bubble expands forever, like ripples of light which travel through space."[2] However, in reality, it is absorbed by the materials of a building, including the people inside, or by the very fabric of the air. Each material has a different absorption rate. Air, wood, adobe, stone, and concrete all absorb and reflect sound differently. Hard stone surfaces often produce an echoing effect where we hear our voice reflected back to us, often taking us by surprise.

## MR. WIZARD

John Reid and I met after John Anthony West suggested I contact him about his sonic research at the Great Pyramid of Giza. I found Reid to be no ordinary scientist. His search for scientific evidence implies a cosmology that resonates with mine, and we share a quest for how sound creates form and shapes consciousness. He makes the science of acoustics come alive.

We were both presenters at a Mensa Conference in Malvern, England. There John gave his world debut demonstrating his Cyma-Scope, a twenty-first century electro-acoustic invention which looks a bit like a six-foot rocket ship. His work is, of course, inspired by that of other scientists: The study of sound creating form began when Hans Jenny, a Swiss scientist, pioneered a study of wave phenomena in the 1950s and called it "Cymatics." Jenny studied and articulated his findings over a fourteen-year period until his death in 1972. He followed in the footsteps of Margaret Watts-Hughes, a Welsh woman, who had begun this work fifty years earlier with her "Eidscope," a device she sang into, thus forming patterns on a sand-strewn India rubber membrane. Both Jenny and Watts-Hughes were inspired by Ernst Chladni, a German scientist who, in 1785, created mandala-like patterns in sand on a steel plate that he vibrated with a violin bow. Jenny's techniques were more sophisticated than those of Chladni or Watts-Hughes because he used a sine wave generator, crystal oscillators, stroboscopes, and other twentieth-century technologies. He investigated liquids, pastes, and powders that, under the influence of vibration, created harmonic shapes. These forms are not static; they exist as long as the vibration exists and change when the vibration changes.

John Reid's research takes the work of these earlier scientists to a new level. His CymaScope has a "super-sensitive thermo plastic membrane, stretched to a precise tension." This membrane can be excited by the human voice, bird song, natural sounds, music, and sacred language, "each sound bearing a unique 'acoustic signature,' or CymaGlyph."[3] At the heart of John's work is an interest in how sound is influenced by sacred space. During his presentation at the Mensa Conference, he invited the audience to make vowel sounds and then watch them magically appear on a screen. When I saw my voice for the first time, I was mesmerized by its changing shapes. At one point there was a petal shape around several concentric circles. With each changing vowel and tone, a new shape appeared. The quartz sand that had been formless and chaotic now took on a beautiful order. John told us that many of the constants of the universe are embedded in these patterns. He showed a slide of a CymaGlyph that he called the "Primordial Egg" generated by a very low frequency sine wave. John believes that life began in the primordial oceans when white noise, from wave action, was filtered by the water, creating an almost pure low-frequency sound at depth. This sound harmonized with low-frequency sounds from hydrothermal vents on the ocean floor, thus creating the "sonic spark" that sang life into being on the surface of microscopic bubbles. The patterns of energy that formed on the bubbles had embedded within them the proportions of the golden mean that created a sonic scaffolding in which life could form. After eons of time, the first organisms increased in complexity, eventually "learning" how to replicate themselves in this "nurturing sonic environment."[4]

Seeing Cymatics in action was like watching the universe being created: A star was born from a drop of water, a flower bloomed and dissolved, a shape like a spine snaked through liquid. Watching such an experiment on John's CymaScope, I imagined that, given enough time, the wiggling wave trains might crawl off the membrane, just like the first fish walked onto the land and became mammals.

If sound can create forms in sand, what effect is it having on our bodies? What forms does it create in our consciousness? Through my work with the Bonny Method of Guided Imagery and Music, I have both experienced and witnessed how listening to classical music in a relaxed state creates vivid visual imagery, body sensations, and emotions ranging from deep grief to states of ecstasy. One man, while listening to Vaughn Williams' *Fantasia on a Theme by Thomas Tallis*, reported worlds being created by light and saw the pyramids being formed. "I can touch the ancient feelings of creation," he told me, "I feel compassion in every cell of my body." We are immediately moved by music because we *are* music, constructed out of the proportions of the golden mean—the architectural building block of every part of our natural world.

## THE GOLDEN MEAN

Once, in a dream, an old alchemist showed me what I thought was a compass and talked about the importance of alignment. He showed me a golden thread that went down through the central core of my body, entering at the crown. At each of the chakras, the thread came out in a horizontal plane. I saw rectangles, triangles, and ovals in my body all interconnecting with the golden thread, which in turn connected the earth to each of the planets. Later, I learned that what I thought was a compass was actually a caliper, an instrument for measuring the golden mean.

What is known as the golden ratio was first studied by the mathematicians of ancient Greece, who recognized its importance in the geometry of pentagons and pentagrams. Discovery of the ratio is usually attributed to Pythagoras. It has fascinated, not just mathematicians, but people in a wide variety of fields including musicians, artists, architects, and biologists ever since.[5] In this ratio, the sum of two quantities is to the larger quantity as the larger is to the smaller. It can be expressed as 1 to 1.618 and is called Phi.

As the twentieth-century French architect Le Corbusier noted, the body itself roughly expresses the law of the golden mean, which you can see by measuring yourself from foot to navel and then from navel to the top of your head.[6] It is a harmonious ratio that unites various sections of a whole throughout creation. The spiral of a nautilus shell, petals whirling open on a wild rose, and the fetus curled in the womb all illustrate this hidden ordering power of the universe. We see it everywhere: in the center of a sunflower, the pattern of a pine cone, and the symmetry of our faces. It is in motion as snowflakes fall from the sky, as a dog chases its tail, and as bees dance around a honeycomb. The golden mean, beauty with a capital "B," is the proportion we find most pleasing. It satisfies our eyes and enchants our ears.

We hear the golden mean in Gregorian chant and the music of Bach and many other composers. It is reflected in the art of Leonardo da Vinci, Botticelli, and other Renaissance masters. The Parthenon in Greece, the Mexican Pyramid of the Sun at Teotihuacán, the Egyptian Temple to Osiris at Abydos, the west facade of Notre-Dame Cathedral, Stonehenge, and other holy places around the world all demonstrate this universal aesthetic.

Hildegard of Bingen, a twelfth-century German mystic, abbess, composer, writer, artist, and herbalist, used the golden mean in many of her compositions. When composer and mathematician Pozzi Escot charted the notes of one of Hildegard's pieces in a three-dimensional form, it resembled a Gothic cathedral, revealing that the "shape of the building in which the chant was sung was the same shape as the chant itself."[7]

The spiraling dance of the golden mean, which lies somewhere between the perfect 5th and minor 6th according to today's accepted standard of tonality,[8] is mirrored in the cochlea of the inner ear, whose shape "corresponds to how chromatic musical octaves appear when graphed as wave lengths."[9]

The architecture of our bodies makes us singing beings. The voice of creation lives all around us, sounding through us like breath blown in a flute. "We drink from the source of Voice," says Silvia Nakkach, director of Vox Mundi in San Francisco. "Sound clears the energy of the body, clears a path, moves through and creates a wide open space like a church. When the sound gets free from the self it becomes spacious. Then the singer becomes sacred architecture, a portable temple."[10]

## SPIRITUAL ACOUSTICS

In *The Book of the Hopi*, Frank Waters tells the story of Spider Woman creating the world through sound. She gives birth to twins and sends them to the earth's poles. As the first twin places his hand upon the earth it becomes solid. The other twin's duty is to keep the world in order. He must "go about all over the world and send out sound so that it may be heard throughout the land. When this is heard you will be known as 'Echo,' for all sound echoes the Creator."[11]

Who has not been enchanted by echoes? They can be heard in canyons and rock outcroppings and near large stone structures, such as cathedrals and pyramids. Send a voice and a voice replies; a delayed ghost returns from the original sound. Clear echoes come from quick claps or short bursts of sound.

Both echoes and reverberation carry spiritual associations. Early people thought of echoes as spirits, mysterious voices coming from a world beyond ours. Since the dawn of time, when people chanted in caves or stone tombs, we have associated the bright sounds of reverberation with ethereal/spiritual atmospheres. Later, we built churches, cathedrals, mosques, and temples that enhanced these types of sounds. Bright sounds heard in the enclosed spaces of stone churches trail off, creating a feeling of infinity. Modern churches need sound systems fitted with reverberation units to create brightness of tone, because sound is dulled by the soft surfaces of heavy drapes and carpets.

Each building has its own reverberation time, "the time, in seconds, required for a sound event to decay to one millionth (60 decibels) of its initial level."[12] Another acoustic phenomenon is called resonance, which is the apparent amplification of the voice when singing or speaking certain notes in an enclosed space, such as a chapel or tomb. Resonance is the frequency at which an object begins to vibrate. Everything has a frequency that sets it in motion, from a bridge over a river, to a rock, to a crystal goblet. Our entire body is a symphony of sound, made of the different resonant frequencies of every organ, bone, and tissue. We each have a sound signature, or personal vibratory rate, that is made up of the composite frequency of all of our bodily systems.[13]

Each covered space has a prime resonant frequency at which it becomes most excited and the least amount of acoustic energy is absorbed. To find the most resonant note of a building, close your eyes and make a slow glissando, sliding your voice from your lowest range to your highest. Try this in your bathroom, often the most resonant room in a house because of its hard, tiled surfaces. Listen for the note that sounds loudest. Even though your voice will sound amplified, in reality no amplification is taking place. You are actually hearing your own voice energy as it is reflected many times around the space. The room seems to come alive with a feeling of presence that is larger than your normal sense of self.

We feel this resonance also in relationships with people. A word, a look, a gesture, the very timbre of our voice can bring us into sympathetic correspondence with someone. Perhaps this resonance is the basis for attraction, where we feel a natural affinity with one another and so feel a sense of enchantment. Similarly, we are drawn to some places and not others. Resonance helps guide us to the people and places where we feel most in tune.

## VOWELS

Pythagoras believed that vowels embody the creative principle. Given that the voice is the only instrument that can produce vowels, he considered it the primal instrument. In ancient Egyptian and Hebrew languages, vowels were sacred and so not notated with writing. To read these languages, one must participate vocally. When the vowels are intoned, words become alive, imbued with magic.

The Bible says, "In the Beginning was the Word. And the Word was with God and the word *is* God" (John 1:1). Creation myths all over the world repeat this same basic truth. For people of the Laguna Pueblo in New Mexico, for instance, it is Spider Woman who shapes the world through humming and singing.

As we change the malleable structure of the voice through sounding vowels, we vibrate different parts of the body. After "Mmm," one of the first sounds we make as babies are vowels containing the emotional content of speech. As babies and early humans we expressed our emotional needs through vowel sounds. A low grunted "Uhhh" is a different experience than a contented "Ahhhh." While some books on sound healing give specific tones to resonate certain parts of the body, I have noticed that everyone experiences them differently due to the unique size, weight, shape, and intention of each person.

But there are commonalities. "Ah," which is expressed through the shape of the mouth on exhalation, is cleansing, like water washing over the body. "Ah" vibrates the heart and is the sound of praise and wonder. Allah! Alleluia! "Ee," on the other hand, lifts up into the head, clearing and stimulating the region of the third eye. "Ou" descends into the interior, vibrating the lower portions of the body. "Oh" explores the deep cavern of the body's core. "Oh," as in *Om* sounds the void and fills emptiness. Perhaps vowels inspired the forms of sacred architecture: *I* for columns, *A* for arches, *O* for domes.

## Harmonics

Singing creates a vessel. Breath moves through the mouth and nose, and natural harmonics are produced that are separated in the tuned resonators of the nasal cavities. These harmonics, or overtones, are what make each voice unique; they are the archetypal matrix behind all music. Just as an oboe sounds different from a flute because of its size, shape, and the materials out of which it is made, the body differences of each of us are what give us our particular timbre.

David Hykes, founder of the Harmonic Choir and the Harmonic Presence work, says that "sound is a living material. Music is a ladder of precise harmonic laws coordinating the ascent and descent of consciousness and matter."[14]

He also remarks, "We prepare for this terrain for sound to come to life by sensing the space in the body in silence. When the sound comes we begin with 'Mmm,' the grain or seed of sound, which becomes charged. Then, the harmonics come, like the flowering of the tree, and can be understood as a flowering of a work that has its roots in the body." Through harmonic chanting, "we can be nourished by, and become part of, a subtle vibrational ecology where sound, breath, listening, silence, space and light become pure elements helping sacred atmosphere to come alive."[15]

In 2006, I attended David's workshop called Harmonic Presence at Esalen, the educational center near Big Sur, California. Though I had taken several overtone chanting workshops over the years with various teachers, I was happy to begin again with an empty cup, humbled by the quality of what this teacher has to offer.

David was born in New Mexico, where his Taos Pueblo godmother sang to him. "We gave you the privilege to sing," she told him later. He is an open, humorous, precise, and demanding man. Like a California cypress, he has been shaped by his listening, honed by a thirty-year meditation practice. His upswept forehead ridge appears as if it might ascend from his head at any moment to reveal sensitive antennae. At the workshop, he wore a brown jerkin over a black shirt, making him look a bit like a woodland elf. His speech was a mixture of poetry, Buddhist philosophy, and pure corn.

To begin the session, David said his work is not just about audible sound: "There are harmonics of breath, harmonics of listening, and octaves of sensation." He asked us to go around the circle, introducing ourselves by whispering our names. Then he asked, "Who remembers a name? Someone sing a name slowly and notice the harmonics in it; float it in the sky like skywriting."

Gi-o-va-ni

So-phi-a

Nee-sa

David reminded us that we don't need to try to shape the mouth to make harmonics; they are intrinsic in the sound of the vowels. We started with the seed sound of "Mmm," placing it below the throat to explore the resonance in the body space. Slowly we opened to "Oh," "Ah," "I," and "E," each vowel displaying its own natural harmonic. As we chanted we moved around the room, sounding like bees making harmonic honey. We explored the sounds carefully, being counseled to listen, not to each individual voice, but to the pure overtones themselves, and then to sing what we heard. As I opened my mouth to sing, I heard the harmonics in my voice merge and arc with the harmonics of others, and we became a being with one voice, creating sacred geometry. I was no longer "I" but part of the Fibonacci spiral of a sunflower, the golden mean between eye and eyebrow. And this was just the first night!

The next morning, David showed slides of Cymatic forms in liquid mercury. One was a slide of four singers in silence that formed a perfect golden ring. The next one, taken after they had begun to sing harmonic chant, looked like a piece of shimmering pyrite. It was an image of the liquid architecture of the shifting voice, a captured moment in time. Another slide revealed ancient faces similar to those of the Green Man and florid decorations of Scotland's Rosslyn Chapel.

As the workshop progressed, again we went into the practice of a new kind of listening. "When the singer gets quieter, the music gets better," David told us. We moved slowly, incrementally from the "Mmm," to the "Oh," hearing how the fundamental tone divides upward to form the second harmonic of the octave. We stopped to water each harmonic like farmers tending a musical garden. As we moved from "Oh" to "Ah," we created the third harmonic of the perfect fifth; from "Ah" to "I," the perfect fourth; and from "I" to "E," the major third. David passed out sheets enumerating the harmonic series and detailed twelve different layers of harmonic singing. All other workshops I had attended taught only what he refers to as the third level, where the mouth is held in a small tight shape and the lower fundamental note stays the same while the harmonics move above, ringing like pure crystal spheres.

(You can easily experiment with overtones yourself by trying this exercise: Hum while quickly changing the position of your tongue, moving it back and forth in the mouth. Then create a small opening in the mouth while keeping the upper lip tight. Cup your hands over your ears and bring them forward. You may begin to hear high, pure sounds of an almost magical quality.)

David is the Leonardo da Vinci of harmonics, a painter of sound. His work is grounded both in musicianship and spiritual practice. He demonstrated several of the levels and, though I watched him while I listened, I couldn't locate the source of the sound. He was singing into himself quietly. He was not just a voice across from me but a voice surrounding me—not a voice projected out but a voice sounding within. He was star mouthed, river tongued, a singing mountain. Flocks of swallows and blue jays chattering outside the classroom accompanied him. I was in "Ah" with him. He was demonstrating through his voice a universal truth.

## TONGUE

Once, in a dream, I saw a pond of frogs and heard them singing. Suddenly there was a hush. From out of the tall grass Grandfather Frog appeared. He was there to teach me the secrets of singing. He taught me that we each possess a wide range of vocal possibilities, much greater than we can imagine. "The tongue is one of the secrets," he told me. He showed me his tongue. On it were pads of many different colors. Each pad, like the indented sections of a steel drum, had a different emotional tone. Each received information from the air and sent it into a related organ in the body. The tongue was like an instrument played by the air. "Get to know your tongue," he told me. For a long time I wasn't sure what he meant. But in my own vocal practice I began to investigate my tongue as I was singing vowels. Each vowel is a complex combination of sounds comprising a main or fundamental tone over-laid by many overtones. I noticed the various overtones were created because of the ways I was positioning and moving my tongue.

When we say someone is articulate, we equate that with intelligence, and it occurred to me that the equation is often valid. The

Down's syndrome children I used to work with had thick, oversized tongues and couldn't articulate consonants well. I talked with a woman working with children with fetal alcohol syndrome who struggled with learning disabilities. She noted that they had speech difficulties because of their tongues. Their mental development was slower than that of most children their age.

The flexible tongue is also a component in achieving higher states of awareness. There are eighty-four acupuncture points behind the teeth and in a row down the hard palate. When chanting sacred languages such as Sanskrit, the tongue hits the points in specific ways that create pathways between the hypothalamus and the pituitary and pineal glands. Out of curiosity I once asked to look inside the mouth of a singer who speaks Sanskrit, Tibetan, and Hebrew. The roof of his mouth looked like the ribbed vault of a cathedral ceiling. Later, when looking at my own journals, I came across an entry recording an old dream in which I had looked inside a man's mouth and found a cathedral.

Aryeh Kaplan, author of *The Sefer Yetzirah,* a Jewish meditative text, tells us that in mystical Jewish writings Abraham, the patriarch of the Jews, was said to have "bound the letters of the Torah to his tongue. . . . He drew them in water, kindled them with fire, agitated them with breath."[16] Kaplan states that there are about a "sextillion possible permutations of all 22 letters of the Hebrew alphabet. This is very close to the number of stars in the observable universe."[17] Hebrew letters equate to numbers, sounds, and notes of the scale. Kaplan says that the letters are to be "engraved" with the voice, "carved" on the breath, and set in the mouth in five places for the five dimensions, the five vowels, and the five phonetic families. The first word of the Torah is *Bereshith,* which means "In the beginning," ushering in all of Creation. *Bereshith* contains five types of sounds: labial, labial-dental, palatal, silibant, and guttural.

Each of the Hebrew alphabet's twenty-two letters has a distinctive sound. "Mmm," for the labial letter *Mem,* relaxes and calms the mind with its mothering hum. Different states of consciousness are associated with each sound related to the ten *Sefiroth,* or "emanations" of the different aspects of God, of the Kabbalistic Tree of Life. *Mem* puts one in touch with the watery world of *Hokhmah*, the principle of Wisdom.

The hissing sounds of "Sh" and "S" express the sibilant *Shin*, which relates to *Binah*, the *Sefiroth* called Understanding. *Hokhmah* and *Binah* are called the mother and father; wife and husband, their union renews the Tree of Life. A sound pathway is created by the recitation of the letters *Mem* and *Shin*. Since written Hebrew usually has no vowels, this formula looks at every possible combination:

> Sho Mo Sho Ma Sho Me Sho Mi Sho Mu
> Sha Mo Sha Ma Sha Me Sha Mi Sha Mu
> She Mo She Ma She Me She Mi She Mu
> Shi Mo Shi Ma Shi Me Shi Mi Shi Mu
> Shu Mo Shu Ma Shu Me Shu Mi Shu Mu [18]

When reciting these divine letters, one alternates between the consciousness of Wisdom and that of Understanding. Hidden knowledge is unveiled through chanting these combinations; the mouth becomes a shrine for the living word, a temple of creation.

Sufi Muslim poet Daniel Abdal-Hayy Moore describes how spiritual text becomes embodied in the posture and consciousness of the practitioner in an excerpt from his poem *Vocalization:*

> During the dawn prayer, reciting
>      Qur'an out loud, I saw
>
> how suited the mouth and voice are
>      for sounding the sacred syllables,
>
> wetness of throat and tongue, tongue
>      hitting teeth,
>           curling and rolling of
>                tongue, shape of cheeks, touch of
>      lips—then how the
> resonance from the heart, like the

core of an up-thrusting geyser, and

the darker recesses of the body-chambers, how they
shape the sounds that are made, and how then

around the sounds the body is shaped like a
reverberant protoplasm, tending to
refinement when the

words are refined.[19]


# BRAIN

The act of singing enhances the cleansing of the cerebral spinal fluid within the cranium. Singing, humming, and shouting massage the brain by vibrating the cranium and allowing waste particles to pass through the blood-brain barrier. Overtones vibrate the skull in ways that normal singing doesn't, reaching deeper into the brain. High frequency sounds stimulate the pituitary gland because of its small mass and positioning directly above the nasal cavity. This master gland regulates the secretions of all the other endocrine glands. Placing the tongue on the roof of the mouth behind the upper teeth also stimulates the pituitary gland. This is the recommended position for tongue placement while meditating.

Overtones are needed for good health. Registered nurse Judith Hitt worked with patients suffering from strokes and other neurological disorders in Vermont. She taught her patients how to produce overtones. She found that overtones created from the vowels "ae" and "ee" resonate the larger areas of the brain, while "the highest harmonics seem to be the most effective on the smaller, more specific neural areas such as the caudate nucleus or cranial nerve junction."[20]

One of the primary ways sound and music influence consciousness is through entrainment, a process where weaker rhythms lock in phase with more dominant ones. When we hear a bass drum in a parade, our feet automatically tap along. When an infant hears its mother's lullabies, it is lulled into sleep. Heart beat, respiration, and brain-wave rhythms can all be influenced by sound and music through the process of entrainment.

Our brain state is a composite of brain-wave patterns. These patterns are measured in different frequency ranges. Beta brain waves (13–30 cycles per second) predominate when we are alert, awake, rational, and engaged with the outside world. The slower rhythms of alpha brain waves (8–13 cycles per second) are generated when we are relaxed. Even slower theta waves (4–7 cycles per second) show up when we are in a trance state where visual images are seen on the screen of our minds. This is a state of deep meditation, the threshold between the conscious and the unconscious. When we listen to the slow sounds of chanted drones we can reach alpha and theta brain waves, matching their rhythms. In deep sleep, or profound states of meditation, delta brain waves (0.5–4 cycles per second) are predominant.

We move in and out of different states all the time through our daily lives. Driving a car, buying groceries, listening to music, working at a computer, talking to a friend on the phone, or taking a walk all create shifts in our brains. Some experiences seem normal, some unusual. We take for granted the complex shift between dreaming and waking, between watching a movie and driving home afterward. Living in a world of electricity, we are used to the altered state of television and movies and perhaps less familiar with internal visionary states beyond dreaming and daydreaming.

At the Menninger Foundation in Topeka, Kansas, I once took a class on guided visualization and brain waves. Each student was hooked up to an EEG machine. As I looked at the strips of paper showing the electrical activity in my brain during visualization, I saw that beta, alpha, and theta waves were intermingled. Sometimes one would predominate with the others interspersed. As my imagery deepened, more theta waves were generated. Sometimes I was in a theta state with my eyes open, which surprised me since I usually associated this state with closed eyes and dreaming. When I lead toning groups, changes in brain wave are easy to track. With its emphasis on breath and the elongation of vowels sounds, toning is a vocal technique that puts people into altered states of consciousness very quickly. When people first arrive they are in a beta buzz of conversation. As we begin to breathe, first in through the nose and then out through the mouth, the group visibly and audibly comes into an alpha rhythm of relaxation. Some people stay there. Others cross over into theta as we tone longer. When we share afterward, people often describe ribbons of color, choirs of angels, and other such images, some fleeting, some part of a detailed journey. Often we find ourselves in a shared landscape, sometimes inside a cathedral. Once we were amazed to find that, unbeknownst to one another, we had all imagined exploring the ruins of a Mayan pyramid together.

Chanting, drumming, and the shaking of rattles have all been used by shamans as sonic driving mechanisms in early cultures. Anthropologist Michael Harner's research shows how drumming creates changes in the central nervous system, which in turn bring about changes in awareness. The low sounds of the drum, which contain many different sound frequencies, transmit more energy to the brain. The Salish Indians of the American Northwest use drum beats of 4–7 cycles per second, which correspond to theta waves.

## BREATH

Song is fueled by breath. When we breathe we inspire and become alive with spirit, which animates all of life. When we breathe we take in the world around us and mingle it with our blood and every cell of our bodies. The same air I breathe was breathed by the aspens in my backyard, by the flicker who rides the wind, and by the coyotes roaming through the sage. It was breathed by Taos Mountain, by my neighbors on Dry Creek Road, and by the people on Hondo Mesa. During the drought one year, I breathed smoke from the fires in Showlow, Arizona, hundreds of miles away. Weather reports show the jet stream moving from place to place. Is there an emotional jet stream, a spiritual jet stream that we also breathe? If so, we can send songs and prayers out into it and perhaps change the emotional weather forecast of the world around us. Prayer and song are connected with our life's breath. In many cultures breath is equated with spirit, with the great unseen mystery that moves through us all.

The Persian mystic poet Kabir says that God is "the breath inside the breath."[21] My experience has been that, when we breathe in song in a sacred place, we receive the imprint of that space into the architecture of our bodies, where it reverberates and awakens our consciousness to new heights and depths. Perhaps, in turn, God breathes us in like fragrance, needing our particular awareness. Perhaps we are each like a flower being breathed by some giant Spirit bee that buzzes through the air, gathering our prayers like pollen to create sonic honey.

How much more simple can it be? We have ears that listen, lungs that breathe, voices that can sing, bodies that vibrate, brains that respond to sound. We are sound technicians creating ourselves anew with every sound we make.

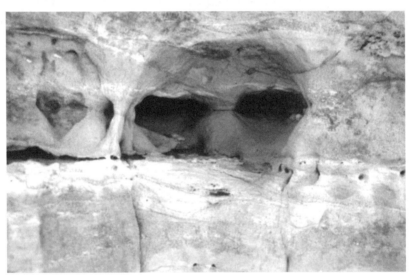

*Sandstone Man cave north of Fort Collins, Colorado*

# ~ *Chapter 3* ~

# CAVES

*It is essential to understand the resonance
of the body and the resonance of the cave.*
—Iegor Reznikoff

As are many people, I have always been fascinated by caves. Before my trip to France, I dreamed about them. In one dream a woman tells me to go to a salmon-colored cave as part of a meditation retreat. I am startled to realize I am inside a throat.

In Les Eyzies, I visited the prehistoric cave of Les Combarelles. I was with a group of tourists and a French-speaking guide whom I could not understand. Etched onto the limestone were pictographs of horses, bison, and even a rhinoceros. Entering this cave I remembered my dream. I longed to sing, but didn't feel it was the right place or time. Sometimes silence is the best song.

Caves are wombs in the earth. In Southwestern Europe alone there are more than two hundred late Stone-Age caves with paintings and bas-relief sculpture. The oldest cave art in Europe dates back thirty thousand years. In Australia cave art is older still, having been created between forty to sixty thousand years ago. Since the 1940 discovery of Lascaux, the French have found an average of one cave a year. It is thought that these caves were never dwelling places but places of ritual. Such rituals were probably not hunting rituals, since the animals painted do not correspond to those that were eaten. We may never know the purpose of these paintings or the rituals enacted; we can only wonder.

"Try to imagine an art gallery," as a *Time* magazine article mused, "that could be entered only by crawling on your belly through a hole in the earth: that ramified into dark tunnels, a fearful maze from the earth's bowels in which the gallery go-er could, at any moment, disturb one of the bears whose claw marks can still be seen on the walls: where the only light came from flickering torches and the bones of animals littered the uneven floor."[1]

Once inside prehistoric caves, we find that they open up into chambers where animals were painted on the walls with charcoal, black manganese, iron oxide, and red, yellow, and brown ocher. This art, aside from that of the decorated body, was the first that we know of; it was an art that extended the human body into the body of the earth itself, an art that could be preserved.

Early artists incorporated the cave's surface to make the animals three dimensional. A prominence in the cave became a swelling in the body of a pregnant mare; another curve became a bison's hump or the haunch of a panther. These images were not painted with brushes but applied by hand, daubed with bits of fur, or sprayed from a bone tube or the mouth itself. According to prehistorian Michel Lorblanchet, director of France's National Center of Scientific Research, this use of the mouth may have had a spiritual dimension: "Spitting is a way of projecting yourself onto a wall, becoming one with the horse you are painting. Thus the action melds with the myth. Perhaps the shamans did this as a way of passing into the world beyond."[2]

Did these early painters sing to the animals after they were painted? There is evidence that sound was an important component in cave art. Although the voice leaves no artifacts, researchers Iegor Reznikoff and Michel Dauvois have found that the images are painted on the most resonant part of the caves. That is, Reznikoff believes that the parts of caves where images are found were chosen specifically for their sound value, confirming that ritualistic chanting was an essential part of cave paintings. These images of such creatures as ibex and auroch were meant, not just to be viewed, but to be experienced and interacted with through rituals that used incantations and rhythm. According to Reznikoff, "There are no societies without songs and chants, and more specifically, there is no rite or celebration which does not use sound, and primarily, recitation and singing."[3] His observation is universally accepted among anthropologists and ethnomusicologists. As Monica Sjöö and Barbara Mor tell us in *The Great Cosmic Mother,* there are traces in Paleolithic cave floors of footprints, "traces of human feet that danced around and around cave paintings...foot marks on the cave floor reveal generations of dancing by all, women, men, children. Dancing to—and with—the spirits of the animals...[is] the most ancient human ceremony that we know."[4]

The three painted caves Reznikoff studied in Southwest France—Niaux, Fontanet, and Le Portel—were highly resonant. He describes them as acoustic pipes with astonishing echo effects. In Le Portel the simple sound vibration "Mmm" produced low sounds that resemble a growl or the lowing of a bison. "This appears comparable to the Inca's acoustic caves, where a jaguar's roar is imitated by amplifying sounds through stone chambers."[5] Other researchers have found that "near the front of the famed Lascaux cave, where the cave art is dominated by horses, bison, and other hoofed animals, a clapping noise gets echoed back and forth among the walks, producing a sound not unlike a stampede."[6]

Jean Clottes, France's foremost paleontologist, has wondered why the hall of the Niaux cave became the main sanctuary: "Is it because it is at the end of a passage, because it is round, because there it has this great echo?"[7] These Paleolithic hunter-gatherers seem to have preferred caves with the best acoustics.

Acoustics engineer Steven Waller and his wife, Pat, lived in France in 1987. Pat, who was studying art history, showed him pictures of cave art and told him no explanation had been found for why early people painted in caves. They went to the mouth of a large cave called Bedeilhac near the Pyrenees Mountains in southern France. Before entering, Pat went back to the car to get a sweater, anticipating that it would be cold inside the cave.

"As I stood there waiting for her," Waller said, "I began to wonder why cavemen would risk their lives to crawl inside caves and paint pictures. I started to try to think like a caveman. Eventually, I realized my wife was taking a long time. When I called out to her, 'Hey, Pat!,' the cave spoke back, '*Hey, Pat.*' The cave's large mouth exaggerated the echo. It occurred to me that if early people heard such an echo they would have no explanation for it. They must have thought spirits were speaking back to them. Suddenly it all came together. In trying to think like a caveman, I had made a paradigm shift.

Waller had read Dauvois and Reznikoff's paper emphasizing that painted images were placed on the cave walls where the resonance was greatest. "They explained this as evidence of ritual and music in the caves." Waller told me. "But at Bedeilhac, as soon as I heard my voice echo, I had the theory that, for the primal mind, echoes were spirits; the pictures that ancient people painted on the rock faces were of what they imagined the echo spirits looked like.

"It wasn't until the fifteenth century that people began to understand acoustics," he went on. "Aristotle talked about air taking on the shape of sound, but the whole phenomenon was still perplexing. Echo as sound reflection is a modern concept. The intuitive approach is to try to forget what you know and experience sound as early people would have done. They must have felt the cave was a place of power where spirits sang along."[8]

One day it may be possible to "replay" the spoken words and songs from the past as they were once voiced in the caves. Acoustics engineer John Reid proposes a hypothetical mechanism based on data storage within the quartz-crystal matrix of rock. His hypothesis assumes the presence of electrostatic charge patterns that are, in effect, encoded sounds that have been recorded in the rock under special environmental conditions. Reid speculates that, when the special conditions are recreated, scientists may be able to decode and replay these patterns using sensitive equipment. Theoretically, the charge patterns may be stored for thousands of years.

Caves are musical in other ways, too. Stalactites and stalagmites are natural xylophones. They sound deep tones when struck and may have been used by the Maya and other ancient people around the world. A friend told me her own story of such an experience at

Cueva de la Pileta, a prehistoric cave in Spain. As the tour group she had joined went through the dark, temple-like cave with only a kerosene lantern, the guide hit each stalagmite and stalactite along the way. The sound resonated through the cave like organ pipes with such intensity that it altered the perceptions of the observers, making the painted animals seem to move. Near one calcite formation was the painting of a mare. "I knew then that mares and music are inseparable," my friend remarked.

## LASCAUX

To visit Lascaux and other nearby caves, I arrive in Les Eyzies and find the old family-run hotel I had booked on a friend's recommendation. A young man at the front desk greets me wearing a dark red shirt and a tie with images of roses. Since I speak only high-school French, I am relieved he speaks English. After checking me in, he leads me to a rose-colored room with roses on the curtains. Surely I am in the right place.

When I ask the young man—whose name is Jerome—how to get to Lascaux on Monday, he replies, "No, Madame, you cannot go to Lascaux on Monday. It is closed on Mondays." I tell him I have an appointment at the cave on Monday at 2:00 p.m. "Madame, it is impossible," Jerome repeats. "The cave is closed on Mondays." He goes on to explain that, although Lascaux is only seven miles from Les Eyzies, no trains or buses go there. "A taxi is the only way, and it would cost over five hundred francs."

After he has told me for the third time that it is impossible for me to go to Lascaux, I realize that he is referring to a reproduction of the cave called Lascaux II, which is indeed closed on Mondays. The *real* cave, on the other hand, has not been open to the public at all since 1963. Over a million tourists had visited it since 1948, bringing with them the green disease of creeping plant growth and the white disease of calcite crystals, caused by carbon monoxide, which threatened the paintings. I had heard, however, that it *was* possible for writers, historians, researchers, and artists to visit the cave through special arrangements. I had written a year in advance and received my appointment for April 15, 1996 at 2:00 in the afternoon—on Monday, only three days away. Finally, I show Jerome my letter in French from the Minister of Culture. "Oh! Oui! C'est formidable!" he exclaims, "You are going to the real cave! I will drive you myself!"

When I offer Jerome the extra pass into the cave I had obtained for someone who was unable to join me, he can hardly contain his excitement. A miniature greyhound underneath the desk begins to bark as he dances around. Jerome was born in this region and has been to every prehistoric cave in the area. It has been his life-long dream to go to Lascaux, but it has been impossible for a young hotel clerk to receive an appointment. I tell him he has an appointment now to accompany me.

At Lascaux on Monday, Jerome and I are in a small group of five. Only five people a week are now allowed entry. Among my group are researchers in early art history from England and Spain. We meet first in a room with a French anthropologist for an hour. There he tells us the seventeen-thousand-year-old history of the paintings and answers our questions. This practice is followed so that when we are the cave itself we can experience it without being weighed down with words. The art historians ask extensive questions about the painting. Jerome sits silently with wide eyes. I ask if there is any speculation that singing has been done in the cave. "No, there are no artifacts." Any music? "Oui, bone flutes and percussive instruments have been found." Does the cave have a natural resonance? "No." May I sing in the cave? "Oui, Madame, but I don't think you'll discover anything."

Finally the questions are over, and we have thirty minutes in Lascaux. We do not have to crawl but are able to walk down into the cave through four different doorways. We enter quickly through each doorway to minimize the entry of outside air. We place our boots in a pan of disinfectant. The moment we are inside, an immediate "Ahhhh" comes from the group. Everything feels primal, yet deeply familiar. Lascaux is not a place of words but of silence, sound, and reverence. The Gallery of Bulls inspires exclamations from each of us. Together, we stand in awe. No more words. No more questions. Only five trembling humans, strangers from different countries and yet now forever linked to this time and place. I stop in front of a bison, taken by his beauty. I breathe in the air of the cave and let it fill me. The cave itself shows me how to sing. I feel the sounds on the roof of my mouth and in the top of my cranium in ways I have never experienced before. I understand something about the human skull in a purely kinesthetic way. As I begin to sing, I feel as if the cave, these animals, and their painters are exchanging information with my breath and voice. When I hear an echo, it seems as if my voice is being reflected back by the bison—no longer just my voice, but the bison's voice, the voice of the cave itself. I want to stay there for hours, for days, but already it is time to go.

As we walk outside, a Spanish woman and I hug with tears of understanding. Jerome takes my hand. We exchange a look of gratitude. The French anthropologist in the group exclaims, "Madame, you made the cave come alive!" I ask if others have sung there. "No one has asked before," he replies. And yet, on that day, we couldn't help but make sound. The "Ohhhs" and "Ahhhs" the group expressed are the beginning of the impulse to sing. The animals of Lascaux were made with breath, as well as touch, long ago. There is music inside the horses and great horned bison. These animals lived inside the creators and were made alive through sound. There is great love here. The cave walls still sing.

*Moss woman in Hoh Rain Forest, Olympic National Park, Washington*

~ *C h a p t e r   4* ~

# EARTH'S BODY

*Nature is like a tuning fork: its space, time, and seasons are marked*
*by an auditory pulse with its variations in echo and penetration,*
*layers of the daily cycles of frog, bird, and insect calls.*
—Paul Shepard

Inside the earth, early humans gave birth to art and heard archaic song-breath resonate through the cave of their mouths against painted cave walls. Outside, the world would have been singing. Everything— every pine tree, oak, and rock—was part of an immense chorus of life. Can you imagine what it would have sounded like without the constant hum of electricity? Without the constant rush of traffic? It is only in the last hundred years that modern technological sounds have enveloped the earth. As Ernest McClain observes, "Assuming that Cro-Magnon man processed sound with the same biology we possess, humans have shared some fifty thousand years of auditory experiences."[1]

But we are far older than fifty thousand years, and music may be older still. In *Origins of the Modern Mind*, Donald Merlin locates music with Homo erectus 1.5 million years ago.[2] Dudley Young, author of *Origins of the Sacred*, believes the impulse to enter into a sacred relationship with the Divine through sound predates humans. It can be heard in gibbons and chimpanzees drumming in the darkness with body rhythms and hooting sounds. "To ponder this stirs us deeply," Young says, "as if a door were opening to allow us back into our first world, something precious. And indeed brief reflection proves this to actually be so: not only do the African Bantu also drum in the darkness, but we can follow the line all the way down, through the Catholic Vespers and Angelus to the Protestant Evensong and 'Taps' on the army bugle, prayers at bedtime to 'protect us from the perils and dangers of this night.' "3

Young believes that, with their drumming and hooting, these primates are not simply warding off predators. "What they are addressing, as they lie in their nests, is above all, darkness descending."4 He believes their sounds to be a way of relieving anxiety by becoming a united voice that expands the individual into a community. Indeed, he wonders if the primates' behavior might be showing us the origin of prayer.

For the ancients, ritual, song, and prayer were inseparable and necessary for survival. Among Australian Aborigines, the oldest living culture on earth, "the definition of a knowledgeable person is the person knowing many songs."5 Canyons, caves, and rock amphitheaters were sought out and sanctified for the purpose of amplifying prayers. Later, sacred architecture was created to house our song-prayers so that Spirit could hear us and reverberate us into stillness—into a living silence where we could listen more closely to the pulse of life.

As Homo sapiens we emerged between 195,000 and 200,000 years ago in the Pleistocene era. Author Paul Shepard believes we are still fundamentally hunter-gatherers who need fire circles, song, and a simpler way of relating to the earth and to each other. Perhaps our shopping malls have made us into shopper-gatherers. Instead of gathering around the fire circle to tell stories and sing, we gather around the fire within the TV set to see flickering pictures move through space.

Not only are we very old as a species, we are also all related. A team of biochemists in Berkeley, California conducted research on the mitochondria within DNA. They reached the conclusion that we can all trace our ancestry "back to a single woman who lived in Africa 200,000 years ago."6 While this date and place are controversial, it is believed that as a species we are very ancient and share a common ancestry.

What did this first Eve hear in her landscape? Here in my New Mexico home, I hear a rooster crow. When I step outside, I hear a grasshopper flit through the autumn grass. The wind rustles through a small grove of aspens, a magpie caws, and a flying crow's wings sound like scissors cutting through cloth. These sounds delight and refresh me, giving me a break from writing the words I hear in my head. But the only sounds linked to my immediate, twenty-first-century survival are the electric hum of the refrigerator, the water running through the pipes, and a clock telling me the time so that I can make my next appointment, which will earn money to pay for the food in my refrigerator. While the sounds of wind and birds are pleasant, they are not part of what I need to stay alive in the modern world.

In Eve's world, things were different. As early humans, we were tuned to the world around us. Our hearing was sensitized to the slightest sound, and we depended on our auditory acuity to help us eat and not be eaten. Hunters were attuned to the sounds of the forest. Knowing bird cries, mating calls, and other natural sounds was necessary for survival. And we did not just listen to the sounds of the earth but mimicked them as well.

One of the things that separate us from the animals we hunted is our use of language. It is speculated that our cousins, the Neanderthals, failed to survive because their vocal tracts did not allow for fully human speech. Neanderthals, like other primates, may have communicated only through vowels. To communicate through vowels alone is to communicate affective but not cognitive experience. Vowels ride on the breath stream. They are perhaps the oldest units of speech. They convey pleasure and pain and express our emotions. But, to be articulate, we need consonants. Through the action of the jaw and tongue, consonants form gates that separate and give definition to vowels, allowing us to create words for our elaborate symbolic thinking. Consonants are what enable us to think in prose. Early speech, on the other hand, was more akin to song.

In order to survive, we had to understand the sounds, movements, smells, tracks, and habits of the animals we ate. And to further insure that we would be successful, we made magic: We invoked, honored, and participated in the animals' mystery through song. Hunting magic is song magic. Amazon people reflect the jungle in their language, which blends animal sounds, "whispers, shouts, whistles, and screams of nature."[7] In the Sharanhua tribe of South America, the women sing the hunters to the hunt. The Amahuaca Indians of Amazon rain forests accompany their hunting by chanting to the forest spirits. The Koyukon Indians of northwestern Alaska believe that caribou "'sing through' human beings when in their vicinity, granting…songs that certain people remember upon waking from sleep. When those persons sing these songs later, their success in finding and hunting caribou is ensured."[8]

## THE SINGING LANDSCAPE

In Eve's time, a sympathetic resonance existed between the human and the natural worlds. We not only sang to animals, we sang to plants, trees, and the land itself. The same is still true of indigenous cultures today. For the Temiar people of the Malay Peninsula, Paul Shepard tells us that the rain forest is "a reflection of social relationship mediated by song."[9] Everything, including the fruits and flowers, is perceived as an essence that can be sung.

Each place on earth has its own song and rhythm defined by the features of the land: lakes, mountains, valleys, hills, rivers, ocean. The red sandstone cliffs in New Mexico sound different from the granite mountains of the Cascade Range. The musical score of a rain forest is different from that of an oak grove. Taos Mountain, where I live now, sends out a different pulse from Sandia Mountain, where I used to live.

Moreover, the places where we live tune us. The sounds of a magpie affect me in a different way than those of a chickadee do. The returning frogs and migrating birds provide not just background; they are tuning the world and the humans in it as well. Martin Prectel, a Native American from Santo Domingo Pueblo who later became a Mayan shaman, says that for the Mayan people "the sounds of birds and bugs had different powers over weathers and destinies. The belief was that the seasons didn't bring the birds, but rather the birds' language of magic sounds brought about seasonal changes in temperature and moisture."[10] Rudolf Steiner also believed that the spring song of birds was the necessary element to bring the plants into bloom. Brooke Medicine Eagle calls this a "sonic bloom."[11] She says it helps to open the stamen of the plant to receive more nutrients. She says even recorded bird song played to plants makes them healthier.

The Aborigines believe that the world was formed in the Dreamtime—that mythic, original time at the beginning of creation—by mythic ancestors who laid down a series of "songlines" between places where the earth emanates magnetic currents. The Aboriginal people sing and dance the legends of their creation story daily. They see features of the landscape as songlines that, when sung, will lead to sources of food, water, and shelter. Through an intimate knowledge of both legend and the song of the land, it is possible to survive.

Listening to each season, one can begin to hear its song. Here in Taos, there is the steady drone of the mountain, the deep bass of the basalt river gorge, the shifting improvisation of bird song, grasshoppers, crickets, frogs, and coyotes who sing with the whistling wind and the rustle of aspen leaves.

Once upon a time, people believed in devas, fairies, elves, and gnomes—elemental natural forces that can still sometimes be seen with "second sight." These beings are not just inhabitants of a child's fairy tale but part of a living tradition for native peoples. Tibetan Buddhists, Japanese Shinto priests, and Celtic pagans all share the belief in such forces. Even Islam and Christianity speak of angels and devils. Until just one hundred years ago, the fairy faith was alive throughout the British Isles, as documented by W. Y. Evans-Wentz at the turn of the century. He spoke to priests, peasants, city-dwellers, the educated and the uneducated, and young and old alike. After hearing their stories he wrote that, for these people, "fairyland actually exists as an invisible world in which the visible world is immersed like an island in an unexplored ocean."[12] Oral tradition has kept these stories alive but, for the most part, they have faded into the background as children's tales.

Fortunately, I was able to meet the late Kip Davidson, a fourth-generation Scottish seer who lived nearby me in Ojo Caliente, New Mexico. Kip saw and heard nature spirits. He heard the song of spring sap rising within trees. He sang to the parched air in a drought and made it rain right over his head. The water spirits told him that the people of New Mexico were misusing water; their forgetting to honor it was the reason for the drought. Sometimes he spoke to rock spirits or to a tree spirit in the forest. He spoke to the air elementals of the wind and to the water devas of streams. He told me there are shamanic honoring songs we may receive when we listen to nature.

Kip taught me a way of introducing myself to the nature spirits by singing one's inner credentials. This technique came from his training as the apprentice of Maria Sabina, a Mexican visionary and shaman whose practices stem from pre-Columbian times. He told me Maria introduces herself to the spirits of nature through chanting. Alvaro Estrada, in a book about Maria's life, shares her ritual approach to nature:

> I am a woman wise in medicine...
> I am a woman wise in herbs...
> I am a hummingbird woman...
> I am a woman with vibrant wings...[13]

The point, Kip said, is for each person to express this litany is in the terms of whatever has been deeply lived, whatever has become part of the fabric of one's being. A flower gardener, for example, might sing: "I am flower woman...I am rose-tending woman...I am blossom woman...I am water-bringing woman." Kip explained that the nature kingdom needs to know who is speaking. Singing is part of proclaiming yourself as human. Kip reminded me of the sacred trust we have with nature. He said that part of our job as humans is to be stewards of the earth, to consecrate it with our love and song.

## TREES

Trees, with their roots in the earth and branches reaching to the sky, were revered by ancient people. Sacred groves of trees were worshipped by druids. Oaks, yews, bristlecone pine, and giant redwoods are among some of the oldest trees on the planet. In *Cathedrals of the Spirit*, T. C. McLuhan says that each grove of redwood trees is "part of an unbroken gene flow originating millions of years ago. Each mature tree is a living history over 2,000 years old. These are very old churches."[14]

Each forest, depending on its genus, has its own keynote. The clarity of reverberation heard in the shaded aisles of evergreens, for instance, became inspiration for the construction of Gothic cathedrals.[15] On one trip to Britain, I drove through the Savernake Forest of ancient oak and beech trees. Some of them are over a thousand years old. Their arching branches reminded me of the cloisters at Gloucester Cathedral and the pillars and fan vaulting of other English cathedrals I had visited.

In Greece the oaks of Dodona were an oracle sacred to Zeus. Thunderstorms were common in this region. "The oracle spoke through the creaking of the boughs, the rustling of the leaves, and the humming of bronze gongs suspended from the trees, accompanied by the cooing of doves and the purling of the sacred spring."[16]

In the Amazon, in a rainforest at sunrise, singer Silvia Nakkach felt trees and plants enclosing her like a temple. "The roof, ground, and walls were made of plants. I was there between twilight and dawn. There was so much sound—and then complete silence. It was foggy and wet. I heard something I couldn't identify and realized it was the sound of the plants breathing."[17]

Author Robin Easton heard the primal voices of other forests. For eight years she lived in Australia, near both the tropical rainforests of Queensland and the subtropical rainforests of New South Wales. She went into the forest every day, at first to cry out her grief about her domestication. She hungered to shed her social conditioning, to heal from its effects, and to take back her true nature.

Initially, she felt afraid and angry because the one place she could go to be alone was also home to deadly snakes, spiders, and leeches. But then she realized that, in order to survive, she needed to shift her way of thinking. It seemed that the earth said to her, "Either get to know me or leave." It reminded her that it was the same earth where her mother lived in Maine.

Over time, Robin extended her cries into guttural wails. She began making sounds she didn't recognize as human, and these primitive utterances eventually led her into the song of the land. She heard her sounds echo off the trees. She felt acknowledged and reflected; she felt the earth as a mother compassionately listening to her daughter.

One day, as Robin sang, she sensed the vibration of the green world becoming part of her. Everything was orbiting with sound. Suddenly, she felt safer here than anywhere on earth. She looked a poisonous snake in the eye and became the snake. She watched ants dragging off a bandicoot, saw a python go after a bush lark, and watched the lark give its life to protect its nest. She saw that the life force is so in love with itself that it consumes itself to create more love. She heard the dream voice of a tree sing to her. She felt the trees as protrusions of the earth, their arms in exaltation worshiping the heavens. Each tree with a different sound, the forest was a full-bodied choir of angels reaching out to the stars to pull their song into the earth.

Many years ago I lived in Sandia Park, New Mexico, next to the Cibola National Forest of piñon, pine, cedar, and alligator juniper trees. One of the junipers was eight hundred years old. I called her Grandma. Looking up into her branches was like looking at the swirls of a Van Gogh painting. Part of Grandma was bare, but part of her was alive with juniper boughs. Some of her limbs were smooth, some covered by square gray chinks—her alligator scales. Her trunk was big enough for two people to join hands around. She was home to ants, beetles, horn toads, squirrels, red foxes, owls, chickadees, flickers, scrub jays, mourning doves, and red-tailed hawks. One bird, which I never identified by sight, sang only in the evenings, just at the moment the pines released their fragrance into the air. This bird made a sound like a tiny golden halo ringing out and circling the sky. Grandma was the matriarch of the forest. She was a steady presence in my life for eight years, an old crone the same age as Chartres Cathedral and the Great Kiva in Aztec, New Mexico. She sang a constant drone while the birds sang harmonies over her bass line. At night coyotes joined in the chorus.

Visiting Grandma was like going to church. I sang into the crevices of her bark and offered cornmeal. I heard Grandma sing through the throats of the flowery Indian paintbrush that grew under her skirts. When I moved from Sandia Park to Arroyo Seco, saying goodbye to Grandma was hard. I stood under her with my feet bare. Asking if she had a message, I saw a shining being, like light on pine needles. This being was cloaked in green. She asked me to sing, to be a messenger, to speak of my love of the forest. In my vision, she placed a wreath of pine cones and wildflowers on my head. Afterward, when I opened my eyes, I looked down and saw at my feet a heart-shaped rock.

Years later in Kent, England, near Canterbury, I led a tour for a group of voice students from the British school Tonalis: Centre for the Development of Music. We went to a forgotten Neolithic earth mound in the forest. Eleven students—from Israel, Denmark, the Black Forest in Germany, New Zealand, Ireland, and all over England—and I walked through a field of mayflowers to the edge of a forest. Here we stopped and chanted before we crossed the threshold onto an overgrown trail deep in the leafy woods. We passed red-tinged mushrooms, sending our song into the earth through our feet. We approached the first part of a circular ring that was once the boundary of a village. The mound was not very high and was covered by centuries of growth. I had heard that this part of England had seen so many invasions that local sacred sites had almost entirely been wiped from memory.

As a group we stood quietly in a circle, offering our ears to the listening space. We heard waves of wind, cooing doves, the piercing cry of a hawk, the silence of the moss-carpeted earth. We sat. I asked the group to place their hands on the ground and silently introduce themselves and their intention for being there. Then the toning of the green leaves rose up from our voices as if we were giving a forgotten village a voice. With the birds above us, we sang from the longing, pain, and love in our hearts, remembering the forgotten places inside us with rolling sounds gently soaring into flight. Feeling a space open in the center, I saw a shaft of green light and a lady clothed in soft green absorbing our sounds. She reminded me of the deva in the forest near Grandma. I heard the word, "Remember," and sang it over and over again. Gradually, the group's tones faded. I passed the heart-shaped rock from Grandma's forest around the circle and asked each person to respond to the phrases, "I heard the earth and she said…"; "I link this place to…"; "I send healing to…"

Our voices mingled: "I heard the earth and she said, 'Remember.'" "I heard the earth and she said, 'I support you,'" or "'Thank you for your song,'" or "'I've been wounded but I'm healing.'" "I link this place to Taos Mountain," or "to the forests in Israel where people are afraid to walk," or "to my garden."

"I heard the earth and she said, 'I will feed you.'" "I link this place to Northern Ireland." "I send healing to my mother," or "to the animals," or "to the children," or "to my family." "I link this place to the Black Forest," or "to the holy wells of Britain," or "to the waters of the world."

"I heard the earth and she said, 'Feel me beneath you.'" "I send this healing to Aboriginal people," or "to the Maoris," or "to my husband." "I link this place with the songlines," or "with my back yard." "I heard the earth and she said,"

*Join me.*

*Singing rock faces, between Gunnison and Saguache, Colorado*

# Mountains

*Investigate mountains thoroughly.*
—Zen Master Dogen (1200–1253)

Before architecture, there were mountains. They reach deep into the ground and far into the sky. They are the meeting place between heaven and earth. Mountains have always been objects of awe and veneration. Like trees they have roots; like birds they have wings; they disappear into the air.

An hour and a half from where I live are the mountains and mesas at Ghost Ranch, the site of one of the richest quarries of the Triassic era that began 220 million years ago. Near Ghost Ranch is the Pedernal, the mesa that artist Georgia O'Keefe painted over and over again in the hope that, if she painted it often enough, God would give it to her. Some of her ashes have been scattered there, and she has become what she loved.

At home, a bowl of mountains surrounds me. To the east is Taos Mountain, one of the seven sacred mountains of the world, according to the Tibetans who have lined the spine of the Sangre de Cristos with stupas, which are mountain-shaped shrines. Taos Mountain is still a place of ceremony, with rituals taking place there that have been conducted for over a thousand years. Non-natives are not allowed on the mountain, and I take comfort in knowing that the mountain spirit is still honored.

Near Taos Mountain are Lobo Peak, El Salto, and Gallina, snow-capped with late October snow. In back of them, but out of view, is

Mount Wheeler, the highest mountain in the state at 13,161 feet. To the south is Truchas Peak, named after the trout that swim in its rivers. To the west are the Jemez Mountains, born from volcanoes. Following the western rim of the circle is *Tres Orejas*, Spanish for "Three Ears." To the northwest is Antonito Peak, a space ship-shaped mound that has become a landmark when I journey into Colorado. To the north, and also out of view, is Lama Mountain, whose trees are still bare from a fire several years ago. Going further north toward Colorado, you can see Mount Blanca, or *Tsisnaajini*, one of the four sacred mountains of the Dineh or Navajo people. All these mountains are part of a vast geography of sacred space. For the Navajo, First Man and First Woman formed the sacred mountains from earth that they brought in a medicine bundle from the mountains of the Third World.

Living in this circle of mountains, I can sometimes hear them sing to one another across the distance. I wonder if the rim of them can be rung like that of a gigantic Tibetan bowl. Singer and sound healer Ani Williams remarks about others who have similar experiences: "At Ringing Rock in California and the *Penal Bernal* (Singing Mountain) in Mexico, the neighboring indigenous people tell of hearing the songs of the earth there.... [They say] that these songs are communicating with all the other stones and hills in the area."[1]

Once, on a high vista coming back from Los Alamos, I saw the scalloped music of the *Sangre de Cristos*, the Blood of Christ, stretched before me like a giant snake. To the south I saw where I used to live near Sandia Mountain, *Oku Pin*, or "Turtle Mountain," as the Tewa call her. The mountain is like an ancient grandmother. Her skin as wrinkled as rocks, her hair as white as the clouds, she sings an old deep song. To the north was Taos Mountain, where I live now. Here the mountain sings loudly; it emits a strong frequency that sometimes makes me long for the flatlands of Kansas. This serpent of mountains rides all the way into Colorado. What I saw was the end of her long tail.

Investigate mountains thoroughly, advises the Zen Master. To investigate a mountain means to encircle it, to walk its trails and climb to its summit, to gaze upon it, to sit on its boulders, to take it within, to sing inside the very mountain itself. I believe the overtone chanting made by Tibetan monks sounds the way it does because they live among the highest mountains on earth. Writing about the Gyoto Monks, Andrew Schelling says, "The notes sound as though they come from granite, from the windswept rock on high mountain passes. Nothing in Western music comes close to these mineral tones."[2]

For the Tibetans, the Dineh, and the Taos Indians, mountains are alive. They are the homes of Holy Beings. In California, the Miwok Indians believe that Mount Tamalpais is a sleeping princess whose body is traced by a long, curving line.

In Tibet, Mount Kailas is the abode of *Chakrasamvara,* a Buddhist tutelary deity.

Sometimes it is the surrounding land that forms the body of the deity. Navajo Mountain, the highest point on the Dineh reservation, forms the head of the earth goddess, *Nahasdzaa.* Black Mesa is her body and Balaki Mesa forms her legs. Walking anywhere in this region, one is walking upon the body of Earth Woman, she who is the beauty of all things.

Voice is one way to create a relationship to mountains and the hidden gods and goddesses who make their home there. Anthropologist Joan Halifax believes that the way to realize "fully the true nature of a place is to talk its language and hold its silence."[3] To know a mountain is to know its songs—not only its lava and granite tones, but the song of the wild rose. It is to speak the language of pine and hear the sonnet of a river, to echo the tongue of the hawk and join the chorus of hummingbirds, to praise the clouds that touch the earth as rain. All these are mountain and belong to mountain. All these are human and belong to human, to the humus from which we are born.

The musical score of nature is written in the veins of leaves, the texture of a ponderosa's bark, the granite grain of rocks, the intricate design of a monarch's wings. Nature is a living scroll, continuously changing and revealing itself. Its patterns are like notes on a page revealing the music within. One can know the song of a mountain by patient listening and by a synesthesia of translating sight into sound, form into sung essence.

As Joan Halifax tells us, "The Dineh understand that all beings, be they star or stone, are solidified vibration. . . . To connect with the medicine, or power, of lightning or star, one must sound them." The Mountain Chant singer knows the language of mountains and "is a specialist who through knowledge of evocative language has access to the natural world."[4]

## STONES: THE BONES OF THE EARTH

We find stones upon mountains, some as big as boulders, others as small as pebbles to hold in the whirl of our palms. As are mountains, stones are venerated by indigenous peoples as the place of the indwelling spirit. They rise from the earth or fall from heaven as meteorites. "In Nigeria," Iegor Reznikoff tells us, "rocks are literally described as dead or alive, according to whether or not they have a voice."[5]

Stones endure. They have been here before we were born and they will be here after we die. Monuments are made of stone to represent eternity. Our ancestors gazed upon the same mountains we gaze upon. Perhaps they held the same stones in their hands.

Both ancient and modern people make pilgrimages to special stones. Each year thousands visit the Oracle of Delphi in Greece— the omphalos or navel stone, which represents a center of the universe. Muslims make the Hajj to Mecca to the Kaba, a sacred shrine that contains a magnetic stone, a black meteorite that fell from the heavens.

Stones contain primordial silence and song. Wallace Black Elk, a Lakota medicine man, learned from the Great Spirit how to find rocks that contain special paints inside. "I learned their songs, but there are many songs out there. There are countless songs. Like the fire . . . has a song. That fire shapes and forms all life, and each shape has a song. And the rocks, the rocks have songs, like the rock I wear around my neck.... All the stones that are around here each have a language of its own."[6]

Stones, sacred in themselves, have been used to create medicine wheels, stone circles, cathedrals, burial chambers, and figures in the landscape. Each type of stone has its own acoustic property. Granite is the most resonant because of its hardness, high percentage of quartz crystal, and ability to retain moisture. As the water content increases, so does the ability to reflect high-frequency sounds.

Granite can also be sculpted into different shapes and "tuned." In Egypt, obelisks, statuary, and the sarcophagus in the King's Chamber of the Great Pyramid are examples of carved granite that sing. In Luxor, one obelisk stands while its nearby companion has fallen. Egyptologist John Anthony West says you can strike the fallen one to hear that it "resonates like a tuning fork with the slightest blow."[7] He believes that obelisks were placed at the entrance of temples to attune "to the 'pitch' of that particular sacred site."[8] Unfortunately, no two pairs of the original obelisks are still in place.

## PAINTED ROCKS

Early peoples carved and painted on stones in Africa; Australia; North, Central, and South America; and throughout Europe and Asia. In Australia there are ten thousand sites with rock images in the Northern Territory in the Arnhem Land Plateau alone. In Tanzania, Mary Leakey discovered paintings in the cliffs twenty-nine thousand years old. She saw groups of dancing women with musical instruments: "A tall red-ochre piper plays with dashed lines falling from the end of her pipe. A singer's open mouth has the same lines falling from it."[9]

Iegor Reznikoff, who studied cave paintings, also studied prehistoric painted rocks in and around three lakes in Helsinki and in the area of Mikkeli, Finland. The rocks, painted with reindeer, elk, fish, hand prints, and geometric designs, were created between 3500 and

2000 BC. Using a powerful, open-air vocal technique, he achieved three or four echoes at each site and concluded that the rocks with images were at locations that produced sound. As he puts it, "We now have a knowledge of how rich, for the prehistoric tribes, were the relations between sound, caves, space, lakes, rocks, and paintings, and how deep and living sound was for them."[10]

Echoes from rock images have also been found in France at Angles-sur-l'Anglin, the Rock Shelter of the Sorcerers, Vallon des Roches, the Vallee de la Grande Beune at Laussel, Commarque, Cap Blanc, and the Orielle d'Enfer. North America also has petroglyph sites where echoes are strong, such as at the Great Gallery in Utah. Acoustician Steven Waller, who goes in search of echoes there and throughout the world, finds that "echoed sound appears to emerge from within the rock, as if coming through the rock surface that seems to act like a permeable veil."[11] Like Alice peering through the looking glass, supernatural beings seem to peer back at him as he gazes at the rocks. He believes that the images of petroglyphs are depictions of these beings "calling out from behind the rock surface."[12] They are visionary pictures of what the people saw when they heard the mystery of the echoes.

"I now listen for echoes whenever I am in caves or at petroglyph sites," he told me, "I love putting myself into the mind-set of early people. I have begun to collect myths from all over the world and have found that they are all very similar." Gertrude Jobes talks of a South Pacific myth claiming that "echo, as the bodiless voice, is the earliest of all existence."[13]

One of Steven's favorite myths is from the Tsimshian tribe about Chief Echo. In the myth, a man wandered into a house and heard many people singing, but he couldn't see them. The house, with a carved front like the side of a cliff, belonged to Chief Echo. "This story is consistent with those of going into the world of rock spirits who live behind the rock," Steven told me. "It may have reflected the belief that echoes were the voices of spirits."

"When I go to petroglyph sites I experiment with sound," he said. "I drum and am drawn into the drumming's hypnotic power. Sometimes when I play my flute, I can hear the notes more clearly because of the echo. Once I sang 'Amen,' but it seemed out of place. Now I make wordless sounds as a natural response to the environment."

## Petroglyph National Monument

From the place of emergence, Masewa, son of the sun, leader of the Acoma tribe, searches for a place called Aako that will be the new home for his people. He wanders, calling loudly, "Aaaakooo!" Sometimes there is no answer. Sometimes a faint voice replies, "*Aaaakooo*," and then the tribe stays to speak to the summoned spirit before moving on. "Aaaakooo!" Masewa calls as they wander. At last, a voice resounds, "*Aaaakooo!*" echoing his own with perfect clarity. On the strength of that echo, Masewa declares the spot his people's new home: "This is Acoma. Aako."

Hence the myth of how the Acoma people found their true home on earth. "Acoma" is both the name of the people and of their pueblo, the multi-storied adobe dwelling place of the village.

Near Sandia Mountain, on the eastern edge of the Acoma pueblo's original territory, in a place now named for a Spanish duke, sits Albuquerque's Petroglyph National Monument on the sprawling west mesa. Not only the Acoma but twenty-three other tribes have affiliation with the monument, including the Hopi of Arizona. Over twenty thousand images, some as old as three thousand years, are carved on black volcanic rocks, including four-pointed stars, birds, frogs, deer, and even crosses of the Spanish conquistadors. The petroglyphs are part of an intricate pattern weaving star alignments, sun and moon cycles, religious myths, and migration stories—an entire sacred library. This is a place of unexpected echoes because Petroglyph National Monument has no tall cliff faces but is rather a series of escarpments with boulders scattered like grazing sheep on the sandy dunes.

In support of Steven Waller's thesis that the petroglyphs were deliberately carved in relation to acoustics, he found that the highly decorated surfaces in Rinconada Canyon, in Boca Negra Canyon, at a location off of Staghorn Drive, and at four separate locations in Piedras Marcadas Canyon all yielded strong echoes.[14] Moreover, the only two locations in Piedras Marcadas Canyon where no petroglyphs do appear *have* no echoes.

The boulders in the park are composed of basalt. John Reid states that few rocks exhibit more musicality than does this substance. When struck with a hard object or another piece of basalt, small, linear pieces sound like a glockenspiel (a percussion instrument similar to a xylophone but smaller and higher in pitch), offering a single high-frequency tone of great purity. The smooth surfaces of large basalt boulders are also excellent reflectors of sound, far better than most rocks, which invariably have rough surfaces that scatter the sound rather than reflect them intact.

Steven urges us to conserve, not only the park itself, but the acoustic environment as well. Petroglyph National Park is threatened by a proposed road that will cut through it to create an infrastructure for more development under the guise that it will ease traffic congestion on the growing west mesa. With increased growth comes increased noise, and the voices of the rock spirits may be lost. A pueblo elder, in opposition to the road, says "Each of these rocks is alive, keeper of a message left by the ancestors.... There are spirits, guardians; there is medicine..."[15]

## HEARING STONES SPEAK

To understand the language of stones, to hear them speak, one needs to remember a different way of knowing. While teaching a week-long workshop at Ghost Ranch—the Triassic-era quarry that is now an educational retreat center in New Mexico—I asked students to find a rock that spoke to them. They were to hold this rock, listen to the music inside the stone, and sing along with it. Some could not make this leap. One woman looked at me as if I were crazy and said, "I have a hard time believing this rock is really alive."

Philosopher and cultural historian Thomas Berry and other ecological thinkers have noted that modern humanity has forgotten how to communicate with other forms of life. We have long since lost a sense of kinship with anything other than our own kind. It is not surprising, then, that the woman in my workshop did not feel a kinship with stones. But later in the week, after a hike to Box Canyon and time alone in the salmon-colored sandstone mesas, she understood. She began to feel a pulse inside her stone. She had created a relationship to the rock in her hand and found her own response. She sang with her rock and to the rock beings she saw in the mesas along the trail. It had only taken a week for her to remember that hers, too, was a voice of the earth. At the closing ritual at Echo Amphitheater north of Ghost Ranch, we sent our names, intentions, and sounds out into its mouth for them to be echoed into the world.

Years later, I returned to the amphitheater with photographer and architect Georgemarc Schevené. We had first met in a gallery in the tiny town of Paonia, Colorado in 1993. He had pulled a black portfolio from underneath a counter and said, "I want to show you something." His portfolio was full of cobalt blue-and-white photographs of the world within stone. In the photos I saw rock devas, guardians, holograms, star-streaked shamans, totems carved in time, ceremonial chambers, a chalice of light, and doorways into the secrets within stones. "I know how to sing these," I said, surprising even myself. I breathed in not only the images I saw but the voices I heard: voices of water and granite; the sound of starlight etched onto rock face; echoes of ocean; psalms of shadow and light. I followed the blueprint of the stones and traced them in the air with my voice. After a moment of silence Georgemarc said, "I've been waiting for you."

Over time, the stones have led Georgemarc and me to many places. We created a ritual performance called "Allegorian Chants" and took it to Colorado, Arizona, and New Mexico. The photos were projected onto white silk. I sang and read poetry in back of the silk. One member of the audience said, "I became part of the art. It evoked the deepest place in me. I had an ageless response. It was like being born a billion years ago, going within stone to the deepest void for discovery."

## ECHO AMPHITHEATRE

Now Georgemarc and I are on another adventure. When we arrive at Echo Amphitheater, wet sheets of rain fall over the rocks, coaxing the rock people out of their hiding places. There they are—a large-breasted, skirted woman, a face with a juniper nose—wise, patient stone faces looking at these two people standing under a tin-roofed shelter in the middle of a rainstorm. The canyon echoes the thunder. Lightning flashes around us.

One at a time the rock people come out, curiously staring back, or like a shy violet, appear briefly before disappearing as the light changes. Some wink at us. Some stand silent. Some have rain and thunder voices. Some echo the white-breasted swift that darts in and out of crevices. Each has a million-year-old story to tell. And yet they also seem to ask, "What do you know? What have you seen? Tell us what's happening down the road."

Song is the only language I know with which to speak to these beings. Sometimes I offer to them:

> Amazing grace...*grace*
> How sweet the sound...*the sound*

And so the rock faces sing back with me as I teach them this two-hundred-year-old human song. This is what we do as humans. We put our thoughts and feelings into words. And sometimes the words are true and lasting. We sing during times of awe and reverence, in places like this when regular speech fails and we remember a familiar song that expresses what we can't say with words.

Sometimes I offer my voice as a reflector of the beauty around me and of what I sense is here: the surface, color, texture, and individual grains that make up whole rocks; the molecules that dance inside still surfaces; the space and light breathed by stones. I hear these sounds and echo them back, so that the rocks can hear themselves, so that I can say, "I hear you. You are beautiful."

Perhaps the rocks don't hear me in this human way. Humans have always anthropomorphized the natural world as a way to try to understand something that the logical mind can never truly comprehend. Rocks don't have ears to hear my offering. But something is given and something received: breath, song, love, vision.

We need each other. humans and stones, children and canyons, men and caves, women and forests, lovers and stars. We are all together in nature's circle, part of the same dance. And if we stay a little longer in the rain, extend our breath a little longer in song, maybe something in our human nature will be stirred, and some ancient way of knowing will be remembered. Perhaps it will be Mother Nature assuring us that we are not alone, that there are rock people waiting to peak around a boulder to say, "Hello."

*Newgrange, Neolithic Monument, County Meath, Ireland*

~ *C h a p t e r  6* ~

# SINGING TOMBS

*The early builders desired to construct a living image of the timeless realm
of the cosmic womb. Thus, architecture, the mother of the arts was born.*
—Miriam and José Arguelles

"Biology is not destiny," write Monica Sjöö and Barbara Mor, "but, like the sea, it is a beginning. The mysteries of female biology dominated religious and artistic thought, as well as social organization, for at least the first 200,000 years of human life on earth."[1]

Neanderthals not only buried their dead, they arranged them carefully in a fetal position. They painted the bodies and bones of the deceased with red ochre, the color of blood, and tossed wildflowers over the grave. The dead body was like a seed taking root to sprout into new life.

In France, at La Ferrassie, a Neanderthal child was found buried in a rock shelter. Over the grave was a stone slab. On the underside, facing the child, were small cup shapes in pairs, possibly symbolizing the mother's breasts.

Tombs were the first architecture. Some were marked by stones carved with what may be vulva symbols. Many had central passageways—birth canals, where a new birth could take place. Was singing done at the burials of early humans?

We know the sounds that accompany birth pangs and attend death today. In ancient Ireland, keeners gave voice at funerals in high, song-like wails to open the doorway of grief. These feelings are universal, biological. The living are torn from the dead in an intensely

59

visceral way. Song is born out of such depths and mysteries—not *lyrical* song as we recognize it but song comprised of sound wrenched from the heart and gut. Sound itself is mysterious, belonging to an invisible realm. It both surrounds and envelops, burrowing inside, evoking many emotions. Sound is atmospheric, creating moods and impressions imbued with magical qualities.

For indigenous peoples today, song is the primary expression of grief at funerals. In New Guinea, Kaluli women weep songs over the dead. In Nevada, the Pauites hold Cry Dances, wailing their grief through song as they dance, holding strips of the clothes the dead person had worn in life.

In Western culture, on the other hand, the intensity of sung grief has been muffled in the process of sanitizing death and removing it from the experience of everyday life. The hymns and popular songs sung at funerals, while comforting, often sentimentalize grief rather than provide a catalyst for joining in the wail. Death confronted early humans in a much more primal way: blood, bone, flesh, rot, stench, fire, ash. Surely their sounds reflected their more intimate experience.

Where do we go when we die? The world's religions are organized around this question, filled with angst and mystery. Christian theology gives one answer, Buddhism another. Early humans must have wondered as well. Perhaps they built the first architecture not only as tombs but also in an attempt to find out where the dead had gone. Perhaps graves were built like stone megaphones, where amplified voices were sent into unseen realms as a way of calling into the darkness to discover what is on the other side.

## VISIONS IN A SCOTTISH CAIRN

Frank MacEowen in *The Mist-Filled Path* describes his experience in a Neolithic burial cairn in the Kilmartin Valley of Scotland. He had entered the cairn in search of a vision. This was a common practice among the Celts of antiquity, when an apprentice poet would spend the night in underground chambers to receive poetic inspiration.

It was a cold night, and MacEowen hummed quietly to himself inside the damp chamber. After a while, he noticed that his chest was resonating, due to the natural resonance of the cairn. The cairn seemed to be humming, too. Then he heard a deeper sound that seemed to have its own source. He later realized that the sound was coming from him, but he felt as if it were connected to something greater. MacEowen states that he was "performing a very powerful kind of throat singing or chant, *sgornan amhranin* in the Gaelic. I was singing like thunder . . . sounds emanated from the stars, from deep within the earth, and activated within me, yet again deeper and deeper tones."[2] He saw a spiral of four spokes made of stars in the form of the Bride's Cross, the ancient symbol of Ireland. "As I absorbed this vision," MacEowen says, "I could ascertain a low drone or humming sound beginning to vibrate again from within the cairn of stars. I knew this to be the Great Song of the Universe."[3]

John Reid considers McEowen's experience significant because of a discovery Reid made in 2001. He found that the sound patterns of many ancient musical instruments closely resemble the iconography of the indigenous cultures with whom the instruments originated. When a didgeridoo was played into his CymaScope, for instance, patterns like Aboriginal artwork appeared on the membrane. Similarly, a Tibetan horn produced a pattern like a Tibetan mandala. Reid suggests that ancient priests may have sensed the sound patterns subliminally, thus influencing the art work of their cultures. Commenting on McEowen's experience, Reid said that many sound patterns feature radial spokes that resemble Ireland's ancient Bride's Cross.

## Acoustic Archaeology

In the 1860s, Herman von Helmholtz developed a metal device that compresses the air within it so that the sound waves oscillate, vibrating at one particular frequency. This apparatus, known as the Helmholtz resonator, produces an effect like the whistling sound that occurs when we blow across the top of an empty bottle.

According to Dr. Aaron Watson, one of the world's foremost researchers in the emerging field of acoustic archaeology, the basic form of prehistoric passage graves is the same as this Helmholtz resonator, in that each grave has its own specific resonant frequency. In his research, Dr. Watson discovered that these resonant frequencies can be reproduced by the human voice and simple instruments such as drums, rattles, and bone whistles.

When continuous pure tones are made at the resonant frequency of a passage grave, the dense stone walls trap the sound so that it forms what is known as a "standing wave." A standing wave is produced by the interference of two waves of the same frequency as they travel opposite directions along the same medium. The result is that it appears to stand still, vibrating in place. One effect is that the perceived volume of the note is dramatically increased. Another effect is that the source of the sound becomes unclear—and thus mysterious. It seems to come from everywhere and nowhere at once, and thus appears to be numinous and otherworldly. Apparently, Neolithic people deliberately designed their graves to produce this phenomenon. They may have used it to enhance the effect of their ritual chanting and drumming in order to carry the spirit of the deceased to the realm of the dead.

In 2004 I experienced this phenomenon myself when John Reid and I visited West Kennet Long Barrow, built in the shape of a goddess with large breasts and hips, near Avebury, England. There we intoned, both individually and together. When he made sounds near the end of the chamber between two rock slabs, I heard overtones emanating from his low drone. They seemed to be coming from many different places. Even knowing where he was standing, I couldn't locate the source of the sound. His voice filled the chamber in an unusual way—now here, now there. It seemed to be right in front of me and then far away, disappearing and then reappearing. Author Paul Devereux has found that many chamber graves in the British Isles have primary resonant frequencies that cluster around 110–112 Hz found in the lower register of male voices. John was certain that only male voices would fully excite the chamber, because the female voice is normally unable to reach low frequencies with sufficient power. However, having sung there once before, I knew that the female voice could also resonate the chamber in unusual ways.

Asking John to remain where he was, I stood at the entrance between two stone slabs, and made a high glissando, waiting to hear which note resonated most clearly. I found one that created a beating in my head between my ears. John later described seeing sparkling white diamond patterns in his inner vision in response to these high-frequency sounds.

I believe both male and female voices may have been used in ritual here, perhaps creating a sonic mating for the purpose of renewal. There are 366 Neolithic tombs dotting the Irish landscape, and many chamber graves in England as well, where couples went to make love until as recently as the late nineteenth century.[4]


## NEWGRANGE

In Ireland's County Meath north of Dublin, Newgrange, also known as *Brugh na Boine*, rises from the landscape near the fertile land by the River Boyne. This Neolithic passage grave, dated at 3200 BC, is older than the Great Pyramid. Rediscovered in 1699, it is one of the oldest roofed buildings in the world. Newgrange was built by a relatively settled and prosperous community of hunters who also engaged in livestock farming, as evidenced from cow, pig, goat, horse, and dog bones found there. Researchers think it took forty years to build the monument. Over a million hours alone were needed to haul the million sackfuls of small stones the people brought from nearby stream and riverbeds.

The facade of Newgrange is covered with thousands of white quartz crystals and gray granite stones that archaeologists found at the site and used during the reconstruction. It is the grandest of some twelve hundred megalithic sites throughout Ireland and is gigantic—265 feet in diameter and 45 feet high—covering almost an acre of land. The Celts used these monuments in different ways over a long period of time. They were not merely tombs; they were also places of ceremony and initiation—temples at which to worship the cycles of sun and moon. They were used, taken down, reformed, reused, and at some point closed off. Over time, different myths, rituals, and purposes evolved.

Ashes and bones of between four or five people were found in Newgrange, thought to have originally been placed in three basins that reside in three small recesses within the monument. Smaller cairns surrounding the passage grave contained greater numbers of burned and unburned human remains, leading to the conclusion that important leaders and kings were buried there.

Legend says that Brugh na Boine was the burial place of the prehistoric high kings of Tara and also the abode of otherworldly beings called the *Tuatha Dé Danann*. This fairy race, the tribe of the goddess Danu, was called the Shining Ones.

And indeed, Newgrange *is* a place of shining. My first sight of it filled me with joy. The white quartz shimmered and sparkled like music from a fairy's harp. I went there in late March 2004 with John Reid and his friend Angela Wood, with whom I had been exploring sacred sites and sounds throughout Britain. As we approached, we passed low rolling hills and craggy granite outcroppings. Blossoms sprang from trees. We arrived at the visitors' center just as it opened in hopes of joining a small group for the first tour. John had called ahead to see if we could be alone to do some research, but was told he would have needed to apply well in advance. Otherwise, all access to Newgrange is by guided tour only.

With tickets in hand, we crossed a bridge over the Boyne River. The ancients thought of the Boyne as an earthly reflection of that celestial river, the Milky Way, which in Old Irish was called the "Road of the Bright Cow." The river was a personification of the White Cow Goddess who inhabits a well at the river's source, thought to confer second sight and the gift of poetry to those who drink from it.

On the day we were there, black rooks with twigs in their mouths were building nests in the oak and ash trees that lined the river.

Delicate leaves unfurled from their bud sheaths. I felt the soft fuzz of pussy willows beneath my fingers. Crows flew against a background of sun-misted air. Green swords of grass were drenched with dew. A constellation of sheep bleated and grazed in nearby fields alongside cows. I hoped I'd see a white cow but didn't. A duo of ducks flew by. John called out to show me a prehistoric beastie on a piece of dark gray limestone. On the same rock was what looked like a tiny, four-leaf clover—a good luck charm for our journey.

We boarded a bus for a short ride that was welcome on that brisk day. Inside, I heard the lilt of Irish voices and was charmed by the different inflections, so different from American accents or the Spanish language I hear in New Mexico. Outside the bus, birds were singing. Angela named them, a poetic litany of green finches, jackdaws, and blue tits with black caps.

When we arrived at the gate to the site, the white facade of Newgrange seemed to glow with a light of its own. It looked much larger than the photos I had seen. The circular stone mound was carpeted with green grass, looking like a place where fairies might dance. But instead of fairies, our guide appeared, and we clustered into a small group of eight.

The guide explained that forty chamber graves still exist in the Boyne Valley alone. We learned that Newgrange was built from a quarter-of-a-million stones. Ninety-seven large stones around the monument weigh up to ten tons each; possibly they were moved by being strapped onto logs and rolled into place. The speculation is that they arrived on logs from the ocean by river—white quartz from the south and sea-rock granite from the north.

Spirals are everywhere at Newgrange, from the spiral vortexes in the River Boyne to the unfurling of spring leaves. Triple spirals dance on the entrance stone and are also carved within the chamber. Speculation abounds as to what the spirals mean, ranging from the cosmic rhythms of sun and moon to the increase and decrease of life cycles and the transformation of birth, death, and rebirth. As with Native American petroglyphs, multiple meanings are possible. Archaeologist Marija Gimbutas sees the spirals as the triple goddess:

mother, maiden, and crone. To me, they are an image of the Irish landscape and of the human landscape of embryo, umbilical cord, fingerprint, ear, cochlea, and the core of our beating hearts.

We walked inside through a narrow passageway, much smaller than it appears in pictures. We crouched under stone doorways and ducked under low-hanging lintels. Were we meant to crawl, humbled on hands and knees, into this earthen womb? I wanted to do so, just as I have entered into Native American sweat lodges, but I walked upright like everyone else. We passed a triple spiral carved on the rock wall along with diamonds, zig zags, concentric circles, and a leafy wand.

After fifty feet or so, the passage opened into a central chamber under a corbelled roof with three adjoining smaller recesses to the east, west, and north. As the guide spoke, I was disappointed that there was no natural resonance. John explained later that the acoustic energy had been diffused by the uneven fragmented ceiling and walls. Sounds fell flat. He was disappointed, too. But this was a place of death. The three smaller chambers once held the burned ashes of the few who were cremated here. In the chamber to the right was a large, white stone bowl with two circular indentations. Were these the breasts of the Mother in her final embrace? If sound was not important here, was silence intentionally built into the space? Was this a place not to sing but to listen to the ancestors? To let the dead rest in quietude after life's cacophonous chorus?

The guide turned out the electric light installed in the monument so that we could see a beam of natural light enter the chamber and form a trail on the earthen floor. She asked us to imagine honeyed sunlight striking the end of the passageway on December 21. This phenomenon of seventeen minutes, when the sun kisses the dark space within through a roof-box, turns everything golden. There is a ten-year waiting list to witness this event.

All too soon the tour was over. As the others left, I explained to the guide our purpose in being there and asked if we could experiment with a few sounds. "No," she said, "that needs to be arranged in advance." I told her we had tried but didn't call soon enough to get permission. "No" was still her answer.

We had to comply, but on the way out the three of us did make soft, low humming sounds in the passageway where the rocks faced each other. "Mmm..." Yes, there was some resonance there. We all noticed it. But if the rocks had been positioned deliberately to produce that resonance, for what purpose? A purification before entering into stillness? An acknowledgment of the bond with Mother Earth? And were there any other sounds that would resonate?

Afterward, as we talked, John wasn't convinced that sound was an important factor in the passageway. I wondered if a priest might stand at the entrance and chant. "Yes," John replied, "but it wouldn't excite the acoustically dead chamber within."

"Perhaps that was the effect wanted," Angela offered, "sending the prayer directly into the earth as an offering for the afterlife journey."

"We may never know for sure," John answered.

Paul Devereux, though, does believe that Newgrange was deliberately constructed to produce acoustic effects. With his instrumentation, he and his team found twelve node and antinode pairs in the passageway where we had hummed that created the effect of a wind instrument. As John suggested, they also found that the sound dissipated once it reached the open space under the corbelled roof. However, near the entrance the team found a separate slab of rock that could be placed or removed as required. If the people had used the slab as a door to shut the chamber at times of ritual, as Devereux observes, "then any sounds they made would have created a more intense standing wave within the passage.... The deep otherworldly sound from the inner sanctum of the mound would have emerged with particular power out through the roof-box, perhaps at the time the winter solstice sunbeam was entering through it. This would have created an alchemical exchange of light and sound."[5] Welsh archaeologist Frances Lynch believes that the acoustic properties of the roof-box at Newgrange may have been used, not only to send the soul on its journey, but also as an oracular device to receive messages from the spirit world.

# DR. WATSON, I PRESUME

After Ireland, John, Angela, and I went to a conference at Malvern in the hills near Hereford. There I met Dr. Aaron Watson, the archaeologist whose work on passage graves I referred to above. It was a wonderful synchronicity, as I had with me a draft of the chapter of this book where I mentioned his research at Stonehenge. He graciously agreed to read the chapter and give his comments. Over the next several days, we had many conversations, both alone and with John and Angela.

Though an archaeologist, Aaron Watson also has an artistic nature. He was at the conference selling his photographs of stone circles and his CD called *Monumental*. With narration and sound effects, *Monumental* demonstrates the transformative power of sound in ancient monuments and draws on research he has done at Newgrange, West Kennet Long Barrow, Maeshowe, Camster Round, and other sites throughout the United Kingdom. As a Neolithic specialist and a native of Britain, Aaron has acquired detailed knowledge and forged a deep relationship with the monuments and land.

"These places drew me in," he told me. "They are the reason I became an archaeologist. The shapes, colors, lines, and land inspire me, and I engage with them on many different levels. When I come to these places, I enact my 'scientific ritual,' though they also speak to me in other ways that I can't always write about academically."

John and I spoke to Aaron of our experience at Newgrange and asked if he had done any research there. Yes, he had measured its basic acoustic properties using "pink noise," a wide band of frequencies that sound like a distant waterfall. He introduced it inside and outside the monument to see how it behaved and resonated. He found that the entrance acted as an acoustic projector that amplified tones in the chamber. This amplification could be heard outside as well, depending on how close the listener was to the entrance.

One of Aaron's most exciting discoveries at Newgrange occurred when he sent sounds from the central chamber into the three smaller alcoves. Upon doing so, he found that standing waves were created.

"The sounds appeared to be coming out from the alcoves," he told me, "as if you were throwing your voice. This gave the supernatural effect of voices coming from many different places." Moreover, he found that the higher frequencies of the voices of women and even of children, while not the dominant resonant frequency, also reverberated within this and other passage graves. This finding suggests that whole communities participated in the ancient rituals at Newgrange, instead of just the men.

One acoustic effect specific to many passage graves is that, through the very nature of their architecture, they create high-amplitude infrasound—extremely low sounds that are inaudible. The way in which the body and brain make sense of infrasound has the potential to cause altered states that may have been used by shamans. As Aaron explains in Neil S. Price's *The Archaeology of Shamanism*, infrasound is not created by the voice or musical instruments but "by the interaction between the propagating sound waves and the structure of the monument itself."[6]

One example of infrasound in Aaron's research is that many passage graves act as Helmholtz resonators. This phenomenon, as discussed above, has the ability to amplify certain frequencies. Aaron discovered as much at Maeshowe, a passage grave in Scotland's Orkney Islands, and has shown mathematically that the same effect might be duplicated at other Neolithic sites throughout the United Kingdom. The amplified sounds are below the threshold of human hearing but affect us nonetheless. Just as we walk daily through ultraviolet and infrared rays of which we are unaware, we walk through a landscape of sound waves below and beyond what we can hear.

Aaron spoke of the changes in interpretation depending on how you are situated as an observer. He said that while Neolithic monuments are sometimes perceived to be full of light and benevolence, many of them can generate uncomfortable and unnerving experiences as well. Taking people with him, he often does his research at passage graves at night, drumming as one way to test the acoustics. The drum sets up certain oscillations in the air around the structures. Drumbeats echo and bind listeners into a common rhythm, sometimes leading to extraordinary experiences. Aaron is embarking upon new research to test some of the unique occurrences he has felt and witnessed. One amazing event occurred while he was drumming in a chamber at Camster Round in Scotland. The drumming seemed to emanate from the earth itself and could be heard within another nearby chamber, although not across the open land between the chambers. At another site, when certain vocal frequencies were used, huge stones appeared to shake and come alive.

As Aaron says on his CD, his findings suggest that Neolithic people were "the first to construct buildings which possessed their own entirely artificial acoustic qualities." The buildings expanded and distorted sounds in a way that sometimes made them seem disembodied. Aaron proposes that many ancient monuments "were constructed not so much to enclose space as to enshrine sound."[7]

"Sound," Aaron continues on the CD, "can fill space with its own architecture. Sound can create worlds." He asks the listener to imagine living always in a world of natural sound and then leaving it for the first time to enter the interior of a monument, where the contrast between the familiar and the uncertain, open space and confined space, fresh air and thick air, and daylight and darkness must have been extreme. We, on the other hand, live in an artificial world where nature is viewed from behind windows. We have to remember that, for Neolithic people, the experience of the interior of a chamber grave would have been completely out of the ordinary, inasmuch as "acoustic effects could not be recreated elsewhere in the landscape." Aaron believes that the Neolithics may have used these monuments to structure the social order, in the sense that only some members of the community would have been given access to the interior. This hierarchy would have created divisions and emphasized the crossing of gateways for some and restriction for others. The monument served as a multisensory theater where there was "an orchestration of the senses at particular boundaries, or thresholds, which constituted the transcendental nature of these places. The architecture of the sound itself may have created points of access into other dimensions and signaled the manifestation of forces beyond our imagination."[8]

A week later, back in the United States, I was sitting by the Rio Grande River a few miles from my home. Black crows flew against a background of turquoise sky. Green leaves unfurled from red willows. Sunlight created diamonds on the water's surface as vortexes spun in the river. As I sat, I listened to the music all around me. From Newgrange to New Mexico, I sang with life's spiraled song.

*Stonehenge, Neolithic rock formation, Wiltshire, England*

# STONE CIRCLES

*The . . . standing stones at Avebury have been described as acting like a
series of giant resonators, amplifying the telluric forces and vibrating
them heavenwards in order to fructify the surrounding terrain.*
—Tim Wallace-Murphy and Marilyn Hopkins

In the sensual Wiltshire landscape, I arrived at Avebury, England on
a bus in early September 2004. The barley and wheat had already
been cut, erasing earlier summer crop circles. As I stepped off the bus
into the cool air, I was struck with how fresh everything looked. It
seemed I was in a Technicolor world where everything was brighter.

The giant sedimentary stones throughout the chalk downs of
southern England are called sarsens. When I first saw them, I felt
as if I were being greeted by old friends. Rock spirits are alive at
Avebury. With the light of the changing sun, shadows reveal faces on
the stones. On the day I arrived, each appeared to have a distinct
persona chosen for its special shape. I recognized one of the stones
by name—The Devil's Chair—so labeled during more puritanical
times. I sat on this throne and felt the rock support and nourish
my body, weary from the long bus ride. A rainbow blessed a sky
of robin's egg blue, which turned a sunset burst of lavender, gold,
and orange.

Avebury is Britain's largest megalithic monument and one of the
most complete Neolithic complexes in Europe. Estimates are that the
Neolithic and early Bronze Age people of western Europe built
between forty and fifty thousand megalithic circles. Stone circles or

standing stones exist all over the world. Hundreds can be found in Africa, Syria, Lebanon, Israel, Jordan, Bulgaria, Japan, Korea, Morocco, Algeria, and Brittany in northern France. Erecting megaliths is one of the earliest forms of sacred architecture. They were built at places that emanate underground currents. By placing stones, called dolmens, on this already-hallowed ground, the Neolithic people moved from worshiping in natural sacred places such as caves and mountains to constructing sacred places for the first time in human history.

Erected between 2600 and 2400 BC, Avebury is over four thousand years old. John Aubrey, the man who first recognized it as a prehistoric site in 1649, wrote that "it does as much exceed in greatness the so renowned Stonehenge, as a cathedral does a parish church."[1]

It is thought that Avebury originally consisted of 183 stones arranged in a circle within a henge, a deeply carved groove in the earth. Two great avenues of stone pairs led out from the circle. From those original 183 stones, only 47 remain. Throughout the Middle Ages and well into the nineteenth century, the great stones were destroyed by villagers and farmers as well as by the church to quell pagan beliefs. People lit fires under them and then poured cold water over them to make them crack. Some of these broken stones can be seen in cottage walls today.

Avebury is part of a greater mythic landscape that includes Silbury Hill, West Kennet Long Barrow, Windmill Hill, the Sanctuary, and other nearby ceremonial sites, all of which were linked to function as a whole within this sacred geography. At Avebury, early people saw the landscape of the entire area as the outline of the body of the Goddess for thousands of years before the stone circle and other nearby ceremonial sites came into being. Rituals moved to different places during the seasonal year to enact the myths of maiden, mother, and crone. Monica Sjöö and Barbara Mor observe that "the monuments were aligned within the 'pubic' triangle"[2] where two streams converge at Swallowhead Spring. This confluence is where the River Kennet is born. This river was originally pronounced "Cunnit," from which the slang word *cunt* is derived. Words now profane were once sacred, imbued with magic.

Michael Dames, in *The Avebury Cycle*, thinks that "the henge was a goddess of love"[3]; and Terence Meaden, author of *The Secrets of the Avebury Stones*, thinks that the "concepts of rebirth, life after death, fertility, myths of creation, and the eternal return of the Earth Goddess's domain motivated the rites."[4] The belief was that, at the summer solstice, a sacred union occurs when the sun's rays penetrate a goddess stone in the North Cove and that, in early May, the sun mates with another female stone in the South Circle. These stones are recognizable images of vulvas, even for those of weak imagination.

According to Michael Dames, Avebury was built during the astrological age of Taurus, a sensual sign relating to the fertile earth. Astrological signs correspond to body parts. Taurus rules the neck, throat, and voice. If the purpose of Avebury was to enhance fertility, I wonder if early people may have used the implied link between sound and sex in some way.

The voice is used to court and woo a mate. During coitus, both sexes moan with pleasure. Breathing in and creating an open throat during orgasm increases the intensity of feeling. Making sound while making love enhances the experience. During childbirth, women groan in pain. Their groans help to open the cervix to allow the baby to push through. Perhaps Neolithic people, who lived closer to their biology and the rhythms of the earth than we do, noticed these connections and made love at Avebury with sound as a way to nourish the land.

Biologically, we know the voice is part of our sexual make-up. In a fetus, the vocal folds grow out of the same matrix as does genital tissue; they differentiate only later. A similar relationship exists between the throat and the diaphragm. Consider the changes the voice goes through at puberty: The high soprano of a boy's voice cracks and deepens. During every menstrual cycle, a woman experiences changes in her voice, though they are less obvious until menopause, when the voice become lower.

Sound brings life. For aboriginal people, sacred sites each had their own song and ceremony. As Paul Devereux describes, these places were "increase centres from which the appropriate ritual could elicit the life essence or *kuraunda* of living things, thus ensuring the fecundity, the increase, of the particular plant or animal associated with the site."[5] Although the Aborigines far preceded the builders of Avebury in time, perhaps they shared similar ideas. We find such beliefs even today in Indonesia, where the Toradja people chant all through the night in rituals around standing stones.

Dolmens are accumulators. They receive energy from the stars above and the earth below and store their charge like batteries. According to Louis Charpentier, they are placed "where the telluric current exercises a spiritual action on man, a spot where 'the spirit breathes.'"[6] Researchers Paul Devereux, Robert G. Jahn, and Michael Ibison found that a common frequency range exists at various stone monuments in England and Ireland. This range is between 95 and 120 Hz—frequencies found in the human voice. They believe these sites to be "tuned" to a frequency compatible with chanting and singing.

What's more, the stones may emit their own music. Paul Devereux has monitored humming sounds and ticking noises from the Whispering Knights dolmen in England. His finding adds evidence to a custom that persisted into the nineteenth century in which young women would put their ears to the hollows of the stones in order to hear whispered answers to their questions. Also, Devereux's team heard deep humming noises at the Machrie Moor complex in Scotland, while the stones at Wicklow in Ireland emitted curious humming sounds. This phenomenon may be caused by natural radiation.

Certain stones emit electromagnetic vibrations to which the temporal lobes of the brain are sensitive. The part of the brain most affected is the hippocampus, a strand of tissue lying deep within the cerebral cortex that houses memory and emotion. When sound activates this area, it is particularly apt to stimulate remembrances highly emotional in character.

Curiously, silence has also been noted in relation to the stones. In some of them, at dawn on the equinox, Geiger counters register a higher level of radiation than on other days. This radiation can even create an ultrasonic barrier. Confirming this finding, Don Robins, in his book *Circles of Silence,* describes experiencing ultrasonic silence within a stone circle. When he moved outside the circle, he heard ordinary sounds of the landscape again. He believes that people in antiquity used this silence for meditation and attuning to cosmic energies.[7]

Neolithic people chose stones with special properties to be part of their monuments. They often used stones with crystal content, for instance, apparently deliberately placing them where underground streams crossed. Barbara Mor and Monica Sjöö point out that "the movement of water through a tunnel in the earth—particularly clay soil—creates a small electrical field, for which the stones act as amplifiers."[8] While early people couldn't have understood this phenomenon scientifically, they nevertheless would have experienced it and arranged their stones accordingly.

They also arranged their stone circles in geometric formations designed to focus and concentrate the energy. While each stone circle has its own particular shape, when lines are drawn between certain key stones the sacred geometry hidden within the monument is revealed. Avebury contains a Pythagorean triangle defined by the ratios 3:4:5, while the lines of Stonehenge create a six-pointed star within a squared circle. These "proportions point to certain characteristic 'resonance signatures' of the sites, which seems to indicate that design in relation to vibration was an important factor for consideration."[9]

## SINGING THE STONES

While I did not have any scientific equipment with me at Avebury, or hear the stones hum, I did conduct my own investigations to see if I could make the stones resonate. Many of the sarsens of Avebury have holes in them. On my second day there I placed my mouth on one of these holes and made a few sounds. But it was a busy Saturday and many people were about. A father pushed a pram with a baby asleep under a white umbrella. A mother called out to her little boy, "Roger, don't climb on the stones!" An elderly man asked his wife if she'd made a wish. Lovers kissed. A woman sang a pretty tune while she sketched. A family shared a picnic. A guide showed a group where one of the fires was lit under the stone to crack it. From a distance, I watched a pagan priestess point a sword to the sky as part of a wedding ceremony. I had come here to sing, but now I felt self-conscious. I did make three low sounds into different stones and noticed that my sound was enhanced. But there was too much going on for me really to let go and listen.

Avebury, once a complete circle of stones, is now divided into four quadrants that one enters through wooden gates. Two busy roads cut through this sanctuary, and the sound of traffic is very present. I walked slowly around the stones and touched them, asking their spirits to teach me their secrets. Immediately, I saw a tiny spider's web over one of the holes. It was like an Aeolian wind harp, vibrating with lines of light. The sun played a rainbow on the strings of the web, turning it into a prismed mandala, a fairy's harp. Enchanted, I showed it to a woman walking past, and we were in awe together. She told me she was an anthropologist. I asked if she knew anything about music being played here. "No," she said, "but there were a set of wooden pan pipes from the Neolithic age found in water nearby." I imagined the rocks themselves as huge pan pipes and wondered if giants had blown into them, creating a giant orchestra of stone—the world's first rock band.

Continuing my journey from one quadrant to the next, I arrived in the northwest quarter called the Cove. It initially had an inner ring of twelve stones that was sixty-five feet in diameter. In the center, three huge stones formed a box-like alcove. Today, few stones are left. Two of the center ones—a tall male stone and its female partner—still exist but are enclosed in a fence awaiting reinforcement, as their bases are unstable. Only two of the circle stones are still erect. Two others have fallen and lie in the field. Within this sketchy circle, I found a stone off by itself near a tree. Few people were around. I walked to this stone and found three crevices in it. One fit my face and chest perfectly. I stood in silence and listened. When I sounded into it, overtones began to ring through me as well as the gray sarsen. The rock supported my body totally, my heart beating against it, my temples cradled against its temple. Singing to the Old Ones, I felt as if I became one with the stone. Then a stone face appeared in my mind's eye. Many faces appeared, looking like the Green Man — those Celtic carvings depicting the archetype of the masculine spirit in nature that we often find in Romanesque churches and in medieval and Renaissance cathedrals. I felt them sing with me, revitalizing my body, bones, jaws, and teeth. The stone I leaned against seemed like a portal, a gateway into the mineral kingdom. As my voice softened, the overtones become stronger. It seemed as if the stone and I exchanged an ancient knowing. After I came to silence, I moved back slowly, thanked the rock spirits for this meeting, and sat for a long time.

## STONEHENGE

Stonehenge sits like a giant's wedding ring on the Salisbury Plain in Wiltshire, just down the road from Avebury. Created over a two-thousand-year period from 3300 to 1550 BC, it is one of the most recognizable Neolithic monuments in the world. Some of the sarsens are from nearby quarries, but the famous bluestones are from the Preseli Hills in southwest Wales, two hundred miles away. Speculation abounds as to how they were moved. Some legends claim that the ancient druids levitated the stones with sound. One myth says it was Merlin himself who brought the stones. Another has it that the stones are giants dancing in a circle frozen in place. In 1979, an experiment took place to prove that two hundred people could move a thirty-two-ton block by using levers, wooden rollers, and ropes. Others have successfully transported the huge stones by river using flat-bottomed boats and rolling logs.

Inasmuch as Stonehenge was built in stages over time, it may have served many purposes, including that of a temple, an observatory for predicting solstices and eclipses, and a giant computer that could determine where the sun and moon were 3,500 years ago.[10] One purpose of the site was to mark and celebrate Midsummer, the longest day of the year. Midsummer was a time of great importance to early agricultural societies in that, following the barrenness of winter, it signified the return of the strength of the sun, upon which survival itself depends. As did the Avebury stones, those at Stonehenge symbolized the mating of the Sky Father with the Earth Mother, insuring another harvest. Through an ingenious placement of the rocks, this marriage takes place at Midsummer's sunrise when the long shadow of the Heel Stone penetrates the womb-shaped center of the ring.

Aaron Watson and David Keating have tested their idea that the sight line tracking the thrust of the shadow into the inner circle might also be a sound line.[11] They found the horseshoe arrangement of stones in the center to be subtly shaped to focus sound in a way "similar to the way that light can be focused by a parabolic mirror."[12] Tests using chanting, speaking, and percussive instruments revealed that the flat and concave surfaces of the broad, close-set stones reflected the sounds, which then bounced back into the center in a way that made the stones seem to come alive.

Many have reported hearing sounds at Stonehenge. One group heard clicking sounds changing into "a whirring noise that suddenly shot heavenwards as if a giant Catherine wheel [circular whirling fireworks] had gone spinning upward."[13] Coming upon Stonehenge at night, the characters in Thomas Hardy's *Tess of the d'Urbervilles* hear a humming noise and the wind playing upon the stones, which produces "a booming tune, like the note of some gigantic stringed harp."[14] Though Hardy's account is fictional, one wonders if it were based on his own experience. Others have heard ringing sounds issuing from the stones.

On the day I visited the site later in 2002, I wondered what I would hear. After my experience at Avebury, I wasn't expecting much. Many people had told me that Stonehenge was crowded and noisy and that I wouldn't be able to get close to the stones. Sure enough, when I arrived by cab several tour buses with running engines were idling in the parking area. A sea of people walked around with cameras and camcorders. Traffic rushed past on a busy nearby road.

Buying my ticket, I walked through a tunnel and caught my first glimpse of the stones. The second I saw them, I felt a profound exchange. I heard a sound and felt it on my tongue—"Ahhhhhh tahhhhhh"—the "T" on the top of my palate, the "Ahhhhh" on my in-breath, and the "Tahhhhh" on my out-breath. It was as if the stones were sending a message, pure, direct, and untranslated. Reverently, I walked slowly around the circle, oblivious to the other tourists. I was glad the stones were roped off, feeling that, were I to walk into the center, I might disappear completely through some invisible portal.

Walking along, I came to a stone with a face and asked it if it had a personal message for me. My father had died ten days earlier. The stone told me his death had left a hole in my middle. Everything about my father, about Father with a capital "F," had been changed, as if the edifice of an old pattern had crumbled to dust. I felt I was receiving a blueprint for a new relationship, not only with my father but with the sacred masculine itself.

Later, I noticed the cab driver who had brought me sitting on a lounge chair near the cafe and asked if he wanted a cup of coffee. "That would be lovely," he said. When I had purchased the coffee and handed it to him, he smiled and remarked, "I'm not a religious man, but I can feel the energy of places like this where people come to pray. When my father was dying, he called me into his hospital room and said, 'Son, I know where I'm going. I've seen it and I'll be gone in a week.' He told me to be kind to people. He died a few days later. I love being a cab driver because of all the people I meet and can help. When I take people to these holy places I feel him here."

I told him that my father had also been a kind man, that he had just died, and that I, too, had just felt *his* presence. One of the gifts my father gave me was the ability to strike up conversations with strangers. The truth I found is that there are no strangers—be they cab drivers or ancient stones with familiar faces on the Salisbury Plain.

*Face of Hathor, Temple of Dendera, built between 125 BC and AD 65, Egypt*

~ *C h a p t e r   8* ~

# EGYPTIAN SONIC TEMPLES

*Give me my mouth;*
*I want to talk.*
*Give me iron words forged in fire*
*That I may speak the language of the Earth.*
—Normandi Ellis

In the beginning, according to Egyptian mythology, the "singing sun created the world with its cry of light."[1] Modern science concurs: As we have seen from the study of wave phenomena called Cymatics, sound creates form. In the beginning, perhaps everything was formed through vibration: sky, earth, oceans. In the Nile Delta, creation gave rise to river, reed, hawk, heron, red sandstone, black granite. The River Nile, like a lotus born from mud, gave life through its rich silt, making a narrow green band along its banks. Here, the civilization we know as Egypt was cradled. From 3050 BC of the First Dynastic period until the Greco-Roman period that lasted until AD 395, the pharaohs ruled and built pyramids, temples, and the enigmatic Sphinx that gazes into eternity. Some believe this civilization to be much more ancient—perhaps over ten thousand years old. Egyptologist John Anthony West agrees. Geologic research has shown that the weathering pattern of the Sphinx is due to water, while all the nearby shrines were weathered by wind erosion. It has been over ten thousand years since the Giza Plateau, where the Sphinx resides, has been under water—hence the rationale of West and of many geologists for redating the age of Egyptian civilization.[2]

Many years ago, while researching sound and Egypt, I had interviewed West. Now, joining his tour in 2006, I would be able to experience the effects of toning in the temples and pyramids for myself.

The flight from New York City was long and tiring. A sandstorm rerouted our plane to Sharm El-Sheikh by the Red Sea. Finally, we arrived in Cairo at 3 a.m. and were taken by bus to the famous Mena House Hotel. Our Egyptian guide greeted us with the words, "Welcome Home."

> Welcome home to the black land by the Nile.
> Welcome home to doves and feathery wands of palms,
>     to spiraling flutes of minarets
>     singing to the dark sky.
> Welcome home to Egypt,
>     to crates of oranges stacked in sidewalk markets,
>     to fires lit on pavement,
>     to a Nile filled with stars.
> Welcome home to magic rugs hung on ropes,
>     threaded dreams carpeting the sidewalk.
> Welcome home to eucalyptus and acacia,
>     to palaces of perfume and a blue scroll of sky.
> Welcome home to honking horns and evening prayer,
>     to Arabic chants hanging in the night breeze like incense,
>     to mud bricks and mosaics,
>     to water buffalo grazing near palm fronds waving hello.
> Welcome home, Immortal Soul.

Awakening at the hotel the next morning, my roommate and I ran to our balcony. The pyramids! There they were, almost close enough to touch. What must they have been like when they were covered in their polished, white limestone casings? The Greek writer Herodotus says that they "glittered in the pure desert air like gigantic prisms."[3] When I first saw them, the pyramids didn't glitter, but they did pulse. I could hear them singing a finely tuned song, as if they were broadcasting stations to the stars.

What *are* the pyramids? Why are they here? Will we ever know? Engineer Robert Bauval believes that the three on the Giza Plateau represent the stars of Orion's belt on earth. Khufu's is the grandest, the most complex, earning the name the Great Pyramid of Giza. Over the centuries, it has been thought to be an astronomical observatory, an almanac, or a telescope. Gnostics, Rosicrucians, Theosophists, and Masons have believed the Great Pyramid to be a center of initiation. Master craftsman and engineer Chris Dunn, who was on the tour, disagrees, thinking instead that it was a power plant where its "crystal edifice created a harmonic resonance with the Earth and converted Earth's vibrational energies to microwave radiation."[4] He believes that every part of its precise design was intended to enhance its acoustics. I would have to wait for my own experience, for our private meditation and toning in it would not take place until the last day of the trip. But on this first day I would be able to sing inside the Red Pyramid at Dahshur, less than an hour from Cairo near Saqqara.

## THE RED PYRAMID

From the windows of our bus we passed pomegranate trees, rows of cabbages, carts of carrots, stacks of hay, an old woman pulling a bony cow through a lane. Other buses with names like Zam Zam, Paradise, and Isis Tours were already in the parking lot. Cream-colored desert dogs greeted us, guardians of these first pyramids, one with a heart on his forehead. Gulls and mud swallows flew overhead. We went first to the Step Pyramid of Zosher and its complex, which included an elaborate, fluted colonnade leading into a great court. Chris wondered if the seventeen stalks of papyrus bound together in the columns related to the seventeen notes of the Arabic scale.

Finally, we arrived at the Red Pyramid, named for the casing of pink granite that covers the stones. This pyramid is not usually on the tourist route, and we had it completely to ourselves. After climbing the steep stairs outside, we descended a ramp into the interior.

We had to duck and walk backwards, holding onto handrails as we went down through the long, narrow passageway. The air was stale; I wore my scarf over my nose. One couple, who had been on the tour before, wore dust masks.

The passage opened into two adjoining chambers, each with a corbelled roof that looked like the inside of a church steeple—or the interior of the nasal cavity. The A-frame shape did not have clean lines but was built in stair steps, with each course of bricks being inset closer together.

In one of these chambers, I led a toning. We didn't have much time, so I didn't prepare the group with my usual speech about how most of us feel shy and awkward about singing or making sounds, especially in a holy place where we are taught to be silent. To get started, I made a glissando, and we agreed that a high note brought out the most resonance. Though my reading had suggested that the acoustics of this pyramid were most suited to the lower registers of the male voice, the stair stepping of the vault suggested a higher note to me. One man, Adam Reed, said that when I sang the room instantly lit up with harmonics. The inner part of the chamber generated overtones from the starting tone, or fundamental pitch, of my voice. The second harmonic of an octave was almost as loud as the room, something that Adam said he had never experienced before. I found out later that he was an acoustics expert.

Strangers just yesterday, still jet-lagged, we travelers from all over the world became fellow pilgrims as we each found our own notes. Soon we became a group voice. As we sang, I had the impression that the granite walls were breathing with us. Each moment in the pyramid became a note in a song that has been sung for thousands of years.

Our tour traveled on. The combination of sensory overload, dreams, visions, and temple dust put me in what seemed an altered state. Nothing had prepared me for Egypt—for sunrise at the Sphinx, for a thousand swallows singing the sun up, for white herons gathered like magnolia blossoms in bushes alongside canals, for the flame trees on Elephantine Island, for Donald Duck speaking Arabic on television, and for the ready laugh of the Egyptian people.

## THE TEMPLE OF MAN

On the east bank of the Nile, past an avenue of sphinxes and twin-throned colossi, sits the Temple of Luxor, skewed on its axis. According to the mathematician and philosopher R. A. Schwaller de Lubicz, the temple reflects the structure of the human body. It reveals an outline of a skeleton whose every part is located within the temple's plan: clavicle walls, colonnade legs, breathing lungs, and the beating heart of the hypostyle hall.

De Lubicz calls Luxor "the cathedral of the Great Teaching."[5] Like a cathedral, it has the equivalent of a nave and a choir, which is placed in the covered area where the high altar sits. Just as in cathedrals Christian choirs sing hymns near the altar where communion is performed, in Egypt the high priest chanted in the temple's "choir" while he circled the sacred barque, symbol of the crescent moon. In relation to the human body, this sanctuary is located at the place of the nasal cavity. At the Chamber of the Annunciation, corresponding to the vocal chords, the king's divine birth is symbolically portrayed in a relief on the west wall. Here he was baptized, and his name was inscribed on stone walls joining the names of the kings who had preceded him.

John Anthony West led our tour group there at night. The temple, illumined by floodlights, had a golden appearance. With the moon almost full, I walked through the Avenue of the Sphinxes to the obelisk. The shadows cast into the carved hieroglyphs brought them forward as offerings: owl, feather, ibis. West began his commentary as we walked through the threshold. I listened first to the bats and rock doves roosting at the top of the columns, their soft rustlings in counterpoint to the dissonant call to prayer from the nearby minarets.

Then I was drawn to West's words: "Luxor is an exercise in harmony and proportion. We are stirred by these places in the same way we are stirred by music. The proportions of Egyptian sacred architecture produce the effect of resonance. We are, in effect, in the middle of a stone symphony. For the purpose of tuning the temple, at its entrance there were always two obelisks cut out of a single piece of granite."

Listening to West explain the temple's reliefs, I was filled with a sense of what a privilege it was to be there. In ancient Egypt, only the pharaoh or high priest was allowed entry into the Holy of Holies. First he would be ritually purified; then he would break the seal guarding the door and enter the inner sanctum containing the deity. Unveiling the image, he would prostrate himself and circle the shrine with incense and incantations. The statue was then bathed, anointed with oil, and dressed in fine garments, with jewelry and other insignias belonging to the deity placed upon it. Then an elaborate banquet would be brought forth. Afterward, the priest, walking backward, would clear his footprints from the floor and close the shrine door, which was then resealed. Through this offering "the underlying fabric of the universe was renewed."[6]

At Luxor, as at other temples, statues of the resident deity were imbued with the qualities of living gods. When a temple was dedicated, its priests performed rituals on every statue, every relief, and every inscription throughout, breathing life into the stones. The temple itself was called a house of utterance and considered a living being. The gods were thought to breathe through stone noses, listen through stone ears, and eat through stone lips.

Now here *we* were at the Holy of Holies—neither priests nor priestesses, but just ordinary people from the twenty-first century. When the group eventually arrived in the inner sanctum, I led them through a toning experience. In *The Serpent in the Sky*, West tells us that the Holy of Holies at Luxor corresponds to the nasal cavity. Its Egyptian name *shtyt* means "sacred" and "hidden." Moreover, the letters *N* and *M* vibrate the nose which is "connected to the sympathetic and vagus nerves."[7] When the nasal cavity is stimulated by sound, altered states of consciousness are possible.

In the inner sanctum, I slid my voice in a glissando to find the most resonant note of my range, and together we toned it with the nasal sounds of "Mmm," "Om," "Nggg," and "Nee." Overtones filled the space. One woman said she was instantly affected and saw vivid colors of gold, green, and blue in her mind's eye. Another said she experienced a perfect harmony with all of our voices, very much like the perfect balance that was created in the Temple of Man itself. She felt her body continue to vibrate even when the toning was over. When we finished, we walked back through the temple in silence.

## DENDERA

Hathor, goddess of music, is the oldest Egyptian deity depicted in art. She was worshipped at Dendera, a temple isolated at the edge of the desert along the banks of the Nile. Though the Ptolomies built it relatively recently—in the first century BC—the site has been sacred to Hathor for over ten thousand years.

Dendera was more than a temple; it was a place to be nourished in body and soul. A center for healing and learning, it housed a papyrus library, a birthing chapel, and a sanatorium where, according to sacred texts, pilgrims would bathe in magic waters while priests uttered trance-inducing incantations. A sacred well offered purified water; laboratories concocted ceremonial perfumes; and the halls rang with singing, hand drums, and rhythmic rattles called *sistrums* that were said to sound like "the cackling of geese or the rustle of papyrus flowers."[8]

Sacred to Hathor and a symbol of her power, the sistrum was like a miniature temple where the goddess resided. Rattling its metal jingles in front of the body when entering the temple helped create a sonic shield of protection and control the rage of wrathful deities. Sistrums give off a significant level of ultrasound—a very high frequency beyond the range of human hearing, but not that of the goddess.

We arrived at Dendera by bus. On the way I saw a baby donkey nursing from its white mother. Black goats gambled down a lane lined with magenta oleanders. An avenue of date palms, reflected in a canal, led toward Hathor's temple, the Great Mother who gives life through her milky breast.

In Egyptian mythology, Hathor is the heavenly cow who nurses the newly dead from her udder. Her pillar-like legs hold up the sky. Her belly is filled with stars. At dusk, the sun, as the hawk Horus, flies into her mouth. She is called Lady of the Stars, Lady of the Sycamore, Mistress of the Desert. She is a goddess of healing and of all things sensual: the touch of a lotus petal, the taste of a pomegranate, the sound of a harp, the scent of musk, the intoxication of red barley beer, the silky fluids of sex.

At each temple, we had time alone before West's guided tour. Dendera's giant, Hathor-faced columns, many defaced, depict the goddess with cow ears. West commented on her unusual face being symbolic of a pregnant womb, with her "ears" depicted at the same level at which fallopian tubes would enter the uterus. While the reason for this appearance may be lost to time, it suggests another link between sound and sexuality.

Inside the temple, the bronze-colored walls are carved with detailed reliefs depicting scenes of Hathor and her consort, Horus. One corridor is inscribed with depictions of dancers, chantresses, musicians, and the instruments they played—harps, lyres, lutes, flutes, double reeds, pan pipes, frame drums, tambourines, cymbals, and rattles. Some reliefs show "conductors" before each musician, with different hand gestures to communicate melodic intervals.

Through studying the harpists' finger positions in these ancient reliefs, we can determine that octaves, fourths, and fifths were part of temple music. We don't know if they were played within or as chords, or perhaps as both. These intervals are common to Western music and to the overtone series. The string arrangement of harps, with the two longest strings being closer together than the others, suggests the use in Egyptian music of drones. Modern dulcimers, and Middle Eastern stringed instruments, have a similar string arrangement. The sound of a drone "generates beat frequencies capable of entraining altered states."[9]

Entranced, I walked through the corridor as it wound up and around to the roof, where Hathor-faced columns created the Chapel of the Union with the Sun Disc. It was here that the New Year was celebrated annually with the rising of the Nile's waters.

Dendera faces the rising of the star Sirius. In ancient Egypt, after being seventy days below the horizon, Sirius's appearance took place at dawn around the summer solstice in June. Typically, this was the time when the Nile began to flood, depositing new layers of its rich black mud so important to the survival of the ancient Egyptians. The corresponding rise of Sirius—called the "womb of Hathor"—heralded this regreening of the desert and so became symbolic of rebirth. The star's appearance marked the first day of the New Year.

Accompanied by flowers, incense, and offerings, Hathor's golden statue was then carried to the roof chapel where I now stood. Hymns were sung as she emerged at the head of the stairs to await the dawn. Outside the temple, below on the ground, her worshipers gathered. As the sun rose over the horizon, Hathor's effigy was undraped, and, naked, she was ritually united with the sun disc, initiating the New Year. A papyrus text proclaims:

> The sky rejoices,
> the earth dances,
> and the sacred musicians shout in praise.[10]

Later in the season, the ancient Egyptians celebrated the Festival of the Beautiful Reunion to ensure the fertility of the land and to give thanks for the flood. A convoy of boats bearing Hathor's statue sailed from Dendera to Edfu, the temple dedicated to Horus. A retinue of musicians, youths, and soldiers accompanied the barge, singing and waving branches along the riverbank. At Edfu, the sacred union of the statues of Hathor and Horus took place over thirteen days in his shrine within the temple. The festival culminated on the fourteenth day at the full moon. Throughout the surrounding villages, the streets were strewn with flowers and fresh herbs. The scent of myrrh and the sounds of chanting floated through the air.

Now, standing in Hathor's sanctuary, it seemed I had been there before. Singing alone, I somehow felt as if I were part of the celebratory throngs who for thousands of years had sung to embody the goddess's gifts of love and music.

# THE GREAT PYRAMID OF GIZA

John Anthony West, who describes himself as a mystic in skeptic's clothing, believes that "each of the pyramids sounds its particular and individual stone note or harmony."[11] As our tour group walked around the Giza Plateau, he pointed out the irregular floor paving around the pyramids and described it as an energy baffle system to amplify terrestrial—and maybe even celestial—energy. My feet vibrated as we walked. Everyone felt something. I heard music in the air, sounding as if it were coming from an Aeolian harp. Music is everywhere in Egypt: in the singing sands, the murmuring doves, and the harmonic proportions of the temples. West believes that ancient Egyptians may have been "practicing a form of musical/magical/spiritual science that has been long lost."[12]

The Egyptians believed that, just as the sun emerges at dawn, the soul rises again after death. Central to Egyptian mysteries of death and rebirth is the myth of the goddess Isis and her brother/husband, Osiris. As the story goes, Osiris was killed by his evil twin Set, who cut his body into fourteen pieces and scattered them far and wide. Isis searched for his pieces and found all but his phallus, which had been swallowed by a fish. Reassembling Osiris's body, she revived him. She fashioned for him a golden phallus and then conceived Horus, the hawk-headed god of the reborn sun.

The god Osiris shone as the most brilliant constellation in the sky. (It's the one the Greeks call Orion.) In the ancient mystery cult, the concept was that the dead were received by and became one with him. It is no accident, then, that the shafts in the Great Pyramid are aligned with the stars in this constellation.[13] The belief was that when the pharaoh died, his soul traveled through the shaft in the King's chamber to join Osiris and become a star.

Perhaps sound was a part of the accompanying rituals of rebirth. Hints of sonic rituals are found in the Pyramid Texts, which are the oldest sacred literature on earth. In one of them, Osiris, Lord of the Underworld, commands his body to rise up:

I come forth by day singing
I am born of sky, filled with light.[14]

In 200 BC, the Greek Demetrius wrote: "In Egypt, when priests sing hymns to the gods, they sing the seven vowels in succession and the sound of these vowels has such euphony that men listen to it instead of the flute and the lyre."[15] John Reid believes that this quotation, more than any other, is the best evidence we have that the ancient Egyptians used sound in their rituals.

In 2001, Reid performed experiments in the King's Chamber of Khufu's Great Pyramid at Giza. Recording the prime resonant frequency of the chamber and its sarcophagus, he found that, not only were these frequencies almost exactly the same, they also match the predominant heart sound of a newborn baby. Reid sees the air shafts as symbolic fallopian tubes and the King's Chamber as a representation of the womb of the sky goddess, Nut; he believes the chamber was the location of a "rebirthing" ritual in which sound played a key role. An instrument called a *pesesh-kaf* was found sealed in one of these shafts. Used in childbirth as a knife to cut the umbilical cord and clear the airways, it was also used in ritual initiations during the "Opening of the Mouth" ceremony where the dead were reanimated.

Reid also conducted Cymatics experiments on the empty sarcophagus in the King's Chamber by stretching a thin, plastic polyvinyl-chloride membrane over it after he temporarily repaired its broken corner. He sprinkled sand on the membrane and excited the sarcophagus with pure tones from an oscillator he had placed inside. Many sound pictures, known as CymaGlyphs, appeared on the membrane, but to Reid's amazement they strongly resembled hieroglyphs. They included Re the sun, the sacred eye of Horus, and the djed pillar—which symbolizes the backbone of the god Osiris. From his subsequent studies of the sound patterns emitted by several ancient musical instruments, he drew an astounding conclusion: All the CymaGlyphs resembled the iconography of the cultures that had invented the instruments! He hypothesizes that the sounds from the instruments, and from the King's Chamber sarcophagus, had impinged upon the ancient scribes and subliminally influenced the design of written symbols.

Before Reid had arrived in Egypt for this research, he had seriously injured his back. He needed help to bring his heavy equipment inside the pyramid and was in pain the entire time. About half-way through his allotted three-hour session, while bending over the sarcophagus to watch the magical Cymatic shapes appear, he realized he had no back pain whatsoever. Later, he was able to carry his suitcases full of equipment back out himself. At first he thought his pain had been relieved by the endorphins generated from witnessing the phenomenon of the emerging hieroglyphs. But afterward, at his hotel, the pain that had beset him for three weeks did not return; nor did he suffer from it on the plane back to England. Why? he wondered.

Several months later, while online, Reid came across Gendel, a company in Northern Ireland that researches cancer therapies. Scientists there have discovered that, if they sensitize tumor tissue with an electric field and then irradiate it with ultrasound, the tumor shrinks. During his own experiments, Reid had, unwittingly, also been bathed in both electrostatic energy and ultrasound, and he believes that the healing of his back is related to his exposure to these forms of energy.

Reid performed his research in part to explore the possibility that the ancient Egyptians chose to construct in granite for its ability to enhance sound. This highly resonant stone, embedded with about 25 percent quartz crystals, stores and gives off a significant electrostatic charge. The hundreds of tons of granite that make up the King's Chamber came from a quarry six hundred miles to the south, at Aswan. That the Egyptians went to so much trouble to acquire this stone seems proof that they considered it to have special qualities. When struck, the sarcophagus sounds like a low-pitched gong. Measuring 20 x 10 royal cubits, it is built in a 2:1 ratio that, Reid states, enhances bass resonances. Did male priests chant here? And was the chanting for the living or the dead? Theosophist Madame

Blavatsky believed that the sarcophagus acted as a baptismal font for initiation. Was the initiate bathed by sound rather than by water?

Reid's findings add credence to theories that the Great Pyramid was used for initiation. Reid, West, and Bauval all affirm the lack of evidence to support the common interpretation that the sarcophagus was a tomb that once contained the pharaoh's mummy. No inscriptions appear inside the King's Chamber to enlighten us as about its use. But now, I would be able to attest for myself that it is the most wonderful place on earth to sing.

## SOUNDING THE SARCOPHAGUS

Our tour ended with a two-hour meditation in the King's Chamber. For years I had listened to stories from other travelers of how, during such meditational periods, the ceiling had opened up to reveal the night sky. Now I would have my own stories to tell. In anticipation of the experience, I wondered if I would feel claustrophobic. But descending through the passageway, I felt ecstatic. I was reminded of Lascaux, of the sense of being deep within the earth. Our group walked quickly down the wooden ramp, and finally we filed into the black granite chamber.

Chris Dunn placed us in three parallel lines to experience the chamber's maximum amplitude. He and I had decided beforehand that the note we would chant would be an "A," the note of the sarcophagus. When he struck its side using his fist like a gong, a deep tone resonated. Together, we all chanted *Om*, and then West instructed the group to sit. He had arranged for the lights to go out for our meditation. It was as dark with my eyes open as it was with my eyes closed. Just then a woman in our group rummaged through her backpack, zipping and unzipping it for what seemed like an eternity. She told me later that she was so scared she needed to shine her flashlight briefly inside her pack just to reassure herself. Someone's stomach growled, sounding like a muffled lion's roar. Then a man fell asleep and started to snore. These were not the sounds I wanted to hear inside the famous King's Chamber.

Finally, we arrived at silence. Every atom in my body became heavier than the stone and then lighter than air. In my mind's eye, I saw Hathor with her cow ears and Isis and Osiris. Their faces shined before me in the dark, along with those of twenty-five Egyptian schoolboys I had met a few hours earlier at the Cairo Museum. I had separated from the tour group and been strolling alone in the sculpture garden when I saw the boys, probably between the ages of seven and nine, sitting on a ledge with their male teacher. One of them waved, and I waved back. Soon all of them were smiling and waving.

Within minutes, twenty-five children had surrounded me. As I began a Basque chant to cleanse the heart called *Oh Shoo Wa*, they clapped, swayed, and chanted with me without missing a note, as if they had grown up with this song. Afterward, they thrust pieces of paper in my face. "Write you name!" I wrote "Susan from New Mexico" over and over on scraps of paper, Egyptian pounds, and even the palms of their tiny hands.

Then several boys had handed me pieces of paper with questions in English from their teacher. "What's it like where you live?" "What kind of writing do you do?" "What do you think of our culture?" I thought for a moment and wrote: "I came to Egypt to experience the ancient sites, but I have fallen in love with the Egyptian people." When this reply was carried back to the teacher, he smiled and waved. One more piece of paper arrived that said simply, "Thank you for speaking with us." Just then my tour group had descended from the museum and walked toward the bus. As the children and I waved goodbye, an armed guard with a belt of bullets around his chest beamed and gave me a "thumbs up."

Now, as I meditated in the King's Chamber, I felt the boys with me again, their faces shining before me like stars circling the sky. I sent prayers to them and to children of all lands and faiths.

When the lights were back on, we took turns lying in the sarcophagus, touching the edges of this "boom box" with our fingertips, chanting *Om* over each other. Each voice became many voices linked together to create harmonic patterns. Finally, it was my turn to lie in the sarcophagus. The *Om* left the mouths of the others in sonic bubbles that funneled into the box and set every crystalline molecule ringing like a miniature galaxy. Three women stayed on the same low drone while another improvised a high melody above. Every part of the King's Chamber—walls, floor, and ceiling—resonated and harmonized with their sounds. I felt I was inside the singing monolith from the movie *2001: A Space Odyssey* and imagined that this was how the pharaoh had become a star.

*Amma giving darshan, California*

~ *Chapter 9* ~

# INDIA'S SOUNDS OF CREATION

*The essence of man is speech.*
*The essence of speech is sacred language.*
*The essence of sacred language is word and sound.*
*The essence of word and sound is Om.*
—The Upanishads

*Om*, the first sound. All sounds have their source in this seed syllable. *Om* is the sound of the expanding universe, the dome of the head opening into a thousand-petaled crown during the awakening of Kundalini, the drone of bees on a summer day, the ocean within a spiral shell, the blood coursing through capillaries.

*Om.* Feel the *O* in the cauldron of your belly; let it rise to the top of your head with the *M*. The body is a laboratory for spirit. Sound *O* and close the lips on *M*; let the sound circulate inside your mouth. Be aware of your body, the alchemist's vessel, and hear the overtones radiate within. Chant slowly, and then speed up the rhythm. Hear the sound *Ma* emanating from *Om*.

*Om Ma, Ma Om.*

For an Orthodox Hindu in Benares, India, the day begins by the River Ganges. Facing east, he sprinkles water on his head, bathes, and then dampens the ground to make it holy as well. He offers flowers, food, and sandalwood paste to the sun god, along with a mantra. Starting with *Om,* he chants a Vedic prayer called the *Gayatri:*

*Om bhur bhuvah svah*

*tat savitur varenyam*

*bhargo devasya dhimahi*

*dhiyo yo nah pracodayat*

*Om Shanti Shanti Shanti*


Earth,

Atmosphere,

Heavens

We meditate on the sacred light of the effulgent source.

Let that inspire our hearts.[1]

According to Karunamayi Sri Vijayeswari Devi, the twenty-four seed syllables of this mantra contain seventy-million supreme mantras to different gods, and all of them merge into the single syllable, *Om*. "Perhaps a whole lifetime is not enough to realize the hidden divine truths of any one of these seed syllables," Devi observes.[2]

India can trace its roots back for at least ten thousand years. Hinduism, its main faith, is thought to be the oldest living religion on earth. Though Hindus worship a vast array of gods and goddesses, they believe they are all like tributaries leading to many streams that flow to the ocean of the One God, Brahman, the eternal reality. Hinduism has no founder, no one holy book.

Hindu temples are centers of communication between the worlds. Alain Danielou tells us that their builders chanted mantras as they placed the temple bricks to infuse them with the god's "rhythmic element."[3] The temples are power generators constructed to receive subtle vibrations and act as a "kind of magnetic center, a yantra which ... crystallizes the cosmic energy."[4] This energy then ripples into the entire countryside. Priests acted as sacred magicians who invoked the deity's presence through ritual and sung formulas. The sexual imagery carved on some temples in the form of voluptuous maidens and entwined lovers reminds us that speech is born from the union of opposites. "The lower lip is the phallus and the upper lip is the vulva."[5] *Om*, often pronounced and spelled *Aum*, is the sound of that union.

## MANTRAS

The Vedas are some of the oldest sacred texts in the world. They were memorized, recited, and passed down through entire families. Vedic mantras such as the *Gayatri* were sung as ritual.

Mantras, sonic formulas used in meditation, are often given to the devotee by a guru. Sometimes they are written on the tongue with a basil wand dipped in honey to insure that all words coming from the mouth are as sweet. Mantras are usually chanted a minimum of 108 times in a sitting. According to yogic traditions, there are many reasons for this number, one of them being that there are 108 energy lines in the subtle body. Mantras feed the chakras with spiritual energy. They vitalize *prana*, our essential life force. Prayer beads called malas are strung with 108 beads, one bead for each utterance. It is recommended that for a mantra to be effective, at least 125, 000 repetitions over time are necessary.

One form of devotional chanting, reciting the names of God perpetually, is called *Japa*. The practice of Japa can be repeated out loud, as a whisper on the lips, or silently intoned. When repetition becomes constant, day in, day out, at waking and in dreams, the words of the mantra disappear and only the subtle sound remains. This is the sound that the poet Kabir, raised in both the Hindu and the Muslim traditions, talks about when he says, "Listen to the secret sound, the real sound which is inside you."[6] Some people spend their whole lives in the practice of Japa without hearing this inner sound. Others may hear it instantly and achieve enlightenment.

"Prayers in Hindu are very sensory," an Indian friend told me, "we give to God all that is good through chanting, ringing bells, and offering garlands, flowers, incense, and food." Hindus worship their many deities with their voice. They chant to Krishna, an incarnation of the god Vishnu, the blue, flute-playing cowherd who embodies the Lord of Love. They chant to the elephant-headed god Ganesha, the remover of obstacles, or to Kali, the dark mother of death and creation.

## CHANTS FROM KALI'S TONGUE

Kali, black with four, blood-smeared hands, holds a severed head in one hand and a sword in the other. Grinning, she stands on top of Shiva's heart as he gazes up at her. Kali is the blood of sacrifice, the blood of death, the blood that forms new life. She is there when a woman screams while giving birth and when an old man sounds the death rattle at his last breath. Her protruding tongue, red as a hibiscus flower, utters the sound that creates the universe.

Kali, the terrible mother, who dances on the cremation grounds, wears a garland of fifty skulls, one for each letter of the Sanskrit alphabet. Each letter is an *akshara*, one of the magic letters that represent the creative power of sound. The letters symbolize the fifty petals of the chakras. "When a Sanskrit mantra is uttered, the petals corresponding to the letters contained in the mantra vibrate in spiritual resonance."[7]

Kali's nine-spired temple sits on the shores of the River Ganges in Dakshineswar. For author Elizabeth Harding, "The building itself seems alive with energy, seems to breathe and watch all who enter the courtyard below."[8] The temple is massive, one hundred feet high and fifty feet square. Inside, a platform surrounds the inner sanctum. Pilgrims ring brass bells to announce their presence. Here, "a family of four sings devotional songs to Kali, and an old woman chants Kali's name loudly as she circumambulates the inner sanctum."[9] A pregnant woman mutters mantras as she smears vermilion powder into the cracks of the walls.[10]

Unlike a Christian church, where silence shows respect, Kali's inner sanctum is cacophonous. Devotees shriek, cry the Mother's name in anguish, chant her mantra, *Om Krim Kali*, and shout until they are hoarse, "*Jai Ma, Jai Ma, Jai Ma, Jai Ma.*" Priests chant, ring cymbals and gongs, beat kettle drums, and blow conch shells. A goddess with a red tongue sticking prominently from her mouth seems to say, "Sing, speak, cry, moan, give me your sounds. Sing your delight and your pain. I am fed by your sounds."

## AMMA

Sri Mata Amritanandamayi, Mother of Immortal Bliss, or "Amma," as she is affectionately known, is called the hugging saint. One of several emanations of the Divine Mother, she welcomes her millions of children into the temple of her arms. Her compassionate embrace is her form of *darshan*, her blessing. Though she lives in India, Amma travels to cities in Europe and the United States every year. I have received darshan many times from her at her ashram in Santa Fe. Inside her Indian ashram, I am told, stands a statue of Kali enthroned between two silver pillars. Amma says that she, the statue, and Kali are all one and the same.

At age two, Amma began singing love songs to Lord Krishna. At five, she was composing her own *bhajans*—devotional songs—and was often deeply immersed in ecstatic trance states. Her parents treated her like Cinderella, making her do all the household chores. Sometimes she slept in a cow shed next to the house. She gave away what little food she had to beggars, for which her parents often beat her.

Amma's public mission began in 1975 when she was twenty-two years old. She made her first trip to the West in 1987 and has sponsored numerous charities in India and abroad. In October 2002, she received the Gandhi-King Award for Non-Violence from the Global Peace Initiative of Women Religious and Spiritual Leaders during a conference at the UN General Assembly Hall in Geneva, Switzerland. Millions of people have received darshan from this hugging saint.

The first time I received darshan from Amma was inside a huge, white tent at one of her ashrams in the middle of a forest near Santa Fe. The smell of piñon mingled with sandalwood incense. By the time I arrived, a crowd was milling around. People greeted old friends, looked at tables full of information, or browsed among the many booths selling malas, photos, books, and CDs. The event was highly organized. Upon arrival, we had all been given tokens to designate our turn with Amma; mine was number 1351. Assistants kept a monitor updated to show what number would next be served, as at a cosmic Baskin and Robbins.

Suddenly two lines formed, and someone initiated the chant *Om Amriteswaryi Namaha*—"I bow to that Supreme Energy which is Immortal Bliss." People swayed and chanted. Soon I, too, was synchronized by the rhythm. Around me I saw babies rocked in their mothers' arms. One little girl hugged an Amma doll. A woman in white danced ecstatically. Another closed her eyes and held her hands in prayer.

Then a three-year-old girl yelled, "Amma's coming!" A few moments later, Amma walked into the tent, followed by an entourage of devotees. She was radiant, dressed in a white sari, with a garland of flowers around her neck and sandalwood paste and vermilion painted on her third eye. She touched the many outstretched hands and smiled before climbing steps to be seated on a cushioned chair.

Devotional singing then started slowly and eventually became feverish in pitch. Laughing, Amma sang and lifted her arms in ecstasy. She seemed to be filling up with divine energy, bringing it down into her soft, round body. We all sat awaiting her blessing. The sounds of chanting voices, finger cymbals, and tablas spun around me, and I joined the chant. *Om Nama Shivaya*. A Swami dressed in orange led us through a meditation, "Feel *Ma* on the in-breath, *Om* on the out-breath. *Ma Om*. Divine Love. Divine Light."

After the meditation, Amma began to welcome her children into her embrace, as in a giant family reunion. She looked like the storyteller doll of the Southwest Indians, or a goddess with a thousand arms. I watched her embrace whole families, her arms wide enough to hug three at a time. Sometimes her face looked pained, as if absorbing their unspoken anguish. Sometimes she greeted people with a laugh or a loving gaze. I watched grown men cry in her arms. A woman wiped tears from her eyes onto her own white sari.

Finally, I moved into the line. Seated on a multicolored carpet, we all slowly inched closer to Amma on our knees. When I was about ten feet away, I could feel her aura. It was clean, cool, refreshing, and sweet like rose water.

At last, I myself was in Amma's arms. She held me to her, rocked me, and gazed into my eyes with a look of utter joy. Then she whispered in my ear, *"Ma Ma Ma Ma Ma Ma Ma."* I cried and laughed at the same time. She showered me with rose petals and placed a Hershey's kiss into my hand. It was like receiving a drop of chocolate milk from the breast of the Dark Mother. Feeling giddy, I made my way to the side of the tent and stood there, empty and full, returning to my breath: *Ma Om. Ma Om. Ma Om.*

Several years later, I saw Amma again at a ceremony in celebration of the Divine Mother called *Devi Bhava.* After a meditation and devotional singing, she retreated behind a white curtain in a makeshift temple in the ballroom of Santa Fe's La Fonda Hotel. A few minutes later, like a quick-change artist in a magician's show, she appeared in the regalia of the Divine Mother. Instead of her usual white sari, she was dressed in red and gold silk. Around her neck was a garland of fresh red roses. Her long black hair flowed free under a golden crown. She was adorned with jewels. A devotee waved a camphor flame before her as the singing rose in intensity. Then she sat and gave darshan until dawn.

After a long wait, it was my turn. On this occasion, I had felt moved to ask Amma for a mantra. Upon receiving my token— number 843—I had been told to say "Mantra" to Amma before she *Ma-ma-ma-ed* me. When I did so, she nodded to an attendant, dressed in white, who placed me over to the side of the stage to wait.

Eventually an Indian man, also dressed in white, led a group of about six of us down the steps over to a circle of chairs. "It is a great gift to receive a mantra from Amma," he told us, "as she is a *Satguru,* one who is in a state of union with God. She transfers some of her divine energy into the mantra, and implants it with her *sankalpa,* or will. This will help to lessen any negative karma you have. Receiving a mantra from Amma means that she is committed to your spiritual progress and enlightenment."

The man told us that we should practice our mantra daily, draw near to Amma whenever possible, and see her in all that we meet, especially those people we have difficulty accepting. He asked us to search ourselves to make sure we were ready for this commitment. A moment of doubt bubbled up. What was I getting into? Who is this woman? Yet everything I had witnessed or heard about Amma over the years had been consistent. This was a woman dedicated to love, a Lady of Roses. I remembered reading her words in a brochure, "Darling children, Mother does not say that you should believe in Mother or a God in heaven. It is enough to believe in yourself. Everything is in you." My doubts subsided, and I felt prepared to accept her as my teacher. We were each given a pamphlet on mantras and asked to write down to whom we pray. Some wrote "Christ." Others, "Buddha." One woman wrote, "The Void." I wrote "Divine Mother."

Soon we were all escorted back to the stage. After a few minutes, a different attendant placed me by Amma's side. She was still giving darshan, still hugging people left and right. She turned and smiled at me from time to time, showering me with rose petals. Then suddenly Amma looked into my eyes. I felt a wave of love as she whispered Sanskrit syllables into my ear. These sounds were private, belonging only to Amma and me. I was linked forever to this moment of sweet sonance and rose petals.

Another woman then whisked me away. She asked me to pronounce my mantra and gave me a slip of paper with the words written in English and Sanskrit. A man led me down the steps over to a different circle of chairs, where a second woman awaited my small group to help us integrate our experience. This woman instructed us on how to meditate, emphasizing that our mantra was a secret link with Amma, a way to call her closer.

Though I have followed a regular morning practice, I also say my mantra inwardly whenever I think about it during the day: in grocery lines, waiting for a plane to take off, driving in my car, at night when I can't sleep. Sometimes, when I start to worry, I catch myself and say my mantra instead. It is becoming a steady stream, a rhythmic presence inside me, like a mother's lullaby.

As is true of many practices, there are times when repeating my mantra is mechanical. Sometimes it is boring. Sometimes I think I'm too busy. Sometimes Amma seems far away. But sometimes she is as close as the air underneath the syllables I utter. Each time I chant my mantra, I am watering the seeds Amma whispered in my ear. I can still feel her breath.

## EMBODYING MANTRAS

One of Amma's children is a woman named Susi who has environmental illness. She had seen Amma for the first time when the Mother had recently been in Santa Fe. Susi hadn't planned to go, but the night before Amma had appeared to her in a dream, saying, "This is part of your life purpose. You have to come and meet me."

Susi and I had met when she had asked for sessions to develop a practice of devotional singing. We began the sessions in her home in El Dorado, east of Santa Fe. She was, however, reactive to my clothing. She had asked if I would wash my clothes in baking soda, but then even my fragrance-free Arm and Hammer detergent was too much for her. Was it the smell of my car from the two-hour drive to her home? Or the smell of the world on me?

She asked if I'd consider wearing her clothes in our sessions. I told her I'd think about it. I wasn't sure. I wondered about boundaries, about being in "her skin." Despite these concerns, I said yes. In her bathroom I took off my worldly clothes and put on hers. She asked me to wrap my hair in a towel. I felt like a priest preparing for mass, or a Buddhist nun donning saffron robes. When I left the bathroom and walked into her living room, I felt I had crossed a threshold into a temple, into a place of purity, into a devotional space of song. Pictures of Amma, Mother Meera, and other representations of the Divine Mother were placed on a simple altar. I told Susi I felt honored. It helped us both to see her world in a different light.

Most of us cannot imagine the life Susi leads. She is like the proverbial canary that the miners send down into the coal mine to test the air. She struggles with things we take for granted. Printer's ink and chemicals used in paper make it hard for her to read. She is reactive to electromagnetic frequencies and has had a special telephone built that reduces these vibrations. She speaks through a tube to gain distance from the electromagnetic frequencies and needs to pause frequently while talking. She is allergic to many foods and many of the materials used in houses. She struggles with fear, anger, and despair.

But though Susi is cloistered from the world, she reaches out through her song in service to us all. She considers herself a song pilgrim and sings to people over the phone. Once she sang an Aboriginal lullaby I had taught her to another environmentally ill woman who was sleepless and considering suicide. The woman was calmed enough to go to sleep. In that moment, Susi became an emissary of the Divine Mother, soothing the fears of one of her children, letting her know that love exists in the world, that her despair had been heard.

Six months after we had started working together, Susi moved to Dallas to be treated for environmental illness at a clinic. After a time she became more connected and grew closer to a spiritual community of Amma's devotees. "Amma's music is here," Susi told me, "Whether I'm well or ill, rich or poor, this is where I need to be for now."

Since Susi moved to Dallas, I've been working with her once a month by phone. We always begin our sessions in silence and tune into Amma. During one meditation, I saw Amma show me a red hibiscus flower, which prompted me to tell Susi what I had been reading about Kali's tongue uttering the sounds of creation. The tongue exercises I gave her to do brought up many repressed feelings.

Susi wanted to learn to chant the *Sri Lalitha Sahasranamam,* the Thousand Names of the Divine Mother, a litany of sacred names that many of Amma's devotees chant. When she had listened to a tape, she been captured by the mantra and felt a deep homecoming. It was so powerful and moved so much energy in her body that she could only listen to it for five minutes a day. It took her two weeks to hear the entire tape, but each time she listened she knew this was a practice she would do for the rest of her life.

Since Susi responds best to homeopathic doses of sound, I proposed she learn just the first name of the Divine Mother, *Om Sri Matre Namah*. The next month, Susi told me she was doing her mantra practice in the morning. I suggested she draw the mantra in the air with her finger. A month later, Susi said she wasn't just drawing the mantra in the air, she was writing it on her body with her finger. She traced *Om Sri Matre Namah*, "Salutations to the Divine Mother, who is Mother of all," onto her heart. She used her feet to trace the sacred letters in the air forwards and backwards. She traced the name with her pelvis and with her shoulders. She traced it with her eyes, feeling subtle shifts inside. She felt the hemispheres of her brain connect, her nervous system calm down, and her energy field expand.

As Susi relayed this experience I remembered reading of a tantric practice called *anga-nyasa*. In it, "the aspirant is asked to consecrate different parts of his or her body to the body of the Mother by placing the different letters, both vowels and consonants, on them. During this practice one is to feel that part of the physical body, with all its biological processes going on within, really belongs to the Mother and not to oneself."[11] When Susi heard this, she was gratified to know that she had intuitively connected to an ancient practice.

During our last session, Susi began to embody the mantra in her cells. She felt the chant helped her enter the poetry of her life. I suggested she use the tip of her tongue to draw the mantra into her mouth, to write it on different places in her upper palate, to use her breath as a paintbrush, painting onto the air the sacred letters of the Divine Mother's name. I'm waiting for my next report.

*Kagya Mila Guru Stupa, north of Questa, New Mexico*

~ *Chapter 10* ~

# CIRCLING THE STUPA

*At almost any hour of day or night,*
*from among the thick crowds in this part of the stupa's grounds,*
*one can hear the deep-throated chants, tintabulations of the*
*bells and cymbals, the booming drums and buzzing shawms,*
*and see the great lama swaying and gesturing upon his silken throne.*

—Peter Gold

Throughout Asia, stupas are representations of the legendary Mount Meru, the central pole between heaven and earth. Some stupas look like mountains, some like breasts. Some have spires, some are like inverted bells, some are gilded, and some are like lotus buds blooming on the earth. All are reliquaries for Buddha's body and a monument to "*parinirvara*—his final transcendence."[1]

When Buddha died in 483 BC, eight kings built eight stupas throughout northern India and southern Nepal to house his cremated remains. Many stupas now house sacred relics of lamas and saints. They are not just monuments but reminders of the spiritual potential that can be awakened within each one of us. They represent Buddha's mind. Some have eyes that gaze into infinite blue sky. Some are symbolic of Buddha crowned and meditating on his throne. All are circled with song.

In Tibet, pilgrims circumambulate the stupa, the center of the universe, walking clockwise and uttering "mantras and prayers while flicking rosary beads."[2] Prayer flags wave in the wind while flames flicker from candles and butter lamps. People read from prayer books, "lightly intoning the sacred syllables and verses like so many bees buzzing in the honeycombs of their hives."[3]

In a legend of a crystal stupa, one day the Bodhisattva Manjushri, riding on the back of a garuda bird, passed over a clear primeval lake. As a thought rose in his mind, a drop of his semen fell into the lake. There a cosmic lotus plant grew and formed a single blossom. Eons passed, and the lotus floated toward an island in the center of the lake. Upon touching it, the lotus opened to reveal within it "a perfectly formed stupa made of gem-like, crystalline material that radiated pulses of light, day and night without stop."[4]

Time passed, and the glow emanating from the stupa reached Manchuria, where a later incarnation of Manjushri noticed its radiance. He returned to the lake. Realizing the need for people to live near such an auspicious place, but also realizing that it was inaccessible to mankind, he cut the lotus-born stupa with his flaming sword and moved it to a valley. There he placed it inside a hill, where its pulsations were felt rather than seen. When the people arrived, they felt the radiance of this crystalline stupa and marked the holy spot with another, golden one, "realizing that both mountain-like monuments were none other than the mind of Manjushri made material."[5] Tibetan Buddhists and others from far-away places still make pilgrimages to the Katmandu Valley in Nepal, where the radiance of the crystalline stupa can still be felt.

## MOUNTAIN STUPAS OF NEW MEXICO

In New Mexico, and throughout the Sangre de Cristo and Rocky Mountains of Colorado, stupas rest at the foot of mountains, mirroring the stupas of Tibet. Tibetans feel a particular affinity to these mountains, which remind them of their exiled homeland. Each stupa has its resident lama. Other lamas appear frequently as they make pilgrimages to these temples along the Rio Grande.

In Questa, a half-hour's drive from where I live, the *Kagya Mila Guru* stupa sits near Lama Mountain. It was built in 1992 as a memorial to Herman Rednick, a meditation teacher who blended Eastern and Western techniques. Many mantras were built into this stupa during its construction, including one for *Chenrezig*, a Bodhisattva of compassion. While most stupas throughout the world are solid, this one houses a small shrine room.

On the way to Colorado I had driven past the stupa several times; one day I decided to stop. It is often windy in the spring in northern New Mexico, and the prayer flags sounded like heavy rain or beating wings. I circled the stupa three times and chanted my mantra, but when I went to open the door of the shrine room it was locked. For a while I sat outside and watched the colored flags sending prayers into the air; then I walked over to an informational bulletin board. One sentence leaped out: "Stupas bless all beings who touch and see them." Some magpies sat on the rope holding the flags. A robin perched briefly on the white spire and flew off. A locust buzzed in a nearby tree. Each was blessed by the stupa; each gave its blessing.

Suddenly a red-haired woman appeared, introducing herself as one of the caretakers. I asked if I could go inside. "Would it be all right to sing?" "Yes," she told me, adding that not only do people chant traditional mantras in the shrine room, but a small group had sung carols there over Christmas as well.

Alone inside the stupa, I spent some moments in awe looking at deities painted on the walls. At the north sat Green Tara, a goddess of mercy with a stringed instrument at her feet. On the altar was a full white rose, tinged with pink. On the ceiling an eight-spoked mandala was home to a dangling spider.

After quieting myself, I heard an "Ah" and began to tone. It was like being inside a Tibetan bell. I heard a beating sound between my ears. Many voices became part of my voice—the voice of a red-hatted Tibetan lama whose picture graced the altar, the voice of the spider. All our voices merged into a radiant pink lotus with vibrating petals.

## GREEN TARA

In Santa Fe, the *Kagyu Shenpen Kunchab* stupa has a shrine room, this one housing a golden Buddha. The main practice there is *Avalokiteshvara*, the Bodhisattva of compassion. Practitioners meditate on themselves as *Avalokiteshvara* and recite the mantra, *Om Mani Padme Hum*, which praises the jewel in the lotus. Green Tara, a widespread practice in Tibet, is also honored here.

Green Tara sits on a white moon inside a fully-bloomed lotus. She is ready to step into the world whenever she is called. She hears the cries of the world, tames the elements, and soothes our fears. She protects, heals, dispels evil, and liberates us from the eight internal fears of pride, delusion, hatred, envy, avarice, lust, doubt, and fanaticism. She protects from the eight external fears, which may also be seen as symbolic, of lions, elephants, fires, snakes, ghosts, floods, demons, and imprisonment. She is the lady of supreme peace, the Mother of All Buddhas, the golden lady of bounty. She is swift, fearless, and spontaneous. Her right hand is held in a mudra of supreme generosity. The mudra of her left hand bestows refuge. She holds a blue utpala flower in each hand and wears rainbow stockings and a jeweled tiara. She was born through one of Avalokiteshvara's tears when he witnessed earth's suffering.

White Tara was born from his other tear. She increases the fortunes and length of life. Green Tara removes obstacles on the path to enlightenment, helping us cross the ocean of suffering into liberation.

Chanting Tara's mantra, *Om Tare Tutare Ture Soha*, brings her to us instantaneously in times of danger or illness. "*Om* is the beginning syllable. *Tare* means that she can rescue from the ceaseless round of cyclic existence and *Tutare* means that she can rescue from the Eight Great Fears. *Ture* means that she has the power to heal us from chronic diseases. *Soha* is the last syllable of the mantra as *Om* is the beginning."[6]

*Om Tare Tutare Ture Soha.* Chant her mantra and see her in front you, a white *Om* at her crown, a red *Ah* at her throat, the blue syllable of *Hum* at her heart. Chant her mantra and see rays of light connect her crown, throat, and heart to yours. Chant her mantra and become her body, her mind, and her speech. Chant her mantra and become active compassion to those who need help: elders in nursing homes, soldiers dying, children crying in the night, whales beached on ocean shores. Send compassionate aid to prostitutes, homeless people sleeping on sidewalks, and cows in cattle yards. *Om Tare Tutare Ture Soha*. Become a temple for Green Tara and surround the earth with mercy's song, swiftly and without delay.


## PEACE PAGODA

In the small town of Grafton, New York, in the Hudson River Valley, a Japanese Buddhist nun of the *Nipponzan Myohoji* order sat on donated land and began to build a pagoda for peace. She began alone, digging the earth with a kitchen spoon. Word spread. People began to show up from all walks of life and from different religions to help her. They donated their time, labor, skills, money, and love to build the peace pagoda and bring it from dream into reality.

Peace pagodas, symbols of nonviolence, have been built for the last two thousand years. Emperor Ashoka of India built the first one. The emperor, a particularly bloody warlord, was reproached by a Buddhist monk after a dreadful battle. He quit his warlike ways, became a devout Buddhist, and began to erect pagodas in the name of peace.

With a group of musicians from New Mexico who were going to perform in Albany, I went to the New York Peace Pagoda for a blessing. We arrived in the late spring. After a short walk through a trail in the woods, we were greeted by Jun Yusada. She welcomed us in her caretaker's home, and we all huddled around a wood stove. The home was simple. The carpet was made of brightly colored squares duct-taped together, and the plywood walls were just draped with colored cloth. And yet the atmosphere was one of a temple. At the front was an altar that Jun Yusada had filled with flowers, fruit, a picture of her teacher, and burning incense.

Motioning for us to sit on pillows in front of the altar, she introduced us to a group of Japanese Buddhists and others who were there for the day. Together, we chanted *Na-Ma-Myo-Ho-Ren-Ge-Kyo,* a sutra from the thirteenth century. It is made up of *Nam,* the Sanskrit word for "dedication"; *Myoho,* Japanese for the "Mystic Law," the essential principle of the universe; *Renge,* Japanese for the pure lotus flower which grows from the mud, the symbol of Buddha; and *Kyo,* Japanese for "sutra," the teachings of Buddha.[7] Sacred syllables, strung together like pearls, joined our hearts and minds together.

The chant ended in a soft stream, like incense dispersing into the air. Jun Yusada bowed to the altar and then to us. She asked if we were all from Albuquerque. "I walked through there," she exclaimed. She had taken part in "The Longest Walk" in 1978, when she joined Native Americans who walked from San Francisco to Washington D.C. Since then she has crossed the country four more times, beating her drum while chanting. *Na-Ma-Myo-Ho-Ren-Ge-Kyo*: each word was a footstep, a heartbeat, a prayer. The chant was a road, a song-line of peace, sacred syllables dropping like lotus seeds onto asphalt.

Jun Yusada handed us all striped Mexican blankets to wear like shawls as we formed a procession and were led outside by one of the men. We made a brief pilgrimage to the pagoda. Some used bare sticks to beat hand drums that looked like skin stretched over small tennis rackets. *Na-Ma-Myo-Ho-Ren-Ge-Kyo.* How many times have these words been chanted by Jun Yusada? By Buddhists all over the world? We circled the pagoda three times, stopping at a white marble Buddha who faces towards the rising sun and at each of the four directions. We chanted and circled past sculptures of Buddha's life. The pagoda is like a giant transmitter, a radio tower to the universe, letting the stars know that on this planet, on this place in Grafton, New York, people are praying for peace. I hope the world receives this broadcast along with the news.

Once we were back inside her home, Jun Yusada offered us all cups of hot tea and cookies. She placed a blanket over a pregnant woman's shoulders who had labored to build the pagoda for four years. It was the woman's birthday and the blanket, a gift. Jun Yusada sang, "Happy Birthday dear Karen-san." We sang with her. It was short distance from *Om* to "Happy Birthday," in her home.

Then Jun Yusada gave gifts for everyone. She passed a bowl full of wooden hearts. Angels danced in the center of each heart. On the back were pins so that we could wear them and always remember this day.

She told us that our group could stay but that she and several others needed to leave. They would be driving to Maine to fast in front of a naval shipyard, joining a Christian group called Plowshares. Together, they planned to fast and chant and beat a nuclear submarine into a plowshare. As they left I sang a chant I had learned years earlier:

> And into plowshares beat our swords
> We shall study war no more.
>
> No more. No more. No more. . . .

*Ariel Freilich blowing the shofar, Rosh Hashanah, 2006*

~ *Chapter 11* ~

# THE TABLE AS TEMPLE

*The time for love has come,*
*my bride: come to my garden*
*The vine is blooming and*
*the pomegranate is budding.*
*Let us rejoice and sing.*
—based on the Song of Songs 6:11

Jewish melodies go straight to my heart. The lamenting minor key that can grow into ecstatic joy mirrors something ancient and deep and moves me in a different way than other spiritual music does. But I did not grow up with this music or these traditions. My family names are Jensen, Bossert, Kempton, and Hawkins. There are no Isaacs or Rachels in my bloodline. Even when I was a child growing up in Arizona and later in California's San Joaquin Valley, the names of my classmates were English, Portuguese, Spanish, and Japanese. It was only in my early twenties, when I moved to Northern California, that I began to meet Jewish friends and to hear the richness and variety of their music. But even then I knew little of Judaism. I always wanted to know more, to find my own way into this faith whose songs struck such a chord in me.

Ironically, it was the Black Madonna who, through the Old Testament story of the dark Shulamite from the Song of Songs, created a doorway. It tells of a woman black and comely, as beautiful as the tents of Cedar, who calls herself the Rose of Sharon. She speaks of a time when the voice of the turtle—a silent creature—will be heard upon the land.

For me personally, Jewish songs embody another melody sung by the Lady of Roses, one that has bloomed in the desert and been forged in exile. And *Shekhinah* is the being that led me into understanding the Sabbath.

In traditional Judaism, Shekhinah is the feminine aspect of the Divine. Present at the beginning of creation as God's consort and bride, she is the indwelling presence of divinity that makes itself available to humans in some form we can comprehend. The Jewish Temple at Jerusalem was considered her dwelling place, and the rituals and ceremonies enacted there were in celebration of her. According to Jewish legend, when the Babylonians destroyed the first temple in 626 BC, Shekhinah went into exile along with her children. Thus, wandering the earth, she became separated from her divine spouse. At times, she may also become separated from her people. The belief is that human acts of destruction and cruelty cause Shekhinah to flee to the higher realms and become hidden from us, while love, good deeds, and the need for comfort bring her closer. [1]

For those growing up in contemporary liberal Judaism, the *Shekhinah* is not widely known. However, the Zohar, Kabbalistic literature, and the current Jewish Renewal Movement are giving a place to her once again.

## SHABBAT

The Friday evening rituals of the Sabbath—or Shabbat—are symbolically designed, through actions, prayers, and lovemaking, to reunite the divine Bride and Bridegroom who became separated when the temple was destroyed. Jews all over the world invite the Shekhinah to join them at the beginning of this sacred period every week in the Jewish faith. The white tablecloth is spread. A braided challah loaf sits on a special plate covered with a white cloth. The table has become a temple. Women light candles, covering their eyes as they pray:

*Baruch atah Adonai.*
Blessed are You, our God,

King of the Universe,

Who has commanded us to kindle the Light of Shabbat.[2]

Shabbat. Shabbos. Sabbath: different names to reflect different branches of Judaism. The word *Sabbath* itself means "to rest." One night every week, tables in Israel, France, Brazil, Argentina, America, Morroco, Turkey, Canada, and South Africa are set with flowers and delicacies, reflecting paradise on a white cloth.

The custom of Shabbat was established in the Ten Commandments, which decreed that a day of rest be set aside in which no work would be done from sundown on Friday until three stars are seen on Saturday evening. This sacred period symbolically reflects the words of Genesis 2:2 that the Creator rested on the seventh day.

Every other day of the week leads toward this holy day of Saturday. The day afterward, Sunday, is not just a day in itself but the first in a new cycle leading to a "sanctuary in time."[3] Week in, week out, Shabbat is part of a rhythm at the very center of Jewish life.

There are three Shabbat meals—Friday night, Saturday lunch, and just before twilight on Saturday. Since no work is permitted during the holy period, the devout prepare meals beforehand, including an elaborate meal on Friday night. As for any wedding celebration, people wear their best clothes. The finest china and silver are laid on the table. Then the hidden Shekhinah—the Bride that awaits her Beloved—is called in through the lighting of candles, prayer, readings from the Torah, and song, all intended to bring the world back into balance again. As the song *Lekha Dodi*, "Come my Beloved," invokes:

Let us greet the bride,

Let us welcome the presence of Shabbat....

Thus the Heavenly Queen "descends once a week to dispense her holiness."[4] She is the matrix behind everything, the white space between the black letters of the Torah. She is that which hides in order to be found.

The Song of Songs is often a favorite theme of Shabbat, filled as it is with its lush imagery of saffron and cinnamon, budding pomegranates, and feeding on honeycombs among the lilies. The beloved has breasts like grape clusters, lips like scarlet threads, a mouth like wine. The songs celebrate the Shekhinah who is "the talking mouth, the word illuminated in living speech, the story that unfolds like fruit from the tree of life."[5]

For singer Consuelo Luz, Shabbat is a time to enjoy everything in a sacred context: food, music, dance, sex. "Everything is more intense and elevated," she remarked. "We imbue everything with sacredness; everything is for God. Ideally, we should live this way every day. We live such a fragmented life during the week, but during Shabbat there is a celebration of oneness."

Consuelo sings at the Temple Beth Shalom in Santa Fe at Friday services. "When the last verse of the Lekha Dodi is sung, everyone turns to the door to welcome in the Sabbath Queen," she told me. "You can feel the spirit entering yourself. I always feel so grateful, so blessed. For me, the Shekhinah is the nurturing aspect of God, the one that brings light, love, and joy. Singing at the temple always bestows the incredible gift of a sense of oneness with others and the Divine; it is one of my favorite places in the world to sing. Temples were built for enlightened purposes. People go to them with the intention of giving energy back to God, so that everything becomes a circle. Sound has the power to crack open the universe. Humanity is dying of the thirst to access other dimensions. Singing is a key."

Consuelo's roots are in the Sephardic tradition, meaning that her family comes from Jews of Spanish ancestry. She sings Sephardic songs in Hebrew and Ladino, the Spanish of the Jews similar to the old Castillian language. "Though I was raised Catholic," she said, "I found out that we were Jewish on my mother's side and related to St. Teresa of Avila, whose family were *conversos*—Jews forcibly converted to Catholicism."

Today, New Mexico has many crypto-Jews, descendants of those who were forced to hide their faith when they came to the New World after being expelled from Spain during the Inquisition in the sixteenth century. At that time, priests would call out along the road-side, appealing to the Jews to accept baptism. But the Jews refused, and their rabbis told the women to sing and beat their drums. Contemporary Sephardic Jews exemplify the reality of the melding of traditions that happened after that Diaspora. Like Consuelo, many of them are reclaiming their roots and gathering to bring their faith into the light once more.

## EXILE

Marjorie Agosin, a poet, writer, and untiring human rights activist, is a descendant of European Jews who escaped the Holocaust and settled in Chile until forced into exile by Pinochet's dictatorship. As Marjorie remembers, "When I heard Hebrew and Yiddish songs as a child in Chile, they were always sung with a Spanish accent. Jewish people have always carried the essence of their identity within them. The music has evolved, but the heart of the song is the same. Today, the songs of Shabbat, Passover, and other Jewish holidays are still Spanish at the core. In them, I hear thousands of years of history. When I hear Spanish, I hear voices of ancient spirits embedded in the language. I realize that I am but a small thread in many threads. Language is a way of hearing these threads, of harmonizing life," she told me.

"In the house where I grew up in Santiago de Chile," she writes, "I heard a Babel of whispers, songs, prayers, and languages. Spanish was my mother tongue. It was spoken in the fiestas, in the schools, and in the poetry books I loved and read out loud, as poetry should be read. My maternal grandparents spoke German and Yiddish. My paternal grandparents spoke Russian and often sang to the music of the balalaika bought in a flea market at the outskirts of our city.

"In school I learned Hebrew and songs in Ladino. At first I seemed to be confused with too many languages, but as the years progressed all of [them became] and continue to be a part of my inheritance as a Jew, as a poet, and as a woman. It was truly enchanting to hear and feel the depth of these many languages that embedded the narratives of the Jewish people throughout our history."[6]

Marjorie says that "Jewish religion and music is about exile and nostalgia and yearning. The music carries a little bit of what was lost." In effect, music gives the Jews a way of naming their world; and the naming is a way of owning, of remembering who they are. This is an important process for anyone who has been uprooted and displaced. It is a claiming of identity. As Marjorie put it, "Naming our world allows us, even in exile, to have inner permanence surrounded by peace. The permanence we long for is the permanence of peace."[7]

## THE TEMPLE

One longing Jews in exile have is for Jerusalem's Temple, which was built in the tenth century BC by King Solomon, destroyed in 626 BC, rebuilt, and destroyed again thirty years later. The Bible describes the temple Solomon built as a tabernacle of gold and silver, with linen veils wrought with fine needlework. The beams and floors were of cedar, and open flowers and palms trees were carved on pillars and overlaid with gold. The altar, in a room called the Holy of Holies, was carved of pure gold. Here, the Ark of the Covenant, containing the tablets of the Ten Commandments, stood on the Rock of Foundation; above it, two cherubim, carved of olive wood covered with gold, stretched their wings. These two angels were the source of prophecy, the revelation of God's voice. And it was here that the Shekhinah dwelled, revealing the radiance of the Divine to her people.

Legend says that, beneath the temple, a network of underground streams spread out to all parts of the country. "Everything done in the temple was amplified and broadcast. The influence of chants and ritual permeated through the veins and energy field of the earth."[8] Lyres, trumpets, horns, cymbals, and drums all sounded within the temple walls. Chronicles speaks of the Levites who, with cymbals, psaltries, and harps, "stood at the east end of the altar, and with them a hundred and twenty priests sounding with trumpets" (Chron. 5:12). In biblical times, singing and the playing of instruments were related to prophecy. When the first temple was destroyed, the whole center of Jewish life was uprooted, leading to the great Diaspora. The secret musical understandings of the Levites, the temple singers, went underground. The Levites lamented, "How shall we sing the Lord's song in a foreign land?"[9]

For some Jews, the loss of the temple is still a cause for mourning; they long to rebuild what was destroyed so long ago. In Jerusalem, the original temple's only surviving element is the western wall, called the Wailing Wall. Here, Jewish men from all over the world gather to pray. Inside the nooks and crannies of the wall, they place small pieces of paper upon which they have written their prayers.

For others, the temple has become an inward place, even as in Exodus 25:8 God says, "Create for me a holy place and I will dwell within you." Not having a permanent home, during the Diaspora the people themselves became God's dwelling place, along with a portable shrine called a *Mishkan*. The tribes of Israel circled the Mishkan as they camped. At this time, "the *Shekhinah* came to represent Jewish longing for an end to exile."[10] She became like the arms of the mother protecting her children. The Mishkan, the prayer shawl or *tallit*, the harvest home or *sukkah*, and the marriage canopy or *huppa* all were symbols of her indwelling presence.

Eventually, however, and although orthodox Judaism still celebrates the Shekhinah as the Bride of the Sabbath, patriarchal dominance forced its mystical tenets and practices to go underground. The Shekhinah was originally one of the seventy-two names of God. Cantor Ira Fein says that "with the emergence of Patriarchal Judaism, names for God that were not masculine were suppressed, or just not taught, and therefore languished in obscurity until they were revived by Jewish Renewal and certain segments of the Reform and Reconstructionist movements." The Jewish Renewal to which he refers is a contemporary transdenominational movement, grounded in the mystical and prophetic traditions of Judaism. Its members strive to bring the balance of the masculine and feminine within themselves for greater wholeness.

One rabbi aligned with Jewish Renewal is Shefa Gold of Jemez Springs, New Mexico. "We try to make our spiritual practice as beautiful as possible to create a container for the really hard work of transformation," Shefa told me. I attended a workshop with her in Taos in preparation for the High Holy Days, beginning with Rosh Hashanah, the Jewish New Year, and ending ten days later with Yom Kippur, the Day of Atonement. The High Holy Days are a time of reflections, forgiveness, and regeneration. The purpose of this sacred time, she told us, is to renew our relationship with God.

Chanting words from the Torah, Shefa led us through a process of Recognition, Remembrance, Reconciliation, Responsibility, and Realignment. "Breathe the energy of the chant into your heart," she instructed. We chanted a song with imagery from the Song of Songs with the intention to give God, the Beloved, the hidden places in our hearts that separate us from the Source. We moved with the chant, bringing our hands to our hearts in a gesture of pulling out our secret failings and giving them to God. As I chanted, I felt as if I were doing my spiritual laundry—lifting out all my soiled, gray doubts that keep me stuck. Shefa uses chanting to find information beyond the conscious mind and plant an intention deep within the heart. This way of praying, she says, serves to "open you with a knife to reveal yourself to God."

Shefa told us how in Deuteronomy 32:1-43 God gave Moses a song and instructed him to "teach it to the Israelites; put it in their mouths, that this song may be a witness. God tells Moses," she went on, "that when they enter into the Land they will become lazy and forget to keep the covenant. When that happens, even though they might ignore every teaching, the song that has been planted within them will not be forgotten, and it will serve as a reminder, as a witness which can help to redirect the hearts of the people towards the One God."[11]

As a member of the Jewish Renewal movement, Shefa believes that Judaism is a living, evolving tradition; each generation reinterprets its essence to reform it into what is newly useful. As we prepared in her workshop for Rosh Hoshana, the Jewish New Year, she reminded us of the three instructions for this holy day from the Talmud, a compilation of all commentaries on the Torah: to eat rich food, drink sweet wine, and share with those who have none. "Chanting together is sharing good rich food," Shefa observed. "It gives strength for the work that lies ahead."

Shefa creates chants by taking a phrase from the Torah. One chant, *Kosi R'vaya*, from Psalm 23, translates as "my cup runneth over." In building the intention for this chant, she invited the workshop participants to be conscious of two dimensions of the word *cup*. As she put it, "One 'cup' is located in the heart. It is the connection to the source of Life and Love within us; and no matter what befalls us, or what 'enemy' faces us from across the table, that inner cup continues to flow and to overflow. The sound of the chant reconnects us with that flow. The other 'cup' is the one that is formed in community. The sound of our voices and the strength of our shared intention create that cup, which both contains the divine flow and serves as a vehicle for our nourishment. As we form the cup of community, we enable each person to access exactly what they need, to drink individually from the flow that we create together."[12]

## SYNAGOGUES

For over three thousand years, Jews have gathered for Sabbath prayers at the synagogue, also called *shule* or "school." The cantor chants the first line of each prayer, which the chorus of worshipers follows. Each service has a different melody or mode called a *nusach*. Entering a synagogue, you can tell the time of day, the holiday, and the particular prayer by the nusach. In the past, the congregation of men rocked back and forth, praying in a melodic recitation called *davennen*. Women were separated from the men by a curtain, sometimes even sitting upstairs. Today, in many temples, men and women worship together, pounding their chests as they pray. A Jewish woman in my writing group remembers the prayers as laments, yearnings that cry out to God, "I want to be with you."

Jewish prayer begins with the phrase *Baruch atah Adonai*: "The Torah itself is called song, and is sung out."[13] The three tenets of Judaism are Creation, Revelation, and Redemption: God created the world, revealed Himself through the Torah, and delivered Jews out of Egypt. He continues to redeem those that live according to the 613 good deeds, or *mitzvot,* that Jews live by. God's presence is not in a temple, not on an altar, and not in the golden idols of Egypt. Rather, God is everywhere—in the heart, in the home, in the soul, in desert and city alike.

> Oh God, you who are concealed;
> Everywhere is God's Presence.
> How can we remember?

Singer Susan Berman told me that this song is sung to remember the spark of God within fanned by the breath. Though her family was Jewish, her father left Orthodox Judaism and she was reared as a Unitarian. Some time ago, a Mayan shaman told her she needed to explore her heritage. Since then she has been ingesting her tradition. "I'm standing on my ancestors' shoulders," she says, "finding my own voice. Judaism is a vocal tradition; it is all about sound. God spoke us into being."

The holiest prayer in the Jewish tradition is called the *Shma:* "Hear, O Israel, God is One." As Susan remarked, "You sing that prayer to wake up your ear as much as your voice, to wake up your heart as much as your mind. In singing it, you create a window through which the divine indwelling presence may enter. I sing to wake myself up, to connect myself, hopefully, to the world around me."

## THE HOUSE OF LOVE AND PRAYER

When I lived in northern California in the late sixties and early seventies, I took a philosophy class from Mr. Druin, a Hasidic Jew. Hasidism, a mystical branch of Judaism from Eastern Europe, speaks of secret melodies that create heaven and earth. From Mr. Druin we learned of *niggun,* wordless musical prayers that often start low and rise higher and higher to lead the singer into realms of ecstasy.

I first heard about "Shabbos"—the Eastern European pronunciation of *Sabbath*—from Mr. Druin. He also told us about the House of Love and Prayer in San Francisco and Rabbi Shlomo Carlebach. I often drove down there whenever Shlomo was in town. What I remember most was his singing and storytelling. We were all mesmerized by his voice. He sang niggun that brought us all to our feet, dancing and swaying together as one. When the dancing reached a peak, Shlomo would gather us into a circle to tell a story: "Friends, friends, this is very deep..." I don't remember the stories, but I do remember falling into the quiet hush of his voice. At the end of the story, Shlomo would break out into an infectious niggun with the simple sounds of "Yi li li li li li," and in a moment we were dancing again together: Jew and gentile, young and old, hippie and business man. Sholmo was a bridge maker. Taking teachings from the Hasidic community into the wider world brought him both love and criticism.

In the early seventies, I felt the full power of Shlomo's impact as a holy singer at a gathering called The Meeting of the Ways at the university in Berkeley, California. Many spiritual leaders from different traditions were present. Swamis, yogis, and philosophers converged. At the end of a long evening of talks, Shlomo got up on the stage with his guitar and, without a word, began to sing, "Dai dai dai dai dai dai dai dai dai dai." The audience, which had been either in a meditative trance or half asleep as a result of the other presenters, suddenly got to their feet and sang with him. As people joined Shlomo on stage, for the first time that night we became one voice. The university auditorium was alive with song and spirit. He ended by singing *shalom*, the Hebrew word for "wholeness." We chanted shalom over and over again, the arms of strangers woven together to create a shawl of peace late into the evening.

## Voices from the Holocaust

According to the Zohar, a mystical text from the twelfth century, angels are made from God's breath to sing his glory. When the people of Israel sing praises to God, angels respond in song. There is a mutual resonance between celestial and earthly songs, an affinity between human and angelic realms. Songs on earth have echoes in heaven.

What happens when voices are silenced? Surely angels weep, and *their* voices are silenced as well. "All of reality is sustained through prayer," says Shava Segal in the liner notes for the CD, *Songs to an Invisible God*. "If prayer did not exist, the world could not exist. But how does one pray after the Holocaust? And what is the voice, the song, the prayer of women emerging from centuries of silence?"[14]

One emerging voice is that of Ruth Wieder Magan, a Jewish singer living in Israel. Both of Ruth's parents were Holocaust survivors. *Songs to an Invisible God* is her CD, recorded at the Ein Karem Chapel in Jerusalem. Though Ruth sings traditional songs, she also improvises and dialogues with the lyrics of traditional songs and the melodies. There is a natural resonance among her voice, her personal story, the story of the Jewish people, and the very stones of the chapel. Ruth's mahogany voice searches, laments, penetrates, trembles, soars and plummets; it cries out in the wilderness and quenches like a desert rain. To me it seems impossible to hear her and not be exposed to the soul's most secret chambers.

Ruth told me about her journey to find the Ein Karem Chapel. "I'm interested in the interchange between the resonance of the inner and outer space," she said. "Being aware of spatial consciousness takes the voice up a dimension; the voice becomes alive in a bigger way. My search began when I was looking for a place to perform an avant-garde theater piece about voices lost in the Holocaust. I went to Catholic churches—places that are not so open to a Jewish woman. One that I loved had once been a temple to Aphrodite. I asked a young priest if I could perform my theater piece there. He talked to the head of the order and then sadly said no. Finally, I came across a little chapel in a women's order of the Notre-Dame de Sion Monastery in Jerusalem, where they let me perform. Later, I found out that this order was particularly concerned with the Holocaust. They had sent nuns to Poland. But I didn't know this when I was performing; nor did they know what my piece was about.

We found out only afterward. That's what I mean by resonance—the nuns and I unwittingly had the same intention. We all wanted to hold a space to be heard and to be received, and together we created a temple with our intentions."

This "temple of intentions" has also been created at Poland's death camps in Auschwitz and Birkenau. In 1996, Bernie Glassman, a Jewish Zen Buddhist teacher and founder of the Peacemaker's Circle, led a five-day retreat there with 150 people of different faiths from all over the world. Included in the group were Holocaust survivors and their children, as well as the children of Nazi and German soldiers. They gathered to bear witness to the souls of the one-and-a-half million people who were exterminated in these two camps. The theme common to all present was secrecy. As is common knowledge in the therapeutic community, abuse instills an intense fear in people that often silences them. Ironically, people who have been severely traumatized usually don't reveal it because they have internalized the voice of the perpetrator, who says, "Keep your mouth shut!" Because of the many talk shows these days focusing on abuse, such secrets are now coming out into the open; but, until recently, the unspeakable horrors of the Holocaust have silenced its victims in profound ways.

The retreat participants intoned the chant called the Buddhist Gate of Sweet Nectar alongside the Kaddish, the traditional Jewish prayer for the dead. The piercing cry of the shofar, a ceremonial ram's horn, sounded at the execution wall where countless Jews had been shot. Its eerie wail reverberated through the camp and broke open the shame, guilt, denial, anger, and horror within everyone's heart.

Together, members of the group lit candles and chanted every name written in the Gestapo's Death Book. Glassman recounted, "As people chanted the names I'd hear them pause. Later, they'd tell me they'd chanted a familiar name, similar to the name of someone they knew, sometimes even a name exactly like their own."[15]

Everywhere the retreat goers went—to the train tracks, the gas chambers, the ruins of a crematorium, and cell blocks large enough only for prisoners to crawl on hand and knee—they recited the

Kaddish and the names of the dead. They sang lullabies in extermination chambers where babies and children had been killed.

I believe that each time a name was chanted a divine spark was restored, and a fragment was thus reunited with the whole of creation. Each name transmuted from the Gestapo's Death Book was stitched into the Book of Life, embroidered with compassion. This group of 150 people who had been silenced, who had been on different sides of the barbed wire fence, became one voice.

It is Friday night. I put down my pen and light a candle. I chant Shalom, adding my voice to Shekhinah's chorus that there may be peace on earth, in every heart, at every table. All over the world, candles are lit in homes, songs to the Bride are sung. Listen. Can you hear them?

*St. Labre Indian School Church and Tipi, Ashland, Montana*

~ *Chapter 12* ~

# FIRST PEOPLE

*The voice that beautifies the land!*
*The voice above,*
*The voice of the thunder*
*Within the dark cloud.*
*Again and again it sounds,*
*The voice that beautifies the land!*
—Navajo Thunder Song

Navajo. Lakota. Crow. Osage. Ute. Chippewa. Seneca. Hopi. Yuma. Yaqui. Comanche. Apache. Pima. Pomo. Pawnee. Like a chant, the litany of native tribal names evokes the sacred land of America. Before Columbus, before the Mayflower, before railroads, settlers, cowboys, and the gold rush, the ancient expanse of America spread from sea to sea.

America: the wide open home of buffalo, beaver, badger, eagle, trout, and crane. The voice of the land: Prairie grass and moon, red willow and dawn, the breathing forest of pine, oak, and redwood. Before the "Star-Spangled Banner," the song of America was heard in chants under the starry sky around council fires and in tipis, sweat lodges, hogans, kivas, and long houses. It was heard on buttes and mountaintops. Songs to the rising sun, rain chants in the desert, and the pueblo drums of corn dances echoed through the air. The drums sounded the pulse of life in praise of beans and squash, thundercloud and lightning, prickly pear and chokecherry, abalone and ocean, deer and elk. Every passage of life was accompanied by song,

135

a gift from the ancient ones. Every change of season. Every full moon. Every sunrise. Every day.

Today, around five hundred tribes live in the United States, comprised of over two million native people. Each tribe has a different language and dress and different rituals, customs, and cosmologies. Tribes in the Pacific Northwest tell stories of Raven and Salmon. Here in the Southwest, the prayer is for rain. A Pueblo story tells of the rain god who has fallen asleep on the mountain. Frogs and locusts try to wake him up by singing. One frog and one locust can't do it alone; but, as their song is heard, others join in, and the rain god wakes up and remembers his duty.

## THE BEAUTY WAY

At Canyon de Chelly, Navajo women in velvet blouses and broomstick skirts still sing as they herd sheep on the canyon floor. Navajos practice *Hozho*, the "Beauty Way," which renews the earth and makes everything holy and lovely again by "the sacred words of the earth."[1]

At dawn, traditional Navajos rise when the planet Venus is on the horizon. They breathe in the dawn four times and offer corn pollen to the deities. Dawn Woman, Talking God, White Corn Boy, and other gods are blessed with breath blown on the nectar of the corn plant as the people chant:

> Beauty before me,
> Beauty behind me,
> Beauty above me,
> Beauty below me,
> I walk in beauty.

Through the dawn ritual, one is aligned with the gods, and body, mind, and voice are made sacred again. Every morning. Every day.

The traditional Navaho home, which still dots reservations throughout the Southwest, is called a hogan. Here, Navahos perform their ceremonies as well as live. According to myth, the first hogan was made by the First Man from sunbeams and rainbows. Sun, Moon, Talking God, and Calling God were in charge of the construction. Talking God gave house songs to human beings. He sang to Earth Woman, Mountain Woman, Water Woman, and Corn Plant Woman, expressing beauty that radiated around the hogan.

The Navajos recreate this first hogan through ceremony whenever they build a new one. A chanter blesses the four directions with cornmeal, while others place the wooden support posts in the earth, accompanied by song. Inside the hogan, whenever disharmony makes a tribe member ill, a chanter or holy man creates a sand painting on the earthen floor.

There are twenty-six different "chantways," or Navajo ceremonial cycles, each with its own songs, prayers, dances, and sand paintings. Each tells a story of origin about a hero or heroine who made "a journey to the land of the gods to acquire special knowledge or healing power."[2] The Navajo Blessingway ceremony, performed over two nights, is one of the most frequent and has been described as "the main beam in the chantway house."[3] Some ceremonies are nine nights long, during which a chanter's song is interrupted only by brief periods of sleep. The chanter creates sand paintings from ground-up flower petals, charcoal, cornmeal, white gypsum, yellow ochre, red sandstone, and other colored rocks. The paintings represent different *yei*, or "gods," who are invited into the sand through the chant. In a chantway, the patient is called the "one sung over"; he or she is "immersed in an amniotic sac of song and prayer and sits surrounded by the osmotic membrane of the sand mandala."[4] As a result, the yei become absorbed by the one sung over, who in turn is thus restored to beauty.


## LAKOTA SONG

The Lakota people live in the vast oceans of grassland on the Great Plains, where the buffalo once roamed freely. An old Lakota song says that the wild rose and all other flowers are songs of Mother Earth:

> All the creatures that live are her songs;
> All creatures that die are her songs;
> The winds blowing by are her songs;
> And she wants you to sing all her songs.[5]

One of Mother Earth's singers is Howard Bad Hand, who comes from five generations of Lakota singers of the Rosebud Reservation in South Dakota. Howard is a teacher, singer, sun dancer, and holy man who blends his native traditions with the ancient Chinese oracular book, the *I Ching*. He lives in Taos and wrote *Native American Healing*, which is structured as a ceremonial song cycle.

The Lakota have no name for God. *Wakan Tanka* is the name for all that can't be named, fathomed, or known. Wakan Tanka is the creative part of life, the greatest relation we can have to the Source. It actually means "to make the connection." Howard said that "any time you make a connection of any kind, it is a sacred moment and event." *Tunkasila*, a word translated by the missionaries as "Grandfather," is the connection to the ancestors from the beginning of time. These concepts are living realities, not easily translated into English. There is a saying in Lakota that even Tunkasila prays to Wakan Tanka.

Howard told me that, as he was growing up, he noticed that the holy people and visionaries around him were musical. When he asked his Grandma Mary why, she said, "These songs that you hear belong to Tunkasila—Grandfather! If you want Grandfather to hear you, teach yourself his songs! If someone sings, Grandfather hears him!"[6]

For the Lakota, song creates a bridge between the spiritual and the material worlds. The holy men not only draw from a wide array of traditional songs, they also create songs for the moment when something particular is needed. "When the spirit gives you songs, you must sing those songs to help the people."[7]

Howard told me that he himself has been given many songs. Once at a sun dance in Fools Crow, South Dakota, he heard the voice of creation come to him in broad daylight. It told him to give his life to Tunkasila as an expression of Wakan Tanka, or the Great Spirit. In his book he writes, "I was to offer myself, offer to *Wakan Tanka* that which is truly my own to make a turning point in my life."[8]

In preparation for the ritual of offering himself to the Great Spirit, Howard asked some friends from Taos Pueblo to cut down a cottonwood tree, considered sacred for its tipi-shaped leaves. After they found and chopped a tree down, they gathered chokecherry branches as a reminder of the fruit given by nature to help with survival. They tied the branches to the tree and then erected it on land north of Taos.

Many family and friends came to support Howard as he pierced the flesh of his chest with hooks that were attached to the tree with rawhide strips. This connection between the man and the tree is called *Cekpa* in Lakota, which means "umbilical cord." Howard prayed to Tunkasila; he offered his life to Wakan Tanka and sacrificed his will. Then he tore himself free from the cord. To those outside the Lakota culture, this sacrifice may appear frightening in its violence. But to those within the culture, it carries great spiritual meaning. Howard saw it as giving of his own flesh to enact a rebirth into a new life to serve the people. Others who have participated in the ritual see it as giving of one's life blood to nourish the earth.

As Howard prayed, a bee buzzed near his head. It called to him by name and asked why he was making this sacrifice. At first, Howard thought the voice came from one of his friends. Then he saw the bee; it flew over his shoulder and buzzed away. He tried to figure out what had happened: "As I was struggling with my need to understand...calmness and quiet came over my whole being. I heard a song!... I realized I had to pay attention, so I began to sing with it. I realized this was a song that I was supposed to receive to unify my being with the Spirit World. This song, I was instructed, was to be used in every ceremony that I was conducting to benefit others."[9]

Howard believes that his job as a holy man is to help people reconnect with their own reality and express themselves through their own creative vibration. "The task given to all humanity is the same," he said. "It is to love and to do good. The role of song is that it inspires enthusiasm. Song is the Creator's language. Songs are the essence of vibration in the universe. The only way we can truly connect with the universe is through song."

Among his people, Howard performs many ceremonies, which can be requested by anyone based on the needs of the moment. A ceremony might be for healing, for mental cleansing, to find a mate, or to say thank you. The friends and family who attend act as a support group for the one on whom the ceremony focuses.

Howard's first act when performing a ceremony is to place his medicine bundle wrapped in a piece of leather or paper on a mound of earth. The sacred objects in the bundle don't have powers in themselves; rather, they are keys that open different parts of the psyche. "Every ceremony is unique," Howard says. "We don't approach any of them as a liturgy; we treat every one spontaneously. We use form to maintain order and create a structure as we delve into the unknown essence. There is no logical sequence. The ceremony is a safe place for the material and the spiritual worlds to interact. It might take place indoors or outdoors. There is no fixed location; the agreement is only for that space at that time. My job is just to show up when the need is there. I don't really have power, but I do have influence. I help to open doors that were closed or to remove obstructions, but then it is the person's job to do the rest."

At the beginning of a ceremony, Howard chants, "*Ho Wana Hocokan ki wecagen kte lo*! Now, I will fix my altar, or center for the voice!"[10] He told me that, "in sending your voice, you are making room for an appearance and for a sacred relationship between the form and the formless to occur. We say 'appearance' rather than 'spirit,' as the former is more open for any avenue of communication. The communication might be from an ant crawling on the floor or from something like that bee buzzing near my head. It might come from an inner image or from a voice I hear. I sing both traditional songs and my own chants to invoke the Spirit Helpers."

When Howard has completed all the songs in the ceremony, a shift takes place in the energy of the room. The Spirit Helpers have descended into the space created for them. The people sponsoring the ceremony pray, asking for help. Then everyone else in attendance prays as well. More songs are sung, and then it is "the Spirit's turn to speak."[11] Everyone who prays receives a response.

"Song truly connects people to the path of least resistance," Howard told me. "My life is a celebration of song and dance. I don't know any other way."

## TAOS PUEBLO

In Taos, Tiwa-speaking native people claim to live in the oldest continuously inhabited pueblo in America. It is the northernmost of nineteen pueblos in New Mexico. Multileveled and built of adobe, it rises in front of Taos Mountain and is divided by the Rio Pueblo. Fed by the waters of *Ma-wha-lo*, "Sacred Blue Lake," the river is believed to be the source of all life "and the final resting place of souls at death."[12]

To protect their religious privacy, the natives do not fully disclose the pueblo's oral history. But there are legends, one of which tells of a chief who, following an eagle to a stream, led his people to this place at the foot of the mountains. When two eagle plumes dropped on either side of the stream, the people knew that this was where they were to build their home. The word *Taos* means "People of the Red Willow," after the plant that grows in abundance in the fields. According to archaeologists, ruins in the area suggest that the Taos Indians have lived there for at least a thousand years, meaning that they were there long before Columbus discovered America. Construction of the pueblo took place between AD 1000 and 1450. Presently around nineteen hundred Indians live on tribal lands, with 150 of them living in the pueblo full time.

In the late winter months, the pueblo is closed to visitors. With only native people allowed access, ceremonies that have been practiced since antiquity are enacted inside six round underground ceremonial chambers called kivas. Here, boys at the proper age undergo their religious education and initiation, and ceremonial dances have their beginning and their end.

When the pueblo is opened in the spring to outsiders again, many ceremonial dances take place that the public can attend. I have often visited this and other pueblos since I first moved to New Mexico in 1984, witnessing the Turtle Dance, Buffalo Dance, Deer Dance, Corn Dance, Eagle Dance, Basket Dance, Butterfly Dance, and Shalako Dance, as well as other events. The sound of drums pulsing through the earth is part of the enchantment of living in New Mexico.

Ninety percent of Taos Indians are Catholic, practicing that religion alongside their own ancient religious rites. On Christmas Eve, the Procession of the Virgin from the San Geronimo chapel, which stands on Taos Pueblo grounds, is held at sunset.

One year for this occasion, my former husband David and I arrive in a stream of fellow Taos residents and tourists from all over the world. It is cold in the gathering dark. While we wait for Mass to be over, a young Tiwa torchbearer looks me in the eyes and says, "Are you ready?" He tells a tourist he is the Statue of Liberty. He jokes in his native tongue to the other torchbearer and flirts with a pretty woman in the crowd. Then the church bells ring, and men fire shotguns into the air and light bonfires. A statue of the Virgin Mary, under a white canopy, arrives in the church courtyard, carried by pueblo men and preceded by the torchbearers and dancers. In some years, the dancers are dressed in deer and buffalo heads. In alternate years, the medieval Matachine dance of Moorish/Spanish origins is held, in which the men wear black masks pointed like bishops' miters and decorated with colored ribbons and black fringe dangling in front of their eyes. Pueblo women follow the procession singing a Spanish hymn to Mary. The women's voices are layered with the sounds of drumbeats, crackling fires, ringing bells, and shotgun blasts.

Throughout the plaza, bonfires burn. Some are twenty feet tall, looking like black ladders ablaze. From them, the smoke braids and billows skyward. Ribbon-thin tornadoes come to life and twist briefly through the night air. Sparks swirl up with the smoke and dance like fireflies. Among the pueblo women wearing colorful, striped blankets like shawls, I catch glimpses of the Virgin under her billowing white canopy. Now and again I see her crown behind a buffalo dancer's shaggy head bobbing up and down. Along with the sounds of gunfire and bells, I hear snatches of Tiwa, Spanish, Swedish, French, and Japanese. Women sing "Santa Maria." A Hispanic woman in the crowd tells a friend, "I sang that as a little girl!"

David pulls me by the hand through the crowd so that we can be closer to the Virgin. When I see the fresh white rose she carries and remember the Lady of Roses, tears well up. I feel I have been found here in the dark, on this cold night huddling by the fire. I smell whiffs of piñon, dust, evergreen, and wood smoke. Friends hug one another around the fires as the procession ends and the Virgin is returned to the altar in the church. A mother calls for her child in the crowd, "Daschel!" I want to add, "On Dancer, on Prancer and Vixen," but I don't. Children laugh, greetings of "Merry Christmas" and "Feliz Navidad" are exchanged by strangers and friends dressed in jeans and down coats, mink coats, sheepskin jackets, cowboy hats, ski hats, scarves, and mittens. Whiffs of perfume and hot chocolate float through the air as snow melts near the fire's circle.

Gradually, the crowd thins. A fire has been lit in our hearts. David and I walk back to his truck. We are ready for home and a hot meal of chicken enchiladas and posole, a traditional, chili-laced corn stew.

On Christmas Day, we return for the Deer Dance. Before the dance begins, sacred clowns, wearing nothing but breech cloths and with their bare skin painted in black-and-white stripes, appear and reappear in different places. There are two groups. One group brings a freshly killed deer's head to the stream and tenderly lowers it for a drink. Then they disappear into one of the adjoined houses. When they reappear, they climb to the roof, while the other group climbs to an opposite roof. Like a flock of birds, the clowns caw and shout at each other.

Once, I saw the clowns go into a police car and mimic driving. One came out and mimed peeing on the tires. One immersed himself in the cold water of the river and splashed himself as if it were a summer day. One year a clown borrowed a fur coat from a woman in the crowd and put it over his back. He bucked and bellowed underneath, making the coat appear to be alive again.

In the native culture, the clowns have many functions. For one thing, they "magically protect the pueblo and its inhabitants from all enemies."[13] They also help the dancers if their costumes need alteration. And they keep the crowd in line, both physically and behaviorally. Pueblo children try to hide behind the adults when the clowns pass by, because, like Santa Claus, the clowns know who's been good and who's been bad.

When the Deer Dance begins, first the women dancers with their long, black hair arrive wearing jewel-colored, off-the-shoulder dresses. In their hands, they hold evergreen branches. I see Alice, the Arroyo Seco Postmistress, dancing in a red velvet dress. The drum pounds while the men chant the same phrases over and over again. There are layers and spaces inside the chant that create doorways into other worlds.

The dance moves to different places in the plaza, with new vantage points and rhythms. A dog walks to the beat of the drums with his red ruff of fur. The sacred clowns smudge themselves with sage using a hawk-wing fan. Wherever you look, there is something different to see.

In the distance, the Deer Dancers appear, walking out of the woods and over the bridge. From another side of the pueblo, more come into view. The women dancers in the plaza create a large, empty space. The clowns then enter it with small wooden bows and arrows and chant while the Deer Dancers move into the space created for them. The Deer Dancers are all men, wearing deer heads whose mouths are stuffed with evergreen boughs. Some of the heads are from freshly killed animals; tongues loll out from the side of their mouths. Some dancers wear buffalo heads. They all wear white crocheted leggings and fox pelts on the back of their white kilts. Sometimes you can see the human underneath the animal; sometimes, you can only catch a glimpse of the animal heads bobbing behind the large crowd, so they appear to be a herd being corralled.

A small boy dances into the center wearing a cougar skin. Women with parrot feathers dance among and around the herd. The clowns make simple but complex sounds, seeming sometimes like herding yells, sometimes like a chant, and sometimes like the animals themselves. We are mesmerized by their compelling din, the drums, the dance, the dust, and the winter sun on Christmas day. The dance is stirring, primal, and foreign, yet deeply familiar. Two old women covered in blanket shawls stand in front of me. This is their ancient heritage. I am just a witness from another land; I don't know what this dance means. Even if it were carefully explained to me, I would never know what it is to be inside the culture, inside the deer head or wrapped underneath a striped blanket. And yet, as I watch, I know the dance is a prayer for everyone: for David, for me, for the woman from Texas with the silly hat, for the mountain and the sea of sage that grows everywhere, for the prairie dog in his burrow and the pope on his throne, for the little boy dressed in a cougar skin and the old women who stand in front of me. Enjoined in the circle of the dance, we have all become part of the same breath.

Potter, poet, singer, and songwriter Harold Littlebird, from the Laguna and Santo Domingo pueblos along the Rio Grande, spoke to me about his participation in ritual dances. "I become a vessel through which creativity flows," he said. "Singing is a teaching place, an honoring that helps my life to continue. When I'm singing, a heat wave arises; it comes from a thankfulness for being in that place. Rituals involve preparation, fasting, and acknowledgment of what has come before. They honor the earth and all the different realms that are part of you as a human being. You create sacred space by your intention. When your intention is clear, helpers who are always available in the place of all living things will come to your aid. The energies invoked are to be harnessed, thanked, and returned. It's necessary to ask permission to harness these energies, so that life perpetuates itself. Taking the time to offer a prayer is the beginning of intention.

"What becomes clear in ceremony is whether the gods have favored you. The voice becomes the instrument through which communion with them takes place. As a singer, you become part of a collective experience. You hear sound that is hundreds and hundreds of years old. You go away from the experience in a different state of consciousness, and later you recall much more than you think you knew."

## SONGS BY THE TONGUE RIVER

When Cecily Schroepfer was a child, her brother told her she sounded like a crow in a tin can. Little did he know that one day this little Anglo girl would be given the right to sing among the Crow people of southern Montana. The Crow receive songs in dreams or visions. Only the person granted the song may sing it, although he can pass it on to another. Cecily was granted the right to sing a Crow song after living among the Crow and the Northern Cheyenne people for fifteen years. A Franciscan sister, she has been part of the Prayer Lodge, a gathering place for women of both reservations. Traditionally, the Crow and the Cheyenne were enemies. At the Prayer Lodge, women from both tribes come together whenever they feel a need for quiet time or to dream, pause, pray, and reflect, alone or with others. This is a community that cares for the earth and lives sustainably with her.

I met Cecily when she moved to Santa Fe to study a bodywork system called Ortho-Bionomy. As she was preparing for the transition, a sister asked, "But how will you continue to give your gift of music?" Having met me briefly several years earlier, Cecily called to inquire whether I had any sort of apprenticeship program. I was just finishing work with my first apprentice, so Cecily's call was timely. I have had many adventures in song with her, but none more meaningful than a workshop we did together in Ashland, Montana in the Rosebud Mountains on the Northern Cheyenne reservation.

Cecily and I drove to the workshop together. When we crossed the Montana border, she got out of the car, kissed the earth, and offered a prayer. In the Wolf Mountains, we passed fields covered with chokecherry trees in blossom, lupine, purple vetch, white chick-weed, and sego lilies. Cecily told me the Mormons ate these lily roots to keep from starving. Though my own ancestors had not come this far north, I thought of my great-great grandmother, who walked alongside a wagon train from Nauvoo, Illinois to Showlow, Arizona. What a tough cookie she must have been! I wondered if she had dined on lily roots.

We stopped in Lodge Grass on the Crow Reservation to see some of Cecily's friends. Then we went on to the Prayer Lodge, where we spent a night and attended a traditional Northern Cheyenne sweat lodge ceremony. The women showed me where sage grew and told me to pick some to take inside. One by one, we crawled on all fours through the door flap and circled into the lodge. As glowing red volcanic rocks were placed in the fire pit, I saw faces appear in the stone people. Water was poured over the rocks, and steam rose into the small, crowded space.

While the medicine man shook a gourd rattle and sang, we all expressed our prayers in groups of two or three. Our spoken prayers mingled with the sound of the rattle and the medicine man's chant. Rattles are often the first instrument given to babies; they help focus concentration and clear static from the mind. Sometimes the layer of sounds reminded me of locusts buzzing on a summer's day, or of crickets singing at night.

Four rounds of prayers were uttered to the four directions. Different herbs were offered at each round and placed on the hot rocks. Sweet grass, cedar, and sage joined the steam and made the air fragrant. We blessed ourselves with the smoke. I was grateful for the washcloth to put on my face and the sage to help me breathe through the searing heat. Between each round of prayers, the flap of the lodge was opened and the precious gift of water was passed from a ladle.

When the sweat was over, I crawled out from the dark womb of the lodge and into the starry cathedral of the Montana sky. We went inside the house and feasted on fry bread and buffalo stew. Cecily had gifts for everyone: blankets, rattles, and jewelry. Then we talked into the night.

The next morning, Cecily and I drove through the Rosebud Mountains and into Ashland, where seventeen of us from Montana, Wyoming, Arizona, Minnesota, and New Mexico gathered at the St. Labre Mission for the workshop. Ranging in age from twenty to eighty years, among the women there were Crow, Cheyenne, Navajo, ranchers' wives, nuns, a music minister, and three mother and daughter sets. For over three days we toned, chanted, danced, and shared ritual and stories.

We began the workshop by singing everyone's name; tears were immediate as women heard their name sung for the first time. We sang both indoors and out—alongside the Tongue River, where fish swam closer as we lined its banks. In a cottonwood grove, Cecily guided us in toning for the children of the reservations whose lives were being lost to drugs and alcohol. The native women gave voice to deep grief. One woman shook and prayed aloud while a friend held her. Another shared a vision of a turtle giving its shell to shield the children. One expressed anger at the drug dealers and the police—who knew where the planes arrived that were loaded with drugs—while yet another prayed for both the children and the dealers. A Crow woman suggested we sing for the families and lift our arms into the air like eagles spreading their wings. We sang a chant about an eagle. Toward the end of it, a bald eagle circled our group and flew off to the east. One woman said, "The Great Spirit has heard our prayers."

The last day of our workshop was on a Sunday, and the women wanted to attend Mass at the St. Labre Indian School Church that adjoined our gathering. Cecily, who knew the priest, asked him if we could tone after the communion, and he agreed.

The church blends Native American and Catholic beliefs. It is a tipi built out of stone; in its chapel the sun shoots through a stained-glass cross like an arrow scattering yellow and blue light. Stations of the Cross are carved like petroglyphs on the walls. Altars and candles are placed according to the four directions; as the congregation enters facing east, they bless themselves with the holy smoke of cedar and sage. A medicine wheel of eagle feathers hangs in front of the altar, as does a figure of Christ carved out of dark wood surrounded by a halo of eagle feathers. He is depicted as a Cheyenne "dog soldier"—the term used for warriors of the tribe who traditionally vowed to sacrifice their lives to protect the people from harm.

On the day we were there, the priest began his sermon by talking about a recent sweat lodge. The music minister and one of our workshop's mother and-daughter pairs sang a song; their voices rose up the four sides of the pyramidal building like sweet-grass smoke. Following communion, our whole group toned, our voices reflecting off the stone walls and seeming to enter another realm. Afterward, people said we sounded like angels. One woman asked how long we had rehearsed. We told her it wasn't a composed song; it had born in the moment. The three days we had spent together had brought us in tune with each other, the land, and the church. If you had told me when I was a young woman—the renegade Presbyterian daughter of an excommunicated Mormon father—that one day I would be singing with native women in a Catholic church, I would have been amazed.

After two years in New Mexico, Sister Cecily has moved back to Montana. She now combines her bodywork with toning and offers private sessions in the city of Billings, at the Prayer Lodge, and on both the Crow and the Northern Cheyenne reservations. Years ago, she had a healing session with an elder named Charles Little Old Man. As his wife, Marcelline Shoulderblade, was praying, she felt a soft breeze come in. Then Marcelline heard a voice give Cecily a Northern Cheyenne name, and later, Charles heard a song for her. Eventually, a naming ceremony was held for Cecily near Lame Deer in the Rosebud Mountains. Here, near a stand of ponderosa pines, this Anglo woman, who once had been mocked for singing "like a crow in a tin can," was honored by her Northern Cheyenne and Crow friends and welcomed into a new relationship with them.

Crow, Cheyenne, Navajo, Lakota, Laguna, Taos, Santa Domingo. In hogans and kivas, in the plaza, in the chapel, and in the sweat lodge, voices rise to purify, beautify, and sanctify the land. From these Native American peoples we can listen once again to the voice of the rose, the cry of an eagle, or a bee buzzing nearby. We can walk the beauty way and raise our own voice in praise of the living earth. We can give praise every change of season, every new moon, every full moon, every sunrise, every day.

*Red Springs at Chalice Well Gardens, Glastonbury, Somerset, England*

~ *Chapter 13* ~

# THE SONG AT THE WELL

*The ancient Isle of Avalon seems to surpass all other places
in Britain for the ability to sound the resonance
between the inner and outer worlds.*
—Nicholas Mann

Glastonbury, or the "Isle of Glass," nestled in the region of Somerset in southern England, is named for the days when an inland sea surrounded its green hills, sometimes obscuring the landscape in mist. A town steeped in myth and legend, it is said to be the burial place of King Arthur and his queen, Guinevere. It is also said to be the holiest earth in Britain, in that Joseph of Arimathaea is thought to have built the first church in Christendom in Glastonbury when he took Mary Magdalene there following Jesus' crucifixion.

Glastonbury is a place where Druids worshipped in an avenue of ancient oak trees that led to a ceremonial path up the Tor, the highest hill in the landscape 518 feet above sea level. It is a place where fires were lit on hilltops at Beltane and a place where holy wells were honored. It is also the place of the legendary Avalon, the otherworldly fairy islet beyond time and space where King Arthur was said to be welcomed after his death.

According to Kathy Jones, author of *In the Nature of Avalon*, Glastonbury itself represents the outer world of daily life, while the coexistent mystical realm of Avalon represents the inner world of the soul. These two worlds are separated by a veil. As Jones tells us, "The veil of Avalon is like mist, like the fog which in autumn and spring often hangs low over the Vale of Avalon, shrouding the sacred land in mystery, hiding familiar landmarks, emphasizing sounds and making us look more closely at the paths we are taking. For the Somerset folk this mist is known as the White Lady, who rises mysteriously up out of the watery Somerset levels at dawn and at dusk, drawing her veil across the landscape hiding her beauty."[1]

Now it is 2002 in the month of *April*, a word which means "to open" in Celtic. All the buds have unfolded, and spring lambs leap in the gently rolling hills. With four women from New York, I am in Glastonbury at Little Saint Michael's Retreat House on the grounds of the Chalice Well Garden, leading a Grail quest. We are here to learn the ancient myths surrounding this unusual town and to sing at its many sacred sites: the Chalice Well; the White Springs; the Tor; Glastonbury Abbey, dedicated to Mary Magdalene; and the two ancient druidic oaks that still remain, named after the biblical Gog and Magog.

I had been to Glastonbury six months earlier, just days before the terrorist attack of September 11 shook America to its roots. At that time, early fall had come to the garden. A fat bumblebee disappeared into a foxglove. The smell of lavender was in the air. The last of the summer roses were lingering. Echinacea, with its Fibonacci spiral center, stood straight, while yarrow stalks waved in the wind.

Now, the four women and I have come to Glastonbury for both personal and collective reasons. Collectively, we have come in search of the Holy Grail; we have come to offer our prayers and songs to heal the wounds of September 11 and our contemporary wasteland. But as the Celtic scholar John Matthews observes, the desire of the quest is always "to penetrate the Grail of one's own being."[2]

The Holy Grail is commonly thought to be a cup, dish, or plate used by Jesus at the Last Supper and then to catch his blood during the Crucifixion. Joseph of Arimathaea was said to have later brought the Grail to England. The quest for the Grail is part of the legend of King Arthur, whose knights go in search of it to heal the wounded Fisher King and so restore his ruined kingdom. The Grail has long been said to reside at the bottom of Chalice Well.

We began our quest with a ritual at the well, drinking from its waters after we had washed away our pilgrim dust from trains and airplanes. We tied white ribbons on the yew trees with our intentions. With few people in the garden, we felt free to sing in thanks for the healing the well brought to us through its minerals. Afterward, we became part of a larger ceremony of community residents. A Tibetan Buddhist lama blessed the well with his deep-voiced chant and holy water and herbs from Tibet.

I can imagine no place as peaceful and healing to both body and soul as Chalice Well, called the Red Spring for its high iron content. When we were there in April, the garden was in first bloom. Tulips of every color, along with bluebells and jonquils, lined the tranquil paths. The birds in constant voice guarded their new nests. One woman in the group said that what had been missing from her life was the sound of the well water there.

Chalice Well Garden has four levels, each with a distinctive atmosphere. At the upper level is the well itself, with two yew trees that act as guardians. In both Celtic and Christian traditions, the yew is associated with death and rebirth because it can regenerate out of its own hollow core. Its red bark bleeds a red sap when cut. Yews are often planted in graveyards, and it is said that the dead are fed by their roots. These trees have always been present in this part of Britain. Excavation of the Chalice Well Garden revealed a yew stump buried eleven feet under the ground that dated from Roman times between AD 43 and 410.

The well has a wrought-iron cover showing two interlocking, perfect circles pierced by a lance. Designed by Frederick Bligh Bond, a resident mystic and archaeologist of Glastonbury, it represents the Bleeding Lance of Christ's Crucifixion "holding together in balance the Visible and Invisible Worlds."[3]

The precise, overlapping circles on the wrought iron cover are called a *vesica piscis*, named for Christ's connection with the symbol of the fish during the Age of Pisces. This natural phenomenon can be seen when two ripples in a pond begin to merge. In sacred geometry the overlapping circles produce an almond shape in the center where a series of exact polygons can be created, based upon the numbers 3, 4, 5, 6, 8, 9, and 10. All the sacred ratios, except for the number 7, exist within the intersection of the two circles. The vesica piscis is symbolic of a vulva, a generative area where inner and outer realms meet and souls become reembodied. Many sacred buildings are based on its geometry, including the Mary Chapel at Glastonbury Abbey.

At the second level, water from the well is piped down into the garden and emerges from a sandstone lion's head. Here you can drink from the waters of the Red Spring. The lion's head seems to say, "Drink from the well, drink from her waters. Rest and be well."

From here, the water cascades down to the third level in a red-stained waterfall into a courtyard called King Arthur's Court. Ancient pilgrims once immersed themselves in a small pool there. The pool is much shallower today, allowing modern pilgrims to bathe only their tired feet. In the courtyard, the ley lines of Michael and Mary meet as one. These alignments of sacred sites stretch across the land-scape in southern Britain. The Michael lines are so named because they lead to high places and towers dedicated to Saint Michael. The Mary lines lead to Chalice Well and other holy wells dedicated to the Virgin Mary and chapels dedicated to Mary Magdalene, sometimes along with the Mother of Christ. The lines also cross on the Tor and at the high altar of Glastonbury Abbey and many other places throughout Britain.

From King Arthur's Court, in the fourth level of the lower garden the water travels down to form a pool that is also shaped like interlocking circles. Chalice Well is fed by a spring that outflows twenty-five thousand gallons of water a day at a constant tempera-ture of fifty-two degrees. This is water that comes from the depths of the earth, from unseen realms not touched by sun or moon. It is not formed from cloud but shaped by subterranean vibrational forces. It is water that holds "the memory of its eternal heat, crystals, minerals, and ores."[4] In its very flow, it represents the intercourse between the inner and outer worlds that is central to the mythology of the place.

In a lecture at Glastonbury, author Nicholas Mann spoke of Avalon as a place that is both current and ancient. As the magical

Otherworld within Glastonbury's enchanted landscape, it is called many things—the land of the Blessed, the land of apples, the land under the waves, the land of women, the land of the dead and of the living, and the place where souls are reborn. To enter Avalon, one must part the veil.

According to legend, the newly dead are met by a woman carrying a silver apple branch. The image may have originated in the heroic tale of the eighth-century Irish chieftain Bran, who was given such a branch to inspire and guide him to the Otherworld. The dead go to a place where birds sing all day and all night. On Samhain, our Halloween, the souls of the dead are taken to the Underworld through the Tor to the home of *Gwynn ap Nudd*, the White Son of Night, king of the fairy folk. Here they feast and make love until they are ready for rebirth. But when they come back to life, it might not be as a human or even an animal. As Nicholas Mann says, "The purpose of incarnation was to incarnate as everything. The dead may be reborn as the song of a bird, a bud on a tree, a light on a wave or the voice of a poet."[5]

When I heard Mann speak in April 2002, it was shortly after my father had died. As I listened, I gazed at the Holy Thorn tree, a descendant of the one planted by Joseph of Arimathaea on his arrival, now decorated with colorful Easter eggs hanging from ribbons on the branches. Christian images of resurrection mingled with Celtic images of rebirth. I wondered whether my father was now the fragrance of the blossoms in the gardens or the sound of water in the nearby well.

Taliesin, the chief bard of Britain who lived in Wales in the sixth century, reflects the same awareness this way:

> I am a salmon in a pool,
> I am a lake on a plain,
> I am the mound of poetry,
> I am a word of skill . . . [6]

In Ireland, the circuit of souls of which Taliesin speaks is called a *tuirgin;* it is where the realm of the ancestors is present in everything.

Chalice Well Garden, where white tulips, bleeding hearts, and forget-me-nots sprang from the earth, was the perfect place to stand in the veil between death and rebirth. Here I was comforted by the nesting music of robins, thrushes, chiffchaffs, and blackbirds. I sang knowing that many others have come here to cry and to ask for healing. Ribbons tied to the yew trees or flying in the wind speak to their hopes. Someone asks for prayers for a friend having surgery. Another asks for prayers for a woman giving birth. The act of tying rags to trees near wells is an old tradition in the belief that, as the piece of cloth disintegrates, so does the ailment in the body. Here, by the oldest holy well in Britain—which has been in constant use for the last two thousand years—I wrote my father's name on a white ribbon and tied it to the tree. Perhaps his spirit had joined with the writing to become his name—Derral Wesley Hawkins—waving now in the wind. As I watched the ribbon, a cool breeze created an Aeolian harp of the trees, playing the branches like strings.

Throughout Britain, holy wells were traditionally places of healing, where people would go to remember the ancestors. According to Kathy Jones, the wells were dedicated to the goddess Brigit, who later became fused with the Christian saint Brigid, or Bride. Brigid was, among other things, the patroness of poetry. A ninth-century poem to her in the Book of Leinster proclaims, "Hear the tuneful ring of your black bent anvils, the sounds of songs on the tongues of bards."[7] In pagan times, bards with branches adorned with tiny bells would go to the wells to be filled with inspiration and commune with the ancestors. Wells were seen as portals to the Otherworld, as places of access to the spirits of the dead. For Christians, the source of power is above and beyond. For the ancient Celts, the Otherworld beneath the earth was the source of all power. Springs and wells were sacred sources of wisdom. The sound of the water induced trance states. Charla Devereux describes a visit to Madron Well in Cornwall, where she was lulled into a state of reverie by the constant sound of the water and the buzzing insects. "The more I listened [to them], the slower the sound became," she writes, "until I felt I could understand what they were saying, although it was impossible to express through words."[8]

Since antiquity, wells have been oracular sites, where incantations of poetic speech, more akin to song than to spoken words, were voiced. In Greece, at Dodona, priestesses heard prophesies in the spring's murmuring sound as it streamed upward from dark and hidden places. Water springing from the earth through the shaft of a well, like song springing from the mouth, was known to bring about ecstatic trance. As Jungian analyst Erich Neumann puts it, "The original utterance of seerdom is the language of water."[9]

In Greece, Demeter grieved Persephone at Maiden's Well. At Eleusis, women danced in circles around the well in an enactment of the Eleusinian Mysteries. At Delagoa Bay in southeastern Africa, women of the Bantu culture strip off their garments and go from well to well, uttering cries and singing songs, to cleanse the wells and pray for rain to fall on the parched earth.

## THE WHITE SPRING

Across the lane from the Red Spring at Glastonbury lies the calcium-rich White Spring. Emerging from a system of honeycombed caves underneath the Tor, its waters rise from the underground dwelling of *Gwynn ap Nudd*, the fairy king. Long ago these two springs flowed into each other near where the lower pool at Chalice Well Gardens lies today.

Their joining held mystical significance. In Christian legends, the red and the white symbolized the blood and sweat of Jesus Christ brought to Glastonbury in two cruets by Joseph of Arimathaea. Before Christianity came to the isle, the two colors represented the mysteries of birth with its red blood and white milk and semen. While blood represents life, it is also symbolic of the shedding of blood at death. Life and death, and the emergence of new life, are part of the mysteries that the two springs celebrate.

In the 1870s the lane was backfilled in order to erect a stone reservoir, and the water from the White Spring was fed into the water mains. The town council made this decision over the need for a safe water supply after a cholera outbreak. Hence, while the Red Spring at Chalice Well continues to be honored, the White Spring has had no public access since the 1870s other than through flowing from the reservoir into a naked pipe. Many of the Holy wells in Britain have fallen into similar disuse.

When I visited in September 2001, the reservoir's stone building was being converted into the White Springs Café.[10] Walking past the cavernous building, I heard a man singing there and leaned inside to listen. When he stopped, I thanked him and asked if I could sing, improvising a Celtic melody. "Come back and sing anytime," he said, "the waters soak up the song."

When I returned to Glastonbury in April 2002, the café was open, and my group and I went to it. Inside, it was dark and beautiful. The White Spring was being honored once again: Candles and flowers were offered to a stone grotto, a rivulet of the spring flowed in a channel in the floor, and a darkened wall was illuminated by designs of light that looked like letters from a sacred alphabet.

We had gone there to write about our quest and offer our songs to the White Spring. We improvised and let our voices flow together. Our sound was carried through the room, out the door, and into the lane. As we sang, one woman, Teresita Castillo, kept hearing the word *holy*. A few days earlier she had experienced a powerful healing when we had sung the sounds "ho-hey-ho" over and over. That night in a dream, she had put her hand to her mouth to cough. She thought a food particle was being dislodged, but it was something else—a block of ice, the exact shape of her throat, fell into her hand and melted. She felt that this block of ice had been there for fifty-two years, preventing her from expressing the freedom of her voice. Now, as she heard us sing the word *holy* in the cafe, it reminded her of the healing in her dream: "Holy is the spring. . . . Holy the water flowing on the floor. . . . Holy the glint in a child's eye. . . . Holy the cake wrapped in a napkin to be eaten later. . . . Where we sit is holy . . . holy, holy, hallow, in this hollow of a café."

Teresita said, "That's really what speech is all about. What we're all really trying to do is to convey 'holy' in every word. What if in every conversation we could say 'holy' to the taxi driver, to the stranger on a train, to a friend on the telephone, to our families, to people in other countries..."

Jungian analyst Linda Sussman links the Grail myth with the power of speech, the power to ask the right question. "Parzival and the initiate-speaker must swim in the deep wild waters of meaning.... The sunken treasure to be found there is the Speech of the Grail."[11]

My group and I walked out of the café/chapel and into the lane, offering our white ribbons to the White Spring as townspeople filled their plastic containers with water. We kept the hum of holy in our steps as we walked past the rush of traffic on Chilkwell Street and back to Little Saint Michael's Retreat Center on this cold spring day. Perhaps someday the waters of the Red Spring and the White Spring will join again. Until then, we have found a way to honor the Grail within our hearts.

*Cloisters, built in fourteenth and fifteenth centuries,*
*Gloucester Cathedral, Gloucester, England*

~ *C h a p t e r   1 4* ~

# GREGORIAN CHANT

*In the sight of the angels will I sing a psalm to you.*
—St. Benedict

One of the first things I did upon arriving at Glastonbury was to visit the ruins of the once-magnificent Benedictine abbey there. Now its gothic arches framed the blue sky instead of stained glass. The two sides of the massive entrance stopped suddenly in the air instead of completing the graceful curve it had once had. There were no roofs. Plants grew on top of the stone walls. Dog-toothed designs were carved on arches. Within the abbey, tendrils and foliage now ornamented the Mary Chapel. The cloisters, where monks once meditated, were now marked paths on green grass. A roped enclosure showed where the high altar used to be. The smell of incense had long since disappeared, but I could still feel why this spot has been described as the holiest earth of England. Near the place of the high altar was where the first Christian choir once sang Gregorian chant.

Gregorian chant was named after St. Gregory the Great, who was pope from AD 590 to 614. He is said to have received the chants from the Holy Spirit in the form of a dove who sat on his shoulder and sang into his ear. The chant is the oldest notated musical tradition of Western civilization. It first appeared in Roman repertory in the fifth and sixth centuries, but its origins can be traced to the first centuries after Jesus's death in the liturgical traditions of Mediterranean countries, where early Christians continued and elaborated on the psalm singing of the Jews. St. Gregory collected chants composed by nuns, monks, and priests from different cultures.

Moreover, Gregorian chant is the earliest example of Western harmony where singers move in parallel fifths above the melody line. The fifth is the first naturally occurring harmonic and has a characteristic open sound that generates a feeling of power and strength. Initially, the monks sang in unison. Musician Kay Gardner believes that they added the harmony of the fifth when, "chanting in highly resonant stone cathedrals and monasteries, [they heard] the fifth naturally occurring as a harmonic above a single melody line... Soon they began singing what they heard."[1]

The rhythm of Gregorian chant is based, not on a strict time signature, but in the body, according to the natural rhythms of the human breath. Prolonged vowel sounds ride the breath out from the mouth and into the air: *Al-le-lu-ia!* As we sing, or even listen, to Gregorian chant, we slow down to match this more relaxed way of listening and breathing. Our thoughts, even the rhythms of our heartbeats, are brought into a state of tranquility.

Christianity is a religion of ascension, as its music and architecture reflect. In song, the interior of the body sounds forth and resonates the interior of the building. Tim Wilson believes that the singers' bones "act like a vibrator exciting the walls of the church," so that the walls then also sing.[2] What makes this resonance possible is the hardness of the surfaces of both our bones and the church walls. Singing bones set into motion singing stones that "create multiple reflections of the higher frequencies." This gives "a feeling of omnipresence, a sense that the sound [comes] not from a single identifiable source but from all around."[3]

Singer David Hykes of the Harmonic Choir, who sang and recorded at Le Thoronet Abbey in France, describes the abbey as an amplifier. "The song is in the space," he told me. "Like the universe, it is filled with all possibilities. Sounding in a sacred space produces a sense of power and grandeur, but it needs to be approached with objectivity and humility. We should ask, 'What is the source of vibration? Where do these vibrations come from? With the art of listening, we become a much more precise instrument for exploring different gradations of space."[4]

Song is a way to arrive at silence. Listening is a way to arrive at prayer. Hykes believes that "the idea is to get quieter and quieter. Cistercian monks were quiet most of the day. They had liturgical times for singing and a one-hour meeting with the abbot, and the rest of the time they were silent." He says that, in approaching sacred sites, "we need to match the vibrations of the space with equal amounts of silence, singing, and then silence again."[5]

Gregorian chant may have also sprung from an earlier tradition of perpetual choirs. British legends speak of holy men in the days before Christianity who chanted twenty-four hours a day and sanctified their society by singing to nourish the land. Glastonbury, Stonehenge, and Llantwit Major in South Wales are three sites mentioned in traditional bardic verses. Interestingly, they are equidistant. John Michell, who has written extensively on these themes, believes there were originally twelve perpetual choirs at sites arranged in a circle. The ancient center, Whiteleafed Oak, is in the middle of the three cathedrals at Gloucester, Hereford, and Worcester—which are also equidistant. Today, these cathedrals take turns hosting Britain's annual Three Choirs Festival.

## OFFICES OF THE MONASTIC DAY

Katharine Le Mée, in her book *Chant*, observes that the official offices of the Catholic Church, seven during the day and the eighth at night, symbolically form a perfect octave (an octave being comprised of eight notes).[6] The offices, also known as the canonical hours, begin with Vigils, followed by Lauds, Prime, Terce, Sext, None, Vespers, and Compline at night. Every day, year in and year out, the monks sing the same words and melodies praising the glory of God and creation at the prescribed times. The offices reflect the hours of the day from predawn to sunset, each symbolic of different spiritual qualities through the choice of text.

Additionally, a final hymn to Mary is sung in the Lady Chapel before the monks go to bed. "The whole day is put to bed with Mary, the Mother of God, tucking you in," says Irish singer Nóirín Ní Riain, who has sung with the monks of Ireland's Glenstal Abbey. Seismic shifts were occurring in her life when she followed the offices of the day with them. "I feel I have a monk within me," she said, "a pure archetype for living in harmony with God. God is between *he* and *she*, between the higher and lower registers of the voice. This is the threshold where heaven and earth meet. When we sing together, our separate distinctions disappear, and we're looking out of the gutter up to the pure drop of divinity.

"God wants us to be all ears," she told me, "I open myself up to the space, listen to the heart of the stone, knock on the door of every stone, and tap into the first one that was ever created. Every space and every stone has a note, if we could but hear it. Even the black hole in space has the sound of B flat, fifty-seven octaves below what we can perceive."[7]

One of Nóirín's most profound experiences in singing Gregorian chant has been at Glenstal Abbey. "Last Easter I sang the *Exultet*, which is a big song of proclamation when Mary Magdalene first sees the risen Christ. I was the first woman to sing this song in the abbey. I sang in darkness with only one lit candle. I was the threshold between the monks and the huge congregation. When I came to the final "Amen," I didn't remember what I had sung; I had left the text and been taken into another state, leaving behind my feet of clay. I felt like Mary Magdalene when she finds the empty tomb. Seeing a man in the garden, she thinks it's the gardener and asks him if he has taken the body of Jesus. Christ says, 'Mary.' In that moment of sound—the sound of our name—we can become transfigured."

## THE SECOND VATICAN COUNCIL

In many communities, Gregorian chant has been silenced. In 1964 the Second Vatican Council changed the ancient liturgical rules to favor the vernacular over the traditional Latin. Gregorian chant and other traditional forms of the Mass slipped into obscurity. The *Liber Usualis*, the book of chants from the Benedictines in Solesmes, France, has gone out of print.

As a result, music in the Catholic Church has changed dramatically. Michael Deason-Barrow, director of Tonalis: Centre for the Development of Music in England, speaks to this issue when he says, "Alas, in masses priests now turn the microphone on to amplify sound into the nave. The voice as vessel has become lost. The dialogue between the voice and the space, and the creation that takes place between them, has been lost. Music is often being used as a kind of filler between the spoken sections of the liturgy. We need to remember that art can also be theology—that music is theology as much as words are. Gregorian chant was sung prayer. Most people may not remember the words of a sermon, but they do remember the spiritual elation of the music."[8]

After the action of the Second Vatican Council, many monasteries stopped singing Gregorian chant. This literally made some monks sick. There is a famous story of a group of Benedictine monks from southern France who observed strict silence and never spoke. When they stopped singing the eight offices of the day, they became depressed, listless, and fatigued, finding it hard to work. Experts were recruited to help them. Some recommended dietary changes, exercise, or new routines. Nothing worked. Finally, Dr. Alfred Tomatis, an expert on the ear, was brought in. As Don Campbell describes in *The Mozart Effect*®, Tomatis determined that the basis for their despondency "was not physiological, but audiological. The monks' enervated state was the result of eliminating several hours of Gregorian chant from their daily routine."[9] Tomatis convinced the abbot to initiate the abandoned Gregorian chant once again. Within six months, the monks sprang back with renewed vigor.

Tomatis's research has shown that one function of the ear is to charge the brain. The frequencies of Gregorian chant are within the bandwidth needed for this charge. The monks were not being fed by the music. According to Tomatis, the monasteries that closed down in the 1960s were the ones where chanting was not practiced anymore.

## THE CHRIST IN THE DESERT MONASTERY

One of the few places in the United States where the entire office of Gregorian chant is still observed is the Christ in the Desert Monastery, nestled in the pink cliffs of New Mexico. I traveled there with a friend in late May 2003. We drove thirteen miles on a winding dirt road past some of the most beautiful country in the world. Mesas striated with colors of cream, salmon, pink, crimson, and rust looked like giant parfaits. Cottonwood trees in their leafy spring dress grew green along the Chama River. New Mexico had enjoyed a good snowfall that winter, and now everything was lush. Even the cholla cactus looked perky. I have seen cholla that looked like it was straight out of hell. This landscape was heavenly. The road came to a dead end in a canyon.

When we got out of the car, what first struck me was the stillness, which enveloped us like a cloak after our chatty, bumpy ride. This is a place of listening, where all are welcomed regardless of faith. It is a place to rest and be nourished. Here, the Benedictine monks meet God in silence, in common prayer, in manual labor and in psalms singing. One hundred and fifty psalms are chanted each week.

We walked to the church made of adobe and stone in the colors of the canyon. Designed by Japanese architect George Nakashima, it sits among red rock guardians and a communion of pines. Inside, the atmosphere was rich in the texture of silence and bird song. I felt the music from the last offices still lingering in the air, as if at any moment the stone altar itself would start singing.

The interior is simple, with walls of mud and straw and a round ceiling made of pine beams laced together with smaller trees. Four windows face the four directions, one toward the canyon, the others revealing the dance of clouds against a turquoise sky. In the center, a square stone altar stands next to a weathered tree branch twisting around a large, white candle. A wooden Christ, carved in the Hispanic folk-art tradition, hangs sorrowfully from a cross and looks down upon the pews.

On the east wall of the church, a Madonna, wearing a red cape and dark blue dress, is painted against a golden background. Cabochons of lapis lazuli and rosy quartz frame her. Christ flares out of her heart like the sun, his hair like solar flames. In front of the Madonna a wooden trough, carved with mermaids and pomegranates, holds sand. Here, we planted honey-colored candles, lit them, and watched our flickering prayers. We were too early to hear the monks sing, and my friend needed to leave before the next office. As we journeyed back down the road toward home, I vowed to return.

A year later in July, I am back on the same bumpy road with a different friend, Alice Fehlau, who completed her apprenticeship with me and presently combines toning with reiki and body work in Santa Fe. Now, the cholla is in bloom and we're here to camp along the Chama River to give us more time to explore.

Before finding our camping spot, we drive to the monastery to gather information. A man working at the gift shop and I talk about my mantra practice, and he says, "Gregorian chant is like a mantra, repeating God's name."

We look around the shop and Alice points to a Black Madonna, the famous Our Lady of Czestochowa from Poland. Her face with its two marks resembling scars epitomizes life's sorrows. Her eyes are pained. Wearing a dark blue mantle, she looks like a bruised heart. "Look more closely at her face," Alice says. "The scars look more like twigs with thorns on them. They go all the way down her neck and disappear under her gown, as if a rose bush is growing out of her heart." Here at the Christ in the Desert Monastery, the Lady of Roses shows me another face. She seems to say that the search for the sacred is not a bed of roses. Sometimes, it is full of thorns.

Camping that night by the river, I wake just before dawn to hear a gentle rain falling on my tent. I sit up and write by flashlight, the shadow of my hand as it moves across the page giving the impression of a feather quill in candlelight. I listen to the deep peace of the earth. Now, while it is still dark, the monks are singing Vigils. I think about the man in the gift shop who said that Gregorian chant is a repetition of God's name. As I listen to the dawn chorus of swallows, finch, blue jay, flicker, and dove, I know that it, too, is the repetition of the name of God—as is the thrum of rain on my tent, the green sheen and swish of the Rio, the cacophony of howling coyotes, the purple four o'clocks and delicate pale trumpets all singing their morning Alleluias.

After breakfast, Alice and I walk to the monastery. We are just in time to hear the bell ring for Terce, where the focus of prayer is on the Holy Spirit. We had agreed that the moment we saw the church we would approach it in silence. Birds on the mesa accompany us. We arrive and find our seats. Slowly the monks and nuns enter and sit facing each other with the altar between them. They alternate verses as they sing—first one side, then the other, as if their voices are threads that weave their offering together on the plain stone altar.

Listening to the beauty of their voices, I search their faces. I want to know how this practice had been woven into them. Just as there are laugh lines and worry lines etched in the face, I wonder if I will see chant lines or lines of peace. Or perhaps there will be the absence of lines. One monk looks serene; another looks sleepy. One nun's face is radiant; another's looks tight. I think about habit—the monks' and the nuns'. When is routine empty? When is it a container for transformation? As I ask myself these questions, I remember the times when in repeating my mantra I have just gone through the motions and other times when it has transported me to place of harmony. The important thing is to be a willing vessel, to take another step at the edge.

The monks depart singing. Mass will be in a half hour. Some people leave but most remained seated, eyes closed in silent prayer. A little boy with a plaid shirt and shorts shyly walks to a side altar and takes a picture of the resident Madonna. The click of his camera reminds me I'm in the twenty-first century, not the ninth.

Once again the bell rings in tune with a simpler time, now for the office of Sext, and I hear the sound of chant. The serene monk enters first, swinging a silver censor and circling the altar with the sweet smell of incense as the monks file in singing. One by one they bow to the center and then take their seats. The priest, dressed in a green tunic over his white robe, looks like a spring leaf. When he sits under the crucifix of the bleeding Christ, the effect is the very image of death and rebirth. The monk continues his censing and then takes his seat as the chanting begins. A shaft of July sunlight strikes the altar and illuminates the spirals of smoke. Galaxies whirl through the air, wheeling and turning as the monks chant. Double and triple spirals form and twirl. A treble clef of smoke appears and disappears as if it is part of a magic act. Sun, sight, smoke, smell, and sound became one.

Entranced, I remember reading about research speculating that the spirals, zigzags, chevrons, and diamonds on the walls of Newgrange may be representations of sound that ancient people could have seen through incense smoke or the water vapor created from using the monument as a giant sauna. Sound waves from the chanting would have vibrated the tiny particles of water and smoke, which, when illuminated by light, would have in effect made the sound appear visible, just as I am experiencing at the monastery.[10]

Slowly tracing each spiral note, I watch the clouds of smoke inside disperse. Through the window, I see the clouds outside billow and bloom. I imagine clouds laden with chant circling the earth with song, enrobing the planet with prayer. When the mass is over, I step out of the church and into the Cathedral of Heaven and Earth.

*Choir, thirteenth century, remodeled fourteenth century; organ, seventeenth century, Gloucester Cathedral, Gloucester, England*

~ *Chapter 15* ~

# ENGLISH EVENSONG

*Anyone who sings, prays twice.*
— St. Augustine

The choral praise of Evensong, a sung service, resounds daily throughout Britain's cathedrals and abbeys. One of the official services of the Anglican Church, this tradition, unique to Britain, has its roots in Gregorian chant. Today it corresponds to Vespers in the Catholic Church, although it was originally formed by combining the offices of Vespers and Compline into one service.

The First Order of Evensong was credited to Thomas Crammer, the archbishop of Canterbury, in 1549. In 1662 it was revised and included as an official service in the Book of Common Prayer.

Evensong services feature a daily psalm from the Book of Psalms, one for every morning and evening of each day of the month. British composers of the Evensong anthems span centuries and include William Byrd, Henry Purcell, Edward Elgar, Benjamin Britten, and Ralph Vaughn Williams. Along with an anthem and a different choral selection featured every Sunday, the "Magnificat" and the "Nunc Dimittis," also known as the "Song of Simeon," are sung along with readings and prayers. The choir stalls are divided into south and north sides. The choir, in two groups, alternates in singing the psalm verses. In medieval times, this weaving of voices from alternating places made more use of the sense of antiphony than is practiced today.

CHAPTER 15

## GLOUCESTER CATHEDRAL

Evensong is accompanied by an organ built to suit the distinctive architecture and acoustics of each cathedral. One Easter Sunday in 2002, I heard David Briggs, one of the great improvisational organists in the world, play at Gloucester Cathedral on his last day as director of music there.

First the Easter bells rang through the cathedral, and it was as if the columns themselves were full of bells. They were like trees bursting with music, a forest full of bird song. The cloisters looked like the spreading canopy of a long row of elegant trunks and branches. Choir boys in their white robes ran among them and chattered like church mice in the same place where the first *Harry Potter* movie was filmed. I knew magic was afoot. Earlier, an elderly gentleman, one of the many volunteer guides, had told me with great relish that he had been a chorister here long ago. His eyes misted over as he remembered his favorite hymn, one by Sir Hubert Parry, and he stood and sang its opening lines:

> My soul, there is a country
> Far beyond the stars.[1]

"The hymn ends with a high G," the man had told me, "and there was an eight-second reverberation through the sixty-eight-foot vault. In those moments, my soul was taken far beyond the cathedral to the heavens."

Now, watching the choir boys take their places in the wooden stalls, I wondered whether they, too, were having mystical experiences that would forever shape their lives. As old men, would they, too, weep at remembering the lingering notes of their voices?

During Easter Evensong I sat underneath the painted organ, built in 1665. The music had many moods and hues. Sometimes it was playful, sometimes mysterious, sometimes like the voice of God. It had a terrible beauty that would just as suddenly sound celestial. The pure sound of the boy choristers lifted me, and, like the old chorister, I soared with the angels far beyond the choir vault.

At the end of the service, we joined the choir in singing a familiar Easter hymn, one I had grown up with in the Presbyterian Church: "Jesus Christ Is Risen Today." As we sang, we strolled with the choir around the cathedral, stopping in front of a cobalt blue and gold window and then continuing into the cloisters, where the hymn stretched and dissolved in the cave-like tunnels. In the Cloister Garth, the choir sang a final hymn beneath the budding trees of March and the gray dome of the sky. Their voices were still beautiful, but more ordinary without the amplification of the cathedral. Afterward, the boys became boys again. The sounds of their giggles echoed through the cloisters as they left.

As I walked back inside the cathedral, David Briggs was still playing. When the organ reached its crescendo, it seemed it was going to erupt through the roof like a musical volcano. As the last note faded, for a moment the man sitting next to me and I locked eyes. Tears were streaming down both of our faces.

## SALISBURY CATHEDRAL

Built on a green field, the foundation stones of Salisbury Cathedral were laid in 1220. Except for the fourteenth-century spire, the entire cathedral was built over a period of thirty-eight years—which accounts for the consistency of its architectural style, called Early English Gothic. The limestone of the cathedral is a matrix full of millions of fossilized seashells and micro-organisms. Ocean song still sings through the pillars and stones.

Michael Deason-Barrow, the director of Tonalis, sang as a chorister at Salisbury Cathedral for four years between the ages of nine and thirteen. He often sang solos and recitals and was a well-known treble star featured on a number of recordings. He even sang for the Queen Mum.

Michael remembers recording at night when the cathedral was pitch-black except for one little light on his music stand and another light from the organ. "I was in this vast, womb-like space, with bats flying around. When you can't see you can listen more," he told me. "Often, after I had sung a solo, priests would say, 'You are an angel. You sang divinely.' I knew I was not an angel. I felt my voice was natural, and yet I also wondered where it came from. I felt it wasn't streaming *out* of me, it was streaming *in* to me. The voice was all around me in the listening space."

He felt that, when he sang, there was no physical separation between his body and that of the cathedral. "I opened up to the sacred space, and the cathedral would sing through me," he said. "I had the strong sensation that the Gothic pillars were mystically connected to my spine. In a cathedral there is a knoblike ornament called a boss at the center of the vault. Besides being a physical place, that center is also a transcendent place where all the lines of energy meet. The boss seemed to be my head. The capital was my neck, the tracery of lines in the vault were my arms, and the pillar my spine."

Michael continued, remembering another occasion, "As I stood in the choir stall with the back of my knees touching the wooden bench, I thought of a line from the old folk song, *Waly Waly*: 'I leaned my back against an oak....' It was as if I, too, was leaning back, supported and carried by the pillar. Singing wasn't in front of me; it was looping back behind me, connecting with my vertebrae. I felt dynamically alive. I didn't have to breathe. The pillars were part of my breathing. My voice would literally stream out into the vast space. The cathedral was breathing me and I was breathing the cathedral."[2]

It is in the lambing time of early April 2004 when I first visit Salisbury Cathedral. The octagonal spire, the tallest in Britain, is like a homing beacon. The exterior of Jurassic limestone is carved with saints. Heads with open mouths greet me over the western door. What they are saying, I wonder. What they are singing?

Once inside, I forget these questions as I stand under the western stained-glass window and look down the endless nave, the longest of any English cathedral, which seems to stretch into infinity. Finally, I walk slowly down the north aisle. There, etched in glass on a side panel, is a flaming rose suspended in the sky near a yew tree. A passing child points to the fiery flower and asks his mother, "Is that God?" She doesn't know how to answer.

In the Trinity Chapel at the eastern end, there is a contemporary cobalt blue window dedicated to prisoners of conscience throughout the world who are imprisoned because of their beliefs. Near a Madonna and Child, a candle surrounded by barbed wire—a symbol for Amnesty International—blazes in the window.

Three tiny blonde girls light candles that flicker in the darkened chapel like the highlights in their hair. As I walk down the south aisle and into the choir, I think of Michael Deason-Barrow as a child in his white ruffled collar, leaning his back against the oak choir stall where carved angels kneel. The harmonic tapestry of all the songs sung here seem to reverberate through the stone columns. When I walk back to the north aisle, I see another etched glass, a twin to the one I had seen earlier. Engraved with another flaming rose are T. S. Eliot's famous words that "all shall be well"[3] when the rose is united with the fire. The image of the blazing rose with its soft petals still intact invite us to reflect upon the mysteries of transformation.

## TEWKESBURY ABBEY

Situated between the confluences of the Rivers Avon and Severn, the abbey in the ancient town of Tewkesbury is one of the finest chapels in England. This twelfth-century Norman and Romanesque church was consecrated in 1121 and is full of the tombs of knights, including the twelfth-century Alan, the Abbot of Tewkesbury, who had been a Knight Templar.

The first thing I hear as I enter the abbey is a finch singing in the courtyard. An ages-old copper beech tree is the glory of the garden. As I look into the halo of its branches, the wind rushes up. The nodding white blossoms of laurustinus with their small wedding bouquets release fragrance into the air.

Before going into the abbey for Evensong, I circle the copper beech with my hands, feeling the nubs of buds, smooth knobs, and craggy whirls around its girth, at least four feet in diameter. Its patterns evoke a green man, a breast, a woman's profile, conjoined twins, an eye, a curve of thigh. Its budding branches fan out like a circulatory system. I remember other trees: Gog and Magog in Glastonbury, the Grandmother tree in Cibola National Forest, a valley oak in California's San Joaquin. This tree looks positively pagan and feels so alive, so pulsing with spring. Its sensual branches are dynamically juxtaposed to this very Christian abbey, as I realize upon entering its interior.

Evensong...what is it? Where are the words for music? "Oh Lord, open thou our lips, and our mouth shall show forth thy praise."

From the Lady Chapel behind me, I hear the voices of the choir begin to sing. A choir of boys enters—a whole gaggle of them with dewy skin. One has blue lenses in his round glasses. There are large boys and very tiny boys. Boys with cowlicks, one screwing up his face in a grimace. A few look like they'd rather be playing cricket or video games. Some look celestial. And their voices are, soaring pure crystalline voices that match the roses in their skin. They wear white robes with high ruffled collars and black stoles. Arcs of music flow between the two choirs facing each other. Sound travels up the pillars and spreads out into a fan.

The choir weaves its spell like the branches of the copper beech. The vibrations of the organ remind me of the pulse of the drums at Taos Pueblo. The choir sings spirituals from Michael Tippett's *A Child of Our Time,* such as:

> Go down Moses,
> Way down to Egypt land,
> Tell my Pharaoh,
> Let my people go...

And again I am struck by a juxtaposition: These songs from America, first sung in slavery by a foreign people adapting to the cruelty of their bondage, are now being sung by rosy-lipped English choir boys in a medieval abbey. When they end the "Magnificat," the sound trails off and lingers in the air, reminding me of the ancient caves, chamber graves, and natural rock amphitheatres where songs have been sung through the halls of time.

Then the Vicar of Tewekesbury, a rather young man whom I would not have taken to hold so high a position, recited a prayer of praise that was full of heart:

Eternal Lord God, Source of all beauty and harmony,
We praise you for the gift of music:
For the inspiration given to those that compose it,
For the skill and devotions of those who perform it,
For the faculties and powers which enable us to enjoy it;
And we pray that, as by the gift our lives are enriched and renewed,
So may we glorify you in fuller dedication of ourselves,
Giving thanks always for all things
In the name of our Lord Jesus Christ.
Amen.[4]

*Labyrinth, stone floor of nave laid AD 1201,*
*Notre-Dame Cathedral, Chartres, France*

~ *Chapter 16* ~

# THE VOICE OF THE CATHEDRAL

*Give space to the heavens and a true music will ring out.*
—Johannes Kepler

Walking into the vast space of Notre-Dame de Chartres was like arriving at heaven on earth. The magnificent rose windows and lancets of stained glass were illumined by the April sun. Someone had told me there was a magnetic current of energy running through the front door into the cathedral. Walking into the nave, I felt the power of the earth beneath me as I was simultaneously lifted, my eyes following the columns as they arched to the ceiling.

Michael Deason-Barrow confirms that, in a Gothic cathedral, "the first thing we do is look up. The main objective of medieval engineers and architects was to maintain the ascension of the upward pointing vaults of the cathedral roof in contradiction to the rounded, barrel vaults of Romanesque churches. The flying buttresses, representing the cathedral's etheric skin, support the ascension of the vaults. But, through the buttresses' arched support, the architectural thrust also points downward. There is a marriage of two different streams, of two lines of force meeting. The energy of heaven and earth flows up and down the pillars."[1]

Chartres was built from AD 1194 to 1220 in the landscape of La Beauce southwest of Paris. Its creation took place during the period of a hundred years when over five hundred churches and eighty

Gothic cathedrals were built, giving the period its name. Contributing largely to this effort were the Knights Templar, a military order of warrior-monks who were involved with the flowering of Gothic architecture through the planning and financing of cathedrals and temples. Founded in 1118 and influenced by the Cistercian abbot St. Bernard of Clairvaux, the Knights went to the Holy Lands in the twelfth century and were said to guard the roads leading to Jerusalem. But inasmuch as there were only *nine* knights, military protection may not have been the real reason the Templars were there. The real reason may have had more to do with their excavation of the ruins of the Temple of Jerusalem. French architect and expert on Chartres Cathedral Louis Charpentier believes that, in the course of the excavation, the Templars found the Ark of the Covenant, secret scrolls, and other key esoteric knowledge. One theory is that Chartres was built as an elaborate reliquary to house the treasures they had discovered.[2]

The construction of Chartres is credited to the guild of masons known as the Children of Solomon, a brotherhood named after King Solomon and instructed by Cistercian monks in the art of sacred geometry. Their relationship with the Templars is unclear, but we do know that both groups were involved with bringing this transcendent cathedral into realization.

Chartres is the only cathedral where no bodies are buried in the crypt and there are no depictions of Christ nailed to the cross. It is a hymn to Our Lady that celebrates birth instead of one that mourns death. There are two statues of the Black Madonna and a third representation of the Divine Feminine in the form of a stained-glass window, Notre-Dame de la Belle Verriere: "Our Lady of the Beautiful Window." In it, a serene Mary holds the infant Jesus on her lap. This twelfth-century window is the largest image in the cathedral. Other windows depict the Tree of Jesse, Christ's birth, the story of Mary Magdalene, the marriage feast in Cana, and the story and miracles of the Virgin—along with her death and assumption—as well as stories of John the Baptist and other saints.

In the nave at Chartres is a labyrinth inlaid in stone with a central rosette of six petals. Most people in medieval times couldn't make the pilgrimage to the Holy Lands. Instead, they would go to one of many cathedrals and walk the meandering paths of the labyrinths there to recreate symbolically the journey to Jerusalem, spiritually uniting with the crusaders as they prayed.

Before the advent of Christianity, the town of Chartres was a place of pilgrimage for both Celts and Romans. It was built upon a Neolithic mound that originally contained a dolmen to mark a strong underground magnetic current and subterranean streams. The mound was a center for initiatory rites in Druidism. There, an ancient, blackened statue of a mother holding a child in her lap was found "carved in the hollowed-out trunk of a pear tree."[3] Made by the Druids, the statue was venerated later by the early Christians. The maternal figure was worshipped as Notre-Dame de Sous-Terre, "Our Lady under the Earth," and housed below in the crypt. The statue was destroyed during the French Revolution, but a copy exists there today.

The Black Madonna is an archetype of the fertile earth—the alchemical *nigredo,* or the darkness that redeems matter. Paradoxically, she is the light in the darkness. Jungian analyst Marion Woodman describes her as "nature impregnated by spirit, accepting the human body as the chalice for the spirit. She is the intersection of sexuality and spirituality."[4] Ean Begg writes that "underneath all our conditioning, hidden in the crypt of our being, near the water of life, the Black Virgin is enthroned with her Child, the dark latency of our own essential nature, that which we were always meant to be."[5]

It is hard to envision what early pilgrims must have endured. Certainly they suffered the trials of hunger and the pains of walking through wind, rain, and sun on roads that were, as Charpentier puts it, "hardly tracks, across rivers that were barely fordable, through forests where the wolves hunted in packs."[6] They had left all the comforts of home and family in order to make a quest to a holy place at least once in their lifetime.

Imagine arriving at Chartres after such a journey and entering into the embrace of the cathedral that, like a mother, welcomed her lost children home. After exhaustion and hunger, now there would be safety, light, and music. My own journey in 1996 had its challenges, too, if less severe. Instead of rivers to cross, I dealt with metros, train stations, fatigue, and the barrier of a foreign language.

Upon entering the vastness of Chartres, it is difficult to take it all in. I first went to the Chapel of Notre-Dame du Pilier—Our Lady of the Pillar. She was carved out of rich, milk-chocolate wood, her face serene. She seemed to gaze directly into my eyes but beyond me at the same time. At her feet were offerings of roses. Beside her, red candles were burning. Lighting one, I asked for a message; what I seemed to hear was like advice from a mother: "Rest. Eat. You are not here yet. There is time."

Rest. Eat. That is also what the early Christian pilgrim did. Afterward, he heard Matins and Mass in a nearby Benedictine abbey. Then, with other pilgrims, he entered the cathedral through the north door, the Door of the Initiates, singing psalms to the Black Madonna. That night, he entered into the crypt, where he heard her story. To my knowledge, no records exist of what story was told. As does any archetype, the Black Madonna has many faces. Jungian analyst Jean Shinoda Bolen and others believe she may have represented the Egyptian goddess Isis. Black stone statues depict Isis with her son Horus enthroned upon her lap.

Chartres is not only a place where music is played. Chartres *is* music. The cathedral echoes the slightest sound. Even whispers sound like angels beating feathery wings through heavenly space.

One factor that might contribute to Chartres's astounding acoustics is the stream that runs under it. Louis Charpentier calls Chartres itself "a musical instrument designed to amplify waves that have some sort of relationship with the underground current of water over which the cathedral is built. The cathedral makes use of resonances: this is certainly why its principle part is emptiness, which constitutes its sound box. All the master craftsmen's art and science went into the tuning of this emptiness, its quality, volume and tension, of the stone that gives dimension."[7]

All instruments, be they guitars or clarinets, exhibit different proportions of both form and emptiness. An instrument's shape, and the material of which it is made, bring out certain harmonics that create its characteristic sound. This is why each voice is different from any other and also why each sacred site has different acoustic properties.

At Chartres, music was built into the cathedral through its sacred geometry. The musical proportions were first laid out on the ground and then realized in the elevation of the walls. The Gothic arch, called an "ogive," is based on the five-pointed star, a number that represents the perfected human and the five senses. As Charpentier observes, "The action of sound waves within an ogive can be controlled, as can the sound from organ pipes of differing length. The degrees of resonance alter with the specification of individual ogives, and Gothic buildings were often tuned in the same manner as, say, a piano."[8]

As did the ancient pilgrims, I, too, went to an evening Mass. Disappointingly, there was no choir, and the Mass was spoken through a microphone, which created a disturbing buzz. Afterward, when few people were left, I walked slowly down the aisle of the nave to the center of the labyrinth, standing where other pilgrims have stood throughout the centuries. Barely audibly, I sang a soft, high Alleluia for just a few moments. My voice circled in the space above me, mingling with the air breathed by the stones, and traveled to the far end of the cathedral and back to where I stood. It felt as if not only my voice was amplified but my prayers and intentions as well.

Michael Deason-Barrow has sung at Chartres with choirs and groups of pilgrims and composed music specific to its architecture, including a hymn to the Black Madonna. Making use of its entire space, he placed his choir in different locations throughout the cathedral. This is a departure from modern practice, in which the nave alone is typically used as the place of worship, with chairs lined up in auditorium fashion. Michael explained that his own musical staging is a return to that of the Middle Ages, when the entire body of the cathedral was used as a worshiping space. Thus, he says, "What is going on in the dramatization of the liturgy was echoed by the specific resonating spaces. Sometimes an intimate space such as the

Lady Chapel or crypt was needed. The musical form of the Mass was guided by the different spaces of the cathedral. There was a linking to every part of the building.

"Once, after hearing my choir, one of the guides said he'd never heard the cathedral sound that way," Michael told me. "Most people tend to sing *at* the space, but he had heard us sing *with* it. This has to do with how you listen. There's an old Italian dictum that says, 'To sing, you inhale the voice.' Singing belongs to the receptive, feminine realm, not to the masculine one of voice projections. But many people force the voice and are taught to project it at, or to, a specific focus.

"The stream of sound includes the space," Michael said, "The cathedral is full of flowing lines of energy. A poem by a participant of a Tonalis course, Peggy Cooper, says it best:

> Here we become the living cathedral—
> made not with the sound of hammers,
> but with the wonder and amazement of our singing.

"The cathedral is full of echoes, and, if you listen well with your whole attention, you can hear the response of the building. It is an act of trust."[9]

Before going to Chartres, I had been fortunate to work with Michael at Findhorn, Scotland. He said that I did not need to sing loudly or project my voice. "The volume of the voice is related to the space we're singing in," he said. "We should be aware of whether the space is intimate, for instance, or the much larger size of a cathedral. When I sing, not just my ears and eyes but all of my senses are working with the space; every joint in my body—even the pores of my skin—are breathing. The size of the resonating space automatically affects my breath, which in turn affects the volume of my voice and the energy and spatial aspects of my voice."

According to Charpentier, the sacred center of Chartres is in the choir between the Black Madonna of the Pillar and the window of

Saint Anne. Astoundingly, underneath the choir, fourteen underground streams converge, charging it with subterranean energy. It is at this center in the choir that the priest originally stood giving voice during Mass. The altar has since been moved to a part of the cathedral called the Crossing. Until the Second Vatican Council decreed otherwise, the priest intoned vowels of Latin as an incantation.

A seven-pointed star, a number related to the Black Virgin, is the hidden sacred geometric figure on which this part of the cathedral is constructed. Is the center of the star at the point where the fourteen streams meet? None of my sources could say for sure.

Charpentier believes that the elevation of Chartres is tuned to a Gregorian mode based on the second note of the scale, *re*, which is called the Dorian mode. The third note of this mode, he believes, is symbolized by the height of the pillars of the choir, the fifth by the height of the cornice under the triforium, and the octave by the height of the capitals in the base of the vault. The Dorian mode is easiest to visualize on a piano. If you start on the note D and play an octave on the white keys, you will hear this mode. The Beatles made use of it in their songs "Eleanor Rigby" and "Norwegian Wood."

"The Dorian mode was used for religious ritual and the one most commonly used in Gregorian chant," Kay Gardner tells us. "Its magical, serene character brought a sense of exaltation to the melodies."[10] It has a particular melancholy sound that is lifted up by the higher notes. Deason-Barrow reflects that "this is because the Dorian mode is one of the few scales in the world where the ascending form and its mirrored descent give rise to the same intervals. It is one of the few scales that balance the inward direction of the minor, i.e., the minor 3rd with the out-breathing quality of the major 6th. Therefore, in music therapy, Dorian is used to help bring about balance between inner and outer, above and below, which are almost always disturbed in illness."[11]

What happens when music is sung in a cathedral? What is its purpose? According to the clairvoyant Theosophist C. W. Leadbeater, it is to create an etheric edifice around the cathedral. He believes that "the whole ritual is aimed rightly at building this form, charging it with divine force, and then discharging it; and each canticle or recitation contributes its share to this work, in addition to the part which it bears in the preparation of the hearts and minds of priest and people. The edifice swells up from below like a bubble which is being blown. Broadly speaking it may be said that the opening Canticle provides its pavement and the Introit the material for its walls and roof, while the Kyrie supplies the subsidiary bowls and cupolas, and the Gloria the great central dome."[12]

The exact nature of the edifice depends on many things: the size of the congregation, the devotion of the priest, the people, and the nature of the service being performed. On hearing the "Veni Creator" sung, Leadbeater described the church as being filled with "a wonderful red glow, a kind of luminous fiery mist.... This celestial fire grows stronger and stronger as the hymn proceeds, and eventually a mighty vortex of it forms over the head of the Bishop, and pours itself down through him."[13]

Cathedral space is perfectly suited for chanting because the voice, too, has immense space, great depths, and soaring heights. The voice can be a nave waiting to be filled with praise, a passageway for the Divine. The voice can be a reflector of silent interiors, a deep well of knowing, an altar to receive communion. Sound travels up through the body. The voice is the place where spirit and matter merge, where heaven is brought to earth.

## THE CRYPT

On my second day at Chartres, I toured the crypt with six others and gained permission from the guide to sing. After I sang a brief song, a Belgian couple came up to me. The man said, "It was you we heard sing last night! Do you know your voice filled the entire cathedral? We went all around looking for you." His name was Franz and his wife's, Beatrice. Since he spoke fluent French, I asked if he would mind asking the guide if I could return to the crypt to sing for a longer time. "Yes," he replied, "and will you allow us to accompany you?"

That afternoon, the three of us had an hour alone together in the crypt. Wordlessly I went to the altar of Our Lady under the Earth. Franz and Beatrice sat on different sides of the aisle. We were silent, each in prayer. I closed my eyes, breathing in the narrow chapel. Then a song of the moment emerged, first with deep blue "Ouuus" that changed into rosy "Ahhhs." The "Ah" became "Ave Maria." From the back of the crypt, I could hear the overtones of my Alleluia resonate off the far wall where the Black Madonna sat. I imagined what it would be like if the room were filled with other singers. Synchronistically, the lights went out, tiny rose-colored lights illuminated the aisle, and a group of about twenty singers entered the crypt, also singing Alleluia. I had no idea of who they were or of why they had come. As they circled around the altar, Franz joined me and together we walked slowly down the aisle toward them. The group opened to include us, and we all sang together in praise of the mystery.

After several songs in Latin, we proceeded slowly up and down the aisle singing Alleluia again. Some sang with their hands over their hearts, others with their hands extended out. Some walked with their eyes closed. Then, without a cue, they left singing. We heard their voices linger in another part of the crypt. Then all was quiet.

Beatrice was crying. I sat in front of the Black Madonna, feeling so small compared with all this glory and beauty. It was beyond my comprehension. The Black Madonna seemed to speak to my heart: "Yes, you are small, tinier than you can ever imagine. Do you know how vast the universe is? You can't begin to understand the powers that move through me. But, at the same time, do you know how much you are needed? Do you know how important it is that we each make our contribution?" Her words both humbled and empowered me. I knew that they were not meant for me alone, but that each of us has our own mission, whether it is singing in a cathedral or driving a cab. We are all much more important than we can imagine. Each of us is needed to give our own unique gifts.

As we were leaving, Beatrice paused for a moment and then went to the altar. She stood silently and then sang a song in Dutch, her voice shaking with emotion and praise.

Later that day, I met the three English ladies who had been on the crypt tour and told them of my experience with Franz and Beatrice. While we spoke, the couple appeared, and Beatrice talked of the song she had sung. She said she had been scared; she had never sung alone but knew it was something she must do. As she translated the song into English, the three ladies beamed, "We know that song! It's written by Rudolf Steiner. We must all sing it together in the center of the labyrinth." Franz replied, "Yes! The cathedral and the human cathedral must meet through the voice!" Together, we walked into the petals of the labyrinth—six of us, from Belgium, England, and America, one for each petal—and sang Steiner's song:

> In Search of the Holy Grail
> Do we wander from land to land...

As I left Notre-Dame de Chartres, that great Lady of Roses, on a bus to southern France, I saw an African woman dressed in a long blue satin gown with a blue satin turban on her head. At her breast was a nursing child. The Black Madonna has traveled with me ever since.

*Carving of angel musicians, Rosslyn Chapel, fifteenth century, Roslin, Scotland*

~ *Chapter 17* ~

# ROSSLYN CHAPEL

*Space is the medium of sound and therefore of the music of praise.*
—William Anderson

On the Celtic holiday of Beltane, May 1, 2002, I arrived at Rosslyn Chapel in Scotland. The glen was fully leafed, covered with a carpet of wild garlic. Gorse was abloom with yellow flames. Rabbits nibbled green shoots. In Scottish Gaelic, *Roslin* means "ancient knowledge passed down through generations."[1] For some, the name refers to the "Roseline," the secret bloodline produced by the marriage of Jesus and Mary Magdalene and kept alive through heretical sects. Here in this glen, nestled in the Pentland Hills in Midlothian just south of Edinburgh, lies this chapel that has been called a "garden in stone."[2] My first glimpse of the chapel was disappointing. It was completely covered by metal scaffolding, both to protect it from the elements and to provide a stairway for viewing the exterior of the chapel from above. Being *inside* Rosslyn, on the other hand, was like being inside the harmony written in our bones and etched in our DNA. There are hundreds of carvings, each one depicting a symbol or symbols from different spiritual traditions. Adorning the walls are 103 faces of the Green Man, the ancient Celtic archetype of the masculine consciousness in nature. The Green Man is "the head that prophesies, that sings and utters verses."[3] Carved plants usher forth from his mouth, symbolizing the union of man with nature and, perhaps—given the cyclic nature of vegetation—knowledge of the mysteries of death and rebirth.

Inside this holy space, originally constructed as a "lady chapel" to a cathedral that was never built, are also carvings of rich foliation. Indian corn and aloe vera, plants of the Americas, were carved on lintels long before Columbus sailed to America, suggesting that earlier trips than his had been made to the new world. Lilies, roses, and stars decorate the barreled ceiling. Egyptian, Celtic, Islamic, Hebrew, Scandinavian, and Masonic symbols twine together through every part of the building. Carvings of angels play bagpipes, drums, lutes, and flutes. Others hold hearts, scrolls, and floriated crosses. Among the images are those of a bound Lucifer, entwined dragons, the head of Christ with the sun and the moon, a salamander, and a mermaid—all parading through the space along with the death mask of the fourteenth-century Scottish king, Robert the Bruce. It was like a dreamscape in which everything is alive and speaks in riddles.

The chapel was built by Sir William St. Clair between the years 1450–1480. Sir Gilbert Haye was also one of the chief designers and builders. His vast knowledge spanned from the ten years he spent in Cathay (the name for China in his time) and the Far East to his position as a librarian to the French King, Charles VIII. Haye was a tutor to St. Clair's children. Together, the two of them built Rosslyn as a symbolic map to the esoteric teachings throughout the world, many brought back by the Knights Templar when they returned from Jerusalem. During St. Clair's time, people who believed in such "heresies" were burned at the stake. It was safer to encode esoteric knowledge in images than in words, so he carved his beliefs in stone. St. Clair oversaw every detail of sculpture and architecture and hired the finest masons in Europe. In *Rosslyn: Guardian of the Secrets of the Holy Grail*, Tim Wallace-Murphy and Marilyn Hopkins describe the result as a "veritable, three-dimensional 'teaching board' of Gnostic, late-medieval initiation."[4]

No historical records exist of Rosslyn being used for initiatory rites. We do know, however, that complex rituals lasting for days were conducted there, including baptisms, weddings, and funerals. Esoteric Freemasons believe that Rosslyn *was* the site of late-medieval initiation into the secret wisdom of that order. The rituals that may have taken place there, and their significance, remain shrouded in mystery. Perhaps the only ones who know the truth are the adepts themselves, but a Mason friend tells me that even they might not fully comprehend the meaning of what they are being taught.

Christian imagery also exists in the chapel, but it, too, is veiled. Jesus hangs from a T-shaped cross, called the "tau cross," a symbol related to the Knights Templar and to the solar god Tammuz who, like Christ, died and was reborn. Moses has upswept hair that looks like horns, symbolic of hidden knowledge.

Wallace-Murphy and Hopkins propose that Rosslyn Chapel was part of an alleged medieval pilgrimage route called "The Field of Stars" or "The Milky Way," as suggested by the late author and esoteric teacher, Trevor Ravenscroft. Modern pilgrims have popularized this route. Wallace-Murphy and Hopkins, who went on the pilgrimage themselves, write that the route traces seven Druidic centers of initiation in relation to celestial bodies and the chakras. The word *chakra* comes from the Sanskrit meaning "wheel"; it refers to seven centers of spiritual energy in the body from the base of the spine to the crown of the head that relate to ascending levels of consciousness. Wallace-Murphy and Hopkins do not say whether sound was used in these initiations, but in yogic traditions Sanskrit letters and sound are related to each chakra.

In the scheme they describe, the first center is Santiago de Compostela in Spain, symbolizing the moon, which is related to the base chakra. The second is Notre-Dame de Dalbade, in Toulouse, France, related to the planet Mercury and to the second, or sacral, chakra. Here the initiate became "the Hidden One or Occultist, who could communicate with Hermes Trismegistus, the thrice-blessed one of the Greek Mysteries."[5]

The third center relates to Venus in the cathedral of Orleans. Here the initiate's solar plexus chakra was activated and, upon the successful passing of this test, knighthood was bestowed. The initiate traveled then to Chartres, associated with the heart chakra and the sun. Next came Notre-Dame de Paris, representing the planet Mars and related to the throat chakra. This is the center "of both speech and inner listening, and is connected with the power of sound."[6] The initiate then went to the Jupiter site at Amiens Cathedral in France, where the brow chakra, or third eye, was opened.

Lastly in the cycle is the wisdom center of Saturn, associated with the crown chakra. "The Crown was the royal symbol of the King of the Grail," Wallace-Murphy and Hopkins tell us.[7] Here, the initiate learned the secrets of time and gained an understanding of the laws that govern the universe. The Saturn initiation was held in the crypt below Rosslyn Chapel.

As must have been true at Rosslyn, song, incantation, and music have been central to initiatory rites through the ages; intonation of sacred words for magical purposes was customary in many cultures. We can trace this practice from the ceremonies of Siberian shamans, Australian Aborigines, Gabon Pygmies of Africa, and Egyptian priests to the Eleusinian and Dionysian mysteries of Greece. The ancients passed wisdom from teacher to initiate through the *oral* tradition, not the written. One reason that vowels were not inscribed in sacred languages such as the Hebrew and the Egyptian is that, rich as they are in harmonics, vowels were thought to be the living spirit of the word. They are what give language its *power*. Hence the utterance of vowels in sacred words was resticted to those initiated into the mysteries and so qualified to handle their force. The full words were not made public because, in the wrong hands, information can be dangerous. Magical words of great power (over brute forces, elementals, devas, animals, and/or human beings) are still carefully guarded in esoteric traditions to this day.

In the Western Mystery Tradition, different words of power were given at every new stage of initiation and needed to be mastered, used only righteously, and spoken discretely. (A Masonic friend says that, while this practice was followed in traditional Freemasonry, it is no longer intact because the true delivery of the words has been lost; now the form consists of substitute words.) The real secrets of initiation concern how to intone the letters, sounds, and syllables correctly in order to make them effective. Is this right use of magical speech what the living plants ushering from the Green Man's mouth was meant to represent?

Sir William St. Clair, the builder of the Rosslyn Chapel, came from a noble family. The St. Clairs were descended from Rollo of Norway, the first Duke of Normandy. Their ancestry is linked not only to the Knights Templar but also to the legend of the Rex Deus, "a hereditary group of families who have exerted great influence over European life from the time of Jesus to the present."[8]

The St. Clair family originally went from Normandy to Scotland in 1057. At that time, William the Seemly St. Clair, along with the knight Bartholomew Ladislaus Leslyn, escorted the Saxon Princess Margaret from the court of Hungary on her way to marry the king of Scotland, Malcolm Cannore. In appreciation, King Malcolm granted St. Clair the lands of Roslin and made him the queen's cup bearer. The chapel depicts the princess's journey with a carving of Margaret sitting on the back of Leslyn's horse carrying the Holy Rood, a piece of the true cross. The Holy Rood Abbey and Palace in Edinburgh is named after this event.

Under the St. Clair family, the area of Roslin became a haven for gypsies and the Knights Templar, who fled France in 1312 to escape the Inquisition imposed by Phillipe le Bel. The knights were safe at Roslin because Robert the Bruce, the Scottish king at the time, had been excommunicated by the pope and so did not have to comply with orders to hand them over. They helped him defeat the English in the Battle of Bannockburn. It is said that from the knowledge the Templars brought from the Holy Lands sprang the esoteric brotherhood of the Freemasons.

The William St. Clair who built Rosslyn also had other distinguished forbearers. His great-great-grandfather had been killed during a battle in Lithuania while fighting with the Teutonic Knights, a Germanic religious military order founded in the late twelfth century. His grandfather was a Templar who died in Spain in 1330 in an attempt to escort the heart of Robert the Bruce to the Holy Land. William himself became the first elected Grand Master of the Grand Lodge of the Freemasons in Scotland.

The Knights Templar are steeped in legend and mystery. Inquisition records state that they committed heresies of spitting on the cross, engaging in sodomy, and worshiping a mysterious head known as the Baphomet. These military monks became wealthy in lands and property throughout Europe and were subject only to the pope's authority. As mentioned earlier, many believe that, contrary to their ostensible purpose of guarding the roads to the Holy Land, they were instead on a mission to retrieve a secret treasure buried beneath Solomon's Temple in Jerusalem. The Templars respected their Muslim brothers because of their bravery and learned much about sacred geometry, architecture, and music from the Islamic culture.

Louis Charpentier thinks that the treasure in question was the Ark of the Covenant and that the Gothic cathedrals that bloomed in France over a fifty-year period were built from knowledge contained within the ark. Others believe that the treasure was the Holy Grail, either as the cup Jesus used at the Last Supper or in the form of written evidence of the legendary bloodline that sprang from his union with Mary Magdalene, in which case her womb becomes a symbol of the Holy Grail. It is also thought that the treasure may have been the head of Jesus himself or a statue of a Black Virgin hidden somewhere.

Both gypsies and the Knights Templar venerated Mary Magdalene and statues of the Black Madonna, who was often thought to be Mary Magdalene herself. The child on her lap was not Jesus but his daughter or son. Hundreds of Black Madonnas can be found throughout Europe, most of them in France. St. Bernard de Clairvaux, the Templars' founder, is said to have received three drops of milk from the breast of the Black Virgin of Citeaux. He wrote many hymns and sermons devoted to her, including 280 sermons on the Song of Songs, which includes the words, "I am black, but I am beautiful, O ye daughters of Jerusalem."

The Black Madonna is also linked to legends of Kali, Isis, and Cybele. The Templars and troubadours who worshipped her were tortured or put to death during the Albigensian Crusades and the Inquisition in France. According to Gnostic tradition, "it was through the Magdalene, rather than through Peter and the male apostles, that Jesus transmitted his secret doctrines."[9] Such an idea was certainly dangerous in medieval times.

Though the Templars took a vow of poverty, collectively they owned wealthy estates and piles of gold. Some believe that their treasure was simply the precious metal and jewels, perhaps even the lost crown jewels and Holy Rood of Scotland. Others believe that the treasure they possessed was not material wealth or a holy relic but knowledge itself, and that the true Holy Grail is found within the human heart. The search goes on.

I myself was on a different search—not for jewels, but for evidence of music written inside Rosslyn. When I arrived, I walked quietly through the chapel, taking it all in. Upon finding one of the many images of the Green Man, I remembered reading that this particular one had eyes that would follow you wherever you go. He seemed to watch me as I moved from one side of the chapel to the other. I found many images related to the Templars: carvings of a five-pointed star; the Templar seal of the *Agnus Dei*, or "Lamb of God"; a dove in flight carrying an olive branch; two brothers on a horse; the head of Christ; and an oriental cross. When these signs appear together, they signal Templar affiliations. Above me were stained-glass windows of different saints. I could make out St. George and St. Michael, the patron saint of the Templars. I saw the carved head of Melchizedek and Saint Margaret on back of a Knight's horse carrying the Holy Rood. Everywhere were symbols to decipher.

Down in the crypt it was cold. Even in May I needed my coat and could see my breath. The crypt housed more mysteries: architectural drawings on the wall relating to sacred geometry and a seventeenth-century stone, called the King of Terrors, showing crowned death with his scythe. On the ceiling were floriated crosses.

Although people were above me in the chapel, no one else was in the crypt. Standing under one of the crosses on the ceiling nearest the altar, I prayed silently for healing. When I asked if I could sing, I didn't hear an answer, but I did see a figure like the Green Man made of twining vines. Sounds rose up, and then it seemed I was singing with the angels carved above me and the Green Man dancing through the space.

Returning to the chapel, in its northeast corner I stood near a group of about seven people circled around a well-dressed, gray-haired guide of some authority. He asked for a volunteer. When a man stepped forward, the guide asked him to stand at the end of a brass memorial plaque on the floor at the head of one of three altars. The guide stood at the other end and asked the man to mirror his hand and arm movements. After several repetitions, he instructed the man to hold his hands in front of him facing each other. The guide then used his own hands to describe what looked like a cube in the space between the other man's hands. As I watched, I felt like Drew Barrymore in the movie *E.T.* just before the little alien levitates fruit into the air. Something was about to happen. The man gave a startled jump and was visibly moved. He said he felt a strong current of energy. We all paused in wonder.

The guide asked if I wanted to try. In following his movements, I felt energy between us; and, when he came closer to work with the space my hands framed, I felt a strong magnetic pull. He then held my right hand and placed his other hand around my right shoulder (a chronic area of tension). He looked into my eyes with profound compassion, and I felt a healing of something I can't articulate. The circle opened to include me, and another man said, "Welcome." Explaining that the people there were members of the Temple Study Group from all over Britain, he introduced me around and invited me to join them for the next two hours. I soon found that our guide was a Grand Mason. It was evident that he loved the place deeply and felt there were many more secrets to be revealed.

The guide took us into the small Lady Chapel in the east part of the building. Here stand three pillars: the Mason's Pillar, a plain central pillar, and the famous Apprentice Pillar, so named for the one who carved it. The story goes that, when the master mason received a model of the pillar, he hesitated to begin work on it until he had seen the original—which was in Rome—for himself. He left at once for Italy. In his absence, his apprentice dreamed the pillar was finished and, upon awakening, set out immediately to carve it. When the master returned and saw the beauty and workmanship, he fell into a jealous rage and killed the apprentice on the spot. The head of one of the men is carved in the southwest corner of the choir, while the other is in the northwest corner.

The story of the murdered apprentice is thought to be a veil for the legendary death of Hiram Abif, builder of the Temple of Jerusalem, who figures prominently in the initiation rites of the the Third—or Master Mason—Degree in Freemasonry. Hiram himself is a mystery. Little is known of him other than his famous murder. Hiram was a master builder who knew many secrets, including the ineffable name of God, which was called the "Grand Masonic Word." To know this word is to have great power. Hiram promised to reveal this and other secrets upon completion of the temple to the other craftsmen, which would have made them Master Masons.

One day as Hiram was leaving the temple, he was accosted by three of his fellow workmen who wanted the secrets immediately. They beat and then killed him by a blow to the forehead with a maul. His body was first hidden and then buried in a grave marked by an acacia branch.

When Hiram did not show up at the temple the next day, King Solomon ordered a search. Hiram's decaying body was discovered after fourteen days. The legend goes that, after three tries, he was raised from the dead. As writers Jim Shaw and Tom McKenney recount, "The first word he spoke was the replacement for the 'Grand Masonic Word' lost at his death, and that word is the one passed down to Master Masons to this day."[10] Many believe this story links Hiram with Osiris, the Egyptian god of death and rebirth, whose body was dismembered into fourteen pieces before being reassembled by Isis.

At the top of all three pillars in the Lady Chapel at Rosslyn, carvings of angelic musicians are interspersed with those of the Green Man, who is also associated with music. In many cathedrals, images of the Green Man can be seen in choirs and choir stalls as reminders to pour forth praise freely in psalms and anthems. The Green Man is nature's singer; he utters the secret language of vegetation. His link to Osiris, the green-faced Egyptian god of agriculture, death, and rebirth, connects him to the ultimate mysteries. Pairing the angelic musicians with the Green Man suggests, not just ordinary music, but music with the power to transform the individual into a greater reality. On the tour, the guide said that there were many musical mysteries at Rosslyn. He felt that the metal scaffolding around the building had changed some of its remarkable acoustics as had the layer of lime and salt painted over the interior to preserve it from deterioration.

The guide then pointed to the stone cubes that appear on the curved arches between the pillars in the Lady Chapel. There are 216 cubes in all, each one etched with a variety of multifaceted carvings. The general belief is that these cubes relate to some kind of musical notation. A number of people have been at work to decipher the code. One expert thinks the cubes may relate to a fifteenth-century musical notation system. Others believe the cubes were created by Cymatics, that is, by producing patterns in sand on brass plates vibrated by a violin bow. They speculate that the stone masons later rendered these patterns in the cubes.

Edinburgh composer Stuart Mitchell thinks that he and his father, Thomas, have definitively cracked the code. Based upon Cymatic patterns and sacred geometry, they have assigned each cube a note in order to create a musical score. The first interval in Mitchell's resulting composition, called "The Voice of Creation," is the augmented 4th or tritone. This interval spans three whole tones. To hear it, play the notes C and F# on a keyboard or other instrument. The tritone was named the infamous "devil in music" and was banned from medieval music by the Catholic Church because of its dissonant sound, which was said to induce visions. Mitchell has found melodies in the ceiling cubes as well, along with old Orkney/Shetland airs distinct to the musical culture of this pagan region of Scotland. However, he and his father think the carvings are not just a musical manuscript of particular songs but a code of frequencies that, when played by medieval instruments, will unlock a secret Rosslyn has been guarding like a dragon would its treasure.

In 2005 the Mitchells realized the original composition given by the cubes in a musical performance. Stuart told me that while the

"Voice of Creation" is a beautiful and aesthetic collection of notes, they need further to research playing the piece with different timing and dynamics to yield the hoped-for results. "Cymatics is the Holy Grail of music," he said. "It's like hearing creation unfold before you. Every note sends out a mathematical signature, a musical ripple, which interacts with the entire environment. We need to find the right wavelengths and the right combination of notes, dynamics, and duration to excite the chapel. We're still searching." [11]

Author and historian Ashley Cowie has produced a musical CD called *The Rose-line Connection*, recorded live at the Rosslyn Chapel and documenting its remarkable acoustics. His research shows that the crypt has a reverberation time of twelve to fourteen seconds, which, to his knowledge, is the longest in the United Kingdom. Long reverberation times extend the sound and make it appear other-worldly, as if the sound stretches to infinity. He writes that "the Lady Chapel is like an instrument itself and creates quite an incredible effect. When instruments are played under the four arches, sweet spots are revealed along the length of the choir, along the east-west axis." During numerous projects with various musicians he and others have lain down under each "sweet spot"—the name for the places of greatest resonance—to listen. "I could see the interrelationships between the sounds and stone, as if the entire structure was designed as a song."[12]

On the tour at Rosslyn, the guide talked of other musical clues waiting to be unraveled. Some people, for instance, are doing research on the finger positions of the angelic musicians to decode which notes they are playing. Perhaps, the researchers speculate, the cubes point to keys or modes and the angels, to notes.

The guide took us next into the crypt, where we chanted *Om*, our mingled voices growing into a powerful single voice. But alas, we only chanted three times, not long enough fully to explore the effects of sound in this magnificent space. Then the guide showed us the most sacred part of the crypt, called the monk's cell. Small, damp, and cramped, it had been a place of penance and ritual. Finally, in a different part of the crypt, the guide pointed out a carving of

St. Matthew holding a key. In Freemasonry the key is a symbol of secrecy. What secrets are waiting to be unlocked? And could the key represent a key in music?

The group invited me for tea, and then I was off to catch my bus back to Edinburgh. At the station I met an American woman who had seen us and asked me about our guide. She was fascinated by the musical clues at Rosslyn. She told me she sings in a choir that performs medieval music, and we agreed to return to Rosslyn together.

When we arrived at the chapel the next day, though, it was crowded. There were several tours offering the standard textbook descriptions, instead of the invitation to experience Rosslyn in the way our guide had facilitated the day before. Many people were listening to recorded messages on audio phones. It was not a good time to sing, and yet, here we were; it was now or never. We experimented briefly, waiting for moments when there were fewer people. I made a few sounds, standing on a brass plaque near the Mason's Pillar and the central pillar under one of the pendent bosses hanging from the ceiling. Listening from the choir, my friend encouraged me to keep going. I went next to the plaque between the central pillar and the Apprentice Pillar, also beneath a boss, and did the same thing. Again she listened and said the sound was rich with harmonics. When I said I wondered if this was the mouth of the chapel, she remarked that the pendulant boss looked like a uvula, the fleshy round protuberance that hangs in the back of the throat.

Then we traded places so that she could sing and I could listen. Yes, the archway did look like an open mouth with a uvula. Actually, *two* mouths were visible, like the open jaws of twin dragons. And I, too, heard sounds rich in harmonics emanating from her voice. We both tried various vowels, trying to distinguish differences between them, but there were too many interruptions and we felt it important not to dominate the space. However, the next day when I returned alone, I felt that "Ah" was the sound most natural to the Lady Chapel. Making it places the uvula in the same position in the mouth as the decorated bosses are in the space. As I made this sound in my midrange, it vibrated the roof of my mouth, creating overtones both within and without. My mouth, arched in an "Ah," sent my voice higher and higher.

Feeling there was much more to discover, I went back to Rosslyn for a fourth day and found the guide from my first visit. In the Lady Chapel I showed him what my friend and I had discovered. He too believed this to be the mouth of the space; he also agreed that the bosses were like uvulas and that the sound "Ah" was important. I said I had envisioned two people in the past standing on the plaques and singing and performing some sort of ritual, perhaps with movement in the four directions. "Yes," the guide replied, "We think there were at least two, maybe three, people."

The number two seemed more important to me: two main pillars, two priests—or a priest and a priestess—singing the notes on the cubes. Though several decorated bosses hang from the ceiling, two in particular are more ornate: One represents the life of the Virgin Mary with a rose in the center of an eight-rayed star, above each side of the star are carvings related to the birth of Jesus. The other boss reminded me of the head of a penis. I said I thought the priest-singers had stood underneath the bosses. "Or maybe at the head of the plaques," the guide speculated. "I need to be off, but you're very close to discovering something else."

Slowly I walked around the Lady Chapel searching for more clues. The air was cold, but as I touched the Apprentice Pillar I felt warmth come into my spine. My feet felt warm for the first time in four days. I already knew this was an important spot; there must be others. Behind the middle pillar at the chapel's center—and so, importantly, central to the space—was a Green Man on a boss. This one did not hang from the ceiling but came forward from the wall, almost like a microphone. Could this area be another initiation point? Perhaps the initiate had faced the Green Man to learn the right sonic formulas in the proper sequence. The expression on this one's face was particularly mischievous; he had an open mouth, as if he were about to speak at any moment. His mouth was in the same smiling shape as if he were saying the vowel "E."

I wanted to experiment with that vowel, but an Evensong service was about to begin. An Anglican priest was preparing an altar in the choir. A few women were taking pictures; one lay down on the central brass plaques to get a shot of the ceiling. I never would have thought to lie down here, but I followed her lead and stretched out on the plaque nearest the Apprentice Pillar. Was I close to the discovery at which the guide had hinted? Here, near the third pillar, perhaps initiates, who symbolically played the role of the murdered Hiram Abif, would have lain to be instructed in the third degree of Masonic wisdom. After all, they were said to be "raised," as in being raised from the dead. Perhaps their rebirth was enacted symbolically as they arose, following the instruction they had received while prone. Authors and Masons Christopher Knight and Robert Lomas believe this ceremony may have had roots in the initiation rites of the ancient kings in Egypt.[13]

Anticipating the service, I took my place in the wooden pews, located in a different section of the chapel called the choir. The pews seemed out of place, and I wondered if they had been part of the original space. If the primary purpose of the chapel had been initiation rather than a church service, perhaps pews had not been necessary.

When the service began, I was disappointed that there was no singing choir. There was only one singer, who chanted briefly while we followed in unison. The rest of the service was spoken.

As I listened, I reflected on initiation and the role that vibration may have played in it. In my twenty-eight years as a music therapist, I have witnessed again and again how sound and music create doorways into altered states of awareness that assist in personal transformation. I wondered what esoteric knowledge of music the Knights Templar brought back when they returned from the Holy Lands. Had this knowledge been encoded in the chapel? Were sacred vowels, and the harmonics they generate, used as they were in Egyptian initiatory rituals? Perhaps the Roseline, after which the chapel is named, refers not only to the secret bloodline of Jesus and Mary Magdalene. Could the true mystical marriage be the sacred union of sound and space within us, merging heaven and earth in our hearts?

Rosslyn poses more questions than it offers answers. As Stuart Mitchell said when I asked him about the chapel's acoustic mysteries: "Rosslyn was created by a secret society to keep the secrets of Rosslyn a secret." I laughed as I remembered the smiling Green Man in the Lady Chapel. Is he one of the keys to unlocking Rosslyn's secrets? As in the search for the Holy Grail, the key lies in finding the right questions to ask.

*Defaced Hathor columns, Temple of Dendera,*
*built between 125 BC and AD 65, Egypt*

~ *Chapter 18* ~

# DESECRATION

*Seeing the hidden and harmonious order built
into body and mind, as it is built into
every flower and leaf, mirrored by the crafts,
echoed by the music, one wonders at the origin of
disharmony and disorder that mars our civilization.*
—György Doczi

The first time I walked into West Kennet Long Barrow, a chamber grave near Avebury in Wiltshire, England, I felt a profound sadness. Here in this ancient Neolithic mound, built in the shape of the body of the Goddess, were tourists walking in and out briefly, snapping pictures and talking loudly. "Ughhh, do you think there are still bones?" At Chartres, as I was sitting and praying, someone turned on what sounded like a vacuum cleaner. The sound roared through the space like an unleashed beast. When I was at Notre-Dame in Paris, there was a constant buzz in the air, and I left after a half an hour. Later, I read that over the last fifty years the cathedral has been stuffed with electric cables to provide electricity. The Grand Gallery in the Great Pyramid of Giza is now lined with fluorescent lights nailed to the wall that emit a constant, high humming noise. At Stonehenge it is hard to meditate because of the sounds of traffic whizzing past. One visitor's comment was, "Nice rocks. Shame about the noise."

Even though traditions of spiritual pilgrimage do still exist, in Western society they have mostly been replaced by tourism. Many people go to look at sacred places and take pictures of them. Cathedrals are reduced in size to a glossy 4 x 6. Camcorders reduce the pyramids to the size of a TV screen. While it is indeed important to view the sacred, Michael Deason-Barrow believes that taking pictures without giving something in return draws energy away from the space: "The cathedral becomes a silent, immutable object and closes down. In the past pilgrims brought offerings. Now we just consume. Once I heard a Bruckner symphony at Chartres. There were huge, monolithic chords in the brass section that rose up and hung like incense in the air. I felt the cathedral was saying 'thank you.' It was as if every nook and cranny in it could breathe again. The cathedral could then allow its spiritual gifts to resonate outward."[1]

In ancient times, ritual in a sacred place involved all the senses and all the arts. Dancing, chanting, drumming, costume, and incense all mingled as part of a ceremonial approach to the Divine. Over centuries, the arts became separate experiences, no longer linked to each other and often divorced from the sacred. One result of this splitting off is specialization, wherein some people are artists and singers but most are not. Thus we give our inborn creativity over to specialists rather than claim it for ourselves.

Further—and as the tourist's camera symbolizes—the eye has replaced the ear as the favored sense. We are now primarily a visual culture, not an auditory or kinesthetic one. In the shift, something vital has been lost, for while the eye objectifies experience as something outside us, the ear embraces experience and internalizes it. When we take a picture, we merely capture something on film. When we sing or hear music in a sacred space, we take in something of its essence and make it part of ourselves.

David Abram, in his book *The Spell of the Sensuous*, points out that it was in the transition from an oral to a written culture that the eye achieved prominence over the ear.[2]

Early written languages such as Hebrew and Egyptian as mentioned previously, were still highly oral in that they were meant to be intoned. They did not depict vowels, the vowels themselves being considered sacred; the spaces between the consonants were where the breath of God could enter. Vowels could be uttered only in speech, turning the strings of consonants into comprehensible words. Hence, in order to understand written text, one needed to engage with it.

Over time, when vowels *were* added to written language, it was no longer necessary to intone it aloud to comprehend its meaning. The act of reading could become a silent and much more internal affair. As a result, we lost the sensuality that a concentration on oral experience provides. We also, in some fundamental way, lost touch with the earth itself. The act of reading creates pictures in the mind. As reading and writing became increasingly dominant, we began to favor these interior experiences over the very ground under our feet.

Alphabet symbols initially referred to natural forms in the landscape. The more abstract writing became, the more its relation to the living land was forgotten.

Thus the invention of writing has played an important role in the desacralization of nature. Over the last few thousand years, the Earth Mother of antiquity has been replaced by the Sky God, who has taken us up and out of our bodies. In the process, sacred groves, holy wells, megalithic monuments, and other natural places of worship have been usurped or destroyed.

Once, while I was visiting the Great Kiva in the town of Aztec in the Four-Corners region of New Mexico, a tour guide explained that the most sacred part of the pueblo, called the "middens," was where food was returned to the earth. The first white settlers, whose religion was one of ascent, saw the middens only as a garbage heap and could not understand why it was considered sacred. Nor could the Puritans of Britain understand the holiness of Avebury. Pagan beliefs survived in Avebury until the thirteenth century. Afterward, during the height of the witch trials, most of it was destroyed. By 1934, only four stones were left standing. Alexander Keiller, a Scottish industrialist, bought the land in 1937 and began to restore Avebury as a sacred site. Before then, the henge had been used as a rubbish dump.

The reasons for such denigration are complex and varied. Conquering tribes often destroy the religious sites of those they conquer or build their own temples or churches on top of the old ones.

Ingrained in this behavior is a "we-versus-they" attitude: Our religion is better than your religion; we are the good guys, and God is on our side. Still tragically common today, such a mind-set and way of behaving can be traced at least as far back as 1352 BC in Egypt, when Akhenaten destroyed images of other Egyptian gods in an attempt to unify Egypt under the worship of a single sun god, Aten. Later, Coptic Christians defaced images of Hathor at her temple at Dendera.

In the Old Testament—a book recognized as sacred by Christians, Hebrews, and Muslims alike—Deuteronomy 7:5 proclaims: "Thus shall ye deal with them; ye shall destroy their altars, and break down their images, and cut down their groves, and burn their graven images with fire." And one doesn't have to believe in the Old Testament to justify destruction. Consider the desecration of Tibetan Buddhist monasteries by the Chinese in the mid-twentieth century. More recently, Buddhist statues in Afghanistan have been destroyed by the Taliban.

In many ways, the history of religion is the history of suppression. In thirteenth-century Europe, the Roman Catholic Church organized suppression in its instigation of the Inquisition, which sought to seek out and punish heretics. The Albigensian Crusades in 1244 culminated in the burning of 225 Cathars in Montsegur, in the Languedoc region of southern France. The Cathars, who preached the Church of Amor, were put to death by the Church of Roma. They preached love through their stress on the principles of helping their fellow man. Though they eschewed sex, women were accorded high status and preached alongside men. The Church of Amor was associated with the principle of courtly love that, celebrated by the troubadours, flourished in southern France at the same time as the Cathars. Courtly love gave new dignity and independence to women and may have been influenced by the veneration of the Virgin Mary.

During this same time period, the Knights Templar, whom Louis Charpentier believes were involved in the building and financing of Gothic cathedrals, were tortured, put to death, or went underground. At that time, southern France had been a fertile ground of ideas shared among "heretical" Christian sects, troubadours, and the followers of Islam and Judaism. To keep the region's rich new culture from spreading, the church crushed it for political and financial reasons. Jungian analyst Robert Johnson believes that the roots of desecration of the earth in modern times can be traced to the thirteenth century when these atrocities took place.

The Inquisition soon moved to Spain, where the Moors—who had built the Alhambra and other sacred places of great beauty—were driven out along with the Jews in 1492, the year Columbus sailed to the New World. Many of these people, both persecuted Sephardic Jews and their persecutors, eventually made their home in northern New Mexico, where I live. A man I know in Arroyo Seco has a carved statue of Jesus in his home that holds a secret compartment where the Torah was kept.

From the seeds of the Inquisition sprang five centuries of witch burnings following Pope Innocent VIII's Papal Bull of 1484. It is estimated that, between the fifteenth and the eighteenth centuries, nine million people were burned as witches in Europe and North America. Eighty percent of those killed were women. Books were also burned. Knowledge went underground or was wiped from local memory.

In this era of suppression, music suffered as well. Because of the role it played in ritual magic, it began to be regulated by the church. The tritone, three whole tones up from the fundamental, was considered to be evil and was called "the devil in music." If we still adhered to these strict rules, Leonard Bernstein's haunting song "Maria" from *West Side Story* would never have been composed. You can hear the tritone if you sing the first two notes of that song.

Before the Renaissance, the Creator was conceived of as sound or vibration. But with the burst of artistry that began in fifteenth-century Italy, "God became portraiture," as R. Murray Schafer puts it.[3] One consequence was that the mystery of the unnamed Divine became reduced to the visual image of an old white man with the white beard sitting in the white clouds.

In the fifteenth century the Catholic Church banned contemplation because contemplation encouraged direct mystical experience. The priest was the only one authorized to be in contact with

God. Walking the labyrinth also fell into disuse. The metal center in the labyrinth at Chartres was torn out to be used as canon fodder.

During the Reformation, under the Suppression Act of 1536, Thomas Cromwell and his men rode into English cathedrals on their horses, which proceeded to defecate on the floors. Henry VIII leveled many monasteries to ruins. By 1540, over ten thousand monks, nuns, and friars had been dispossessed and eight hundred monasteries destroyed. Gregorian chant, which once rang throughout the cloisters, sounded no more. These actions put an end to pilgrimage in Britain.

The Puritans of sixteenth-century England believed that space in itself was meaningless: Spirituality lived inside of man, not in an ornate church. Many Puritan sects banned music as well as disapproved of Gothic architecture. As Mor and Sjöö point out, "It was Protestant moral rationality that finally forced European music into the constricting framework of the major and minor scales, and the tick-tick or marching rhythms of 2/4 and 4/4 time."[4] The modal scales and complex rhythms of pagan music were considered to be of the devil.

According to Morris Berman, in the seventeenth century the philosopher Marin Mersenne moved "music theory away from the affective and ecstatic and towards the abstract and analytical." Mersenne believed that sound was "nothing more than the movement of air, and thus amenable to mechanical and mathematical treatment."[5] Thus, the spirit of music was reduced to acoustics. *Neume* refers to the basic element in musical notation denoting the pitch. Etymologically, it is linked to *pneuma*, or spirit, and has to do with bringing the living breath into the music. Early musical notation in medieval Europe instructed both pitch and manner of performance. Michael Deason-Barrow believes that in much popular music of today "the neume of Gregorian Chant has been reduced to a note, the spirit has been lost. Many people read the notes of music without understanding the spiritual life that animates them. Notes then become knots."[6]

The great mythologist Joseph Campbell once observed that "you can tell what's informing a society by what the tallest building is."[7]

When approaching a town or city in France, the cathedral spires, built before the Inquisition, were the first thing I saw. Political palaces replaced the cathedral as the tallest building in the eighteenth century. In America, as in other Western industrialized countries, banks and places of commerce now dominate the landscape. Church services are held on TV and in shopping malls where the choir is amplified through speakers. Music bounces off the walls in right angles, which deadens the sound.

"The size and shape of interior space will always control the tempo of activities within it," writes R. Murray Schafer. "The modulation speed of Gothic or Renaissance church music is slow; that of the nineteenth and twentieth centuries is much faster because it has been created for smaller rooms or broadcasting centers.... The contemporary office building, which also consists of small, dry spaces, is similarly suited to the frenzy of modern business, and thus contrasts vividly with the slow tempo of the Mass or any ritual intended for cave or crypt."[8]

Modern skyscrapers are like file cabinets that, according to Keith Critchlow, an expert on sacred architecture, are "very efficient at filing human beings and filing objects and filing technologies, but they have very little to do with what we would call the fuller or meaningful dimensions of being human."[9]

In short, over the last mere five hundred years in the long history of the human race, sacred harmony has given way to muzak.

*Cityscape*

~ *Chapter 19* ~

# DISSONANCE

*As roads and railroads and flat-surfaced buildings*
*proliferated in space, so did their acoustic counterparts in time;*
*and eventually flat lines in sound slipped out across the countryside.*
—R. Murray Schafer

In the last hundred years the landscape has changed dramatically. Freight trains and railroads, cars and freeways, telephones and telephone lines, radios and radio stations, televisions and satellite dishes, computers and modems, and cell phones and cell-phone towers have altered the face of the earth forever. Everywhere the horizon is broken by roads, fences, and electric lines.

Even when we can find an unmarred landscape, it is hard to escape civilization's mechanized hum. Gordon Hempton, professional sound tracker, has tried. As an Associated Press story reported, "Fifteen years ago, Hempton documented 21 spots in Washington State where he could reliably capture 15 minutes of natural sounds uninterrupted by the likes of roaring jets, humming trucks or barking dogs. Now he finds only three."[1]

In *The Soundscape*, R. Murray Schafer talks about the acoustic reality of "flat lines"—continuous, artificially produced drones introduced by the Industrial Revolution. Nature does not produce flat lines; they are emitted only by electricity. Every appliance in our homes, electrical wires, and even our light bulbs emit their own flat line. Schafer says they not only affect our consciousness, they also become a narcotic to the brain. Since these sounds are continuous, we often don't notice them. Nevertheless, our bodies and brain waves register and respond. Schafer has done an interesting experiment to prove this point. After leading students into a deep meditative state, he asks them to sing the tone they hear inwardly, the one that seems to arise naturally. In America, students often sing B natural, the resonant frequency of 60 cycles per second, which is the sound of our electric current. In Europe, the tone often sung is centered on G sharp, which is the sound of the 50-cycles-per-second current of European electricity.

In Taos, citizens fought the air force to prevent routine fly-bys over the mountains to train bombers. At the heated town-hall meetings, we were told by the air force that we would adjust to the noise. We won the argument, but only eventually.

Adjusting means entrainment, through which we automatically begin to synchronize with the most powerful rhythms and vibrations around us. This is why we tap our feet to rock music and feel soothed by Gregorian chant. We become the sounds we hear. When we shop at Big Box mega-stores, we become entrained by Big Box consciousness. The high frequencies of electricity play through us because we are highly sensitive acoustic soundboards. As we entrain with the sound of the flat line, on some level our state of mind changes and becomes flat. We speak of people who have "flat affect," meaning that they don't express emotion. Certainly there are many causes of flat affect, but our exposure to flat lines may well be one of them. We receive sound through our skin, ears, and bones and play back the continuously emitted noise in the form of increased stress. Stress affects our heart rate, respiration cycle, brain waves and other bodily rhythms, thereby changing our behavior.

Physician John Diamond states that "the ill effects of noise are cumulative...and noise-induced hearing impairment is permanent."[2] Steven Halpern cites a study done over two years among people living within a three-mile radius of the Los Angeles International Airport. Noise levels of 90–115 decibels occurred about 560 times a day. The results were compared to the condition of people living within a nine-mile radius of the airport. "The mortality rate from all cases among the near-airport residents was 20 percent higher than those living further away; admissions into mental hospitals were 31 percent higher; and cases of cirrhosis of the liver due to drinking were 140 percent higher."[3]

On a busy street in Seattle, Washington, I heard a VW Bug playing rap music over a booming sound system. It sounded like a heart attack on wheels. Each beat pulsed through the pavement and into my chest. Dr. Diamond has done research to show that the stopped-anapestic beat of most rock music goes against the natural beat of the human heart. It overpowers the body's own internal rhythm. This beat can become addictive over prolonged exposure. As is true with other unnatural addictive substances, he says, "It is as if the body can no longer distinguish what is beneficial and what is harmful."[4]

Our sonic landscape has changed throughout history and continues to change as more and more people become plugged in, wired to the dissonance of the techno-world. In Eve's time, we sang in caves, imitated birds and beasts, and improvised with the changing acoustic landscape that each season and new environment brought. As we moved from a nomadic to an agrarian life style between ten and twelve thousand years ago, our soundscape was fundamentally altered. Harvest songs, street cries, sounds of farm animals  chickens, pigs, cows—and the ever-present barking of dogs set the tone. The blacksmith's hammer and anvil rang throughout the town in time with church bells. People sang in the streets; choirs sang in cathedrals. In the fourteenth century, the mechanical clock ticked for the first time, accompanying the sounds of sawmills and paper mills.

R. Murray Schafer observes that "before the Industrial Revolution, work was often wedded to song, for the rhythms of labor were synchronized with the human breath cycle, or arose out of the habits of hands and feet." He goes on to say that "singing [on the job] ceased when the rhythms of men and machines got out of synch."[5] That is, in the process of entraining with the dominant rhythms and sounds of machines, we lost the connection with the natural rhythm of our breath. Most people do not sing at their jobs anymore. Today, work is most often accompanied by the sounds of computers, cell phones, and piped-in music.

Hence, over the centuries, singing evolved from engaging in duets with nature to singing songs in the parlor accompanied by piano. Music became audible through machines. Thomas Edison's invention of the phonograph in 1877 gave rise to the music industry; and slowly, as beautiful voices emerged from his startling new device, we began to compare our voices to others. The radio, and later the TV, replaced the ever-present piano, and we began to sing along with our favorite artists. Though many people still sing, most of the thousands I've worked with as a music therapist sing only in the shower or car where no one can hear them. As a species, we are becoming listeners rather than singers. In the last few decades, the Walkman, the boom box, and now the iPod have created private sonic environments that we can plug into in order to tune out what's in front of us.

Big business uses music to manipulate us. Fast food restaurants play fast music to get customers in and out quickly so that they can sell more burgers. Many department stores use muzak to lull shoppers into lingering in the aisles. Cell phones can connect us immediately to any place on the planet. Will the next technological advance involve implants which can connect us to each other without the need for any sort of external device at all?

In Vancouver, B.C., I met a psychic who told me of the future scenarios he sees. The one that scared him most was that we would become so hypnotized by shopping malls and movies and sounds of computers that we would become like a hive of drones, losing touch with our individual selves. Philosopher David Abram writes that, at computers, "our nervous system synapsed to the terminal, we do not notice that the chorus of frogs by the nearby stream has dwindled to a solitary voice, and that the song sparrows no longer return to the trees."[6]

Listen to the words *flat line* and *terminal* as reflectors of our modern world. These are words of death. In earlier times humans lived within the circular forms of caves, cliff dwellings, huts, yurts, igloos, hogans, and tipis. As author Christopher Day says, "It is no accident that a world made only of rectangles is death to the soul."[7] Black Elk, the Oglala Sioux warrior and medicine man, expressed it another way: "The Wasichus [white people] have put us in these square boxes. Our power is gone and we are dying, for the power is not in us anymore."[8]

Years ago I dreamed that, at one time, every hundred miles along the Canadian border, natural power spots had existed where singing was practiced. These places had absorbed the songs and broadcast them to the rest of the earth. They were places that protected the planet. Looking at a map in my dream, I was sad to see that these power spots have now become shopping malls. I was told it is time to go to these places to sing again.

I believe the earth is nourished by the sonic energy and intent in our voices, just as we are nourished by listening to birdsong or the sound of a waterfall. My dream resonates with the Aboriginal belief that the land is a series of songlines—sacred places between which the ancestors once walked. In singing the features of the landscape, the Aborigines entered into a communion with nature. The rise and fall of the terrain was like a musical score that could be sung. Could it be that the whole earth is made up of songlines? If so, what might be the effect of our modern road systems? How many freeways cross over songlines today?

In Britain, songbirds living near highways can't sing their natural and territorial songs anymore. The constant rush of traffic, a flat line foreign to the rolling hills of Britain, has interfered with their auditory senses. According to research by the British Ecological Society, "Birds, ranging from wrens and blue tits to woodcocks and pheasant, are so off-key that they cannot ward off intruders from their territory or attract a mate."[9] One study in England has shown that "songbirds have begun to mimic cell phone melodies."[10]

Wireless cell phone towers do more than just confuse songbirds. They kill them. An article in *The New Mexican* newspaper said that an estimated five to ten thousand Lapland long spurs were found dead on the ground near a cell tower because they had become disoriented and flown into it. The article went on to say that, for the newest upgrade of cell phones, we will need towers and antennae every half-mile or so within five years. "Think of a grid with a dot every half-mile... in each direction."[11]

David Abram speaks to this loss: "As technological civilization diminishes the biotic diversity of the earth, language itself is diminished. As there are fewer and fewer songbirds in the air, due to the destruction of their forests and wetlands, human speech loses more of its evocative power. For when we no longer hear the voices of warbler and wren, our own speaking cannot be nourished by their cadences."[12]

But it is not just songbirds and our language that are in peril. As physiologist René Dubos believes, "It is questionable that man can retain his physical and mental health if he loses contact with the natural forces that have shaped his biological and mental nature."[13]

With all of our astounding scientific knowledge, can't we find a way to tune our technology to the rhythms of the earth? Imagine, for instance, what the world would be like if our alarm clocks sounded like meadow larks. What if lawn mowers sounded like wind chimes and computers were completely silent? What would life sound like if we all decided to unplug for a day and no one drove a car, watched television, or used a machine? I imagine the earth would breathe a deep sigh, like a mother who finally has a day off and can hear herself for the first time in a very long while.

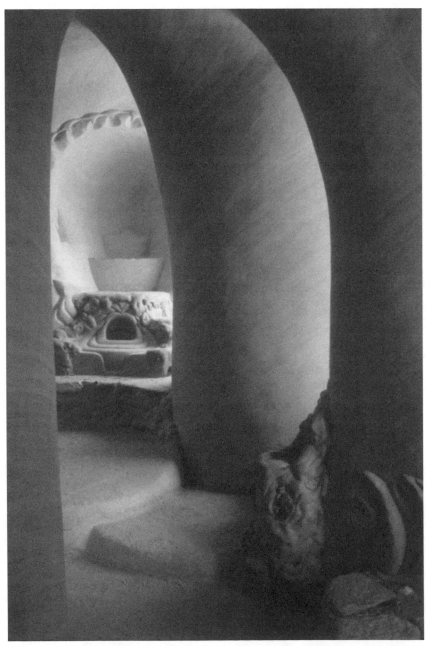

*Sandstone Shrine, Rancho de San Juan Country Inn, Ojo Caliente, New Mexico*

~ *C h a p t e r  2 0* ~

# Return to the Temple

*You can't kill the spirit*
*She is like a mountain*
*Old and strong she goes on and on and on.*
— Naomi Littlebear Morena

We have a genuine hunger for the sacred. Many yearn to reclaim sacred space, sound, and silence and to become part of the music of the spheres. One purpose of making a pilgrimage is to transpose the energy of a sacred place you've visited to wherever you are. The cathedral, cave, or temple becomes part of your living tissue. Singing is one way to plant the vibrational seed of a place into one's self and then "pollinate" other people and spaces.

Because many sacred places today are frequented by tourists, it is a risk to sing in them. In Western society, we have no context for sudden bursts of song in public places. Most people would consider singing in public a bit crazy, especially when it comes to improvised sounds rather than a familiar song. One of my teachers, Susan Osborn, used to say, "You have to be out of your mind to sing."

And it's true: Singing does take you out of your mind and into your heart. Many people are afraid of the emotions that singing generates. Memories of the Inquisition and witch hunts still echo in the collective unconscious, making us afraid to stand out and be different, to speak our truth and share our beliefs. For centuries, much of orthodox Christianity has communicated messages that we are not worthy to approach the Divine. Yet many people long to sing as a way of becoming a part of something greater than they are.

Encoded in the earth, encrypted in our bodies, and built into temples is a knowledge that wants to live again as music. There are musical and spiritual layers, as well as geologic and historical ones, that have been covered over by centuries of ignorance and fear. About sacred sites, Michael Deason-Barrow laments, "I find it nearly impossible to offer these places something true, objective, heartfelt, and spiritual without exploring what is living there."[1] Sometimes it is difficult to gain access to these places outside the regulations of a guided tour and to have time alone really to listen and offer what is in our hearts, especially when we are in a foreign land. We go in search of healing to places full of their own religious traditions and rules. For some people, singing in a sacred site may seem an impossible dream.

A question is essential to a quest. Parsival did not receive the Holy Grail until he first asked the wounded Fisher King, "What ails thee?" Ask and you shall receive. When I asked a Native American guard if I could sing in the reconstructed kiva at Coronado National Monument in Albuquerque, I received a smile and a hug.

Shannon Frediani had a similar experience at Chartres when her husband asked the tour guide if she could sing there by herself. "On the tour I sang but stopped myself short out of consideration for other people. Later, I was given the opportunity to sing in the crypt alone. I know well the red lights along the stone walls of the north corridor. As I came down the corridor singing, I was filled with the company of pilgrims of all ages through time singing with me."[2]

Michael Deason-Barrow says the best time to visit a sacred place is at twilight, when often other visitors have gone. He goes to West Kennet Long Barrow in the silence of midwinter when frost is on the ground. Then, he says, it has a "special potency, an enclosed energy that is dark and silent."[3] He feels the barrow to be a place of birth, not death, and envisions it as a place of shining. He believes it needs to be left alone for long periods of time in order to rest from the penetration of attitudes that do not belong to the space.

## SONG PILGRIMS

Jungian analyst Jean Shinoda Bolen believes that many people are drawn to go on pilgrimages to sacred sites to retrieve "something that is missing not only from our own lives but from the culture as well."[4] She believes that as we share our stories we each contribute to returning the Holy Grail that is absent from our world. Song pilgrims all over the world are learning to listen and ask, What ails thee? How may I serve?

Singer and sound healer Ani Williams of Sedona, Arizona has sung and played her harp at Stonehenge and Chalice Well in Glastonbury, England; Machu Picchu in Peru; the King and Queen's Chamber in the Great Pyramids of Egypt; Palenque in Mexico; and Black Virgin sites in France. She approaches sacred space by listening. "Sometimes I will literally hear to tune my harp a certain way. I use music and song as a communion. Once in Machu Picchu I was with a Tibetan lama who saw deities and told me the life energy of the place was being increased by the gift of music. Each time we sing we add to a beneficial sound bank for anyone who needs it. The more people sing, the more it gives others permission to sing and feel."[5]

Singer and recording artist Jenny Bird of Taos leads Alchemy of the Voice workshops with author Mirabai Starr in the Yucatan. She says that you must always ask permission from the space. "Be mindful and respectful. There's often a protective shield around a sacred place. There are guardian energies that we must ask."[6] She believes it is important not to impose a structure onto a space but to listen for what is needed, creating a relationship.

Sometimes one can form a deeper relationship not just with the place but with the people in it. Sound healer Jonathan Goldman thought he was alone when he chanted in the crypt at Rosslyn Chapel. The crypt reflected, amplified, and enhanced the harmonics in his voice. When he stopped singing, he noticed a tearful woman behind him, who said, "Now I finally understand how sound was used in Egypt to heal."[7]

We never know what comfort song can bring, or how the ripples we send out may change someone's life. But we can see the gratitude in the people we meet when we have the courage to sing. When I was singing alone at the Great Kiva of Aztec in New Mexico, a woman passing by heard me and came inside. She said her father had just died and asked if I would sing "Amazing Grace," his favorite song. Our voices rose together in the sun-illuminated dust, dedicating a song prayer to her father's spirit.

The urge to seek out resonant spaces to sing and play music is a natural human impulse. In Glastonbury, after the local board of directors had destroyed the sacred white spring and cave, musicians played their instruments into a large hole in the stone façade, even though it was dark and dank. In Llano Quemado, near Taos, one night a band of people climbed into an empty water tower to sing. On Earth Day, singers and musicians in Albuquerque sought out the long, tunnel-like corridors in an Art Deco shopping center to hear their voices reverberate and send their music into the street. Like grass growing through concrete, this fundamental need to hear our sounds echoed is persistent. The most resonant place in our homes is our tiled bathrooms. Most people sing there, even if they are too shy to admit it.

While no such place—a water tower, a shopping center—would be found on a pilgrimage to sacred sites, they *can* be consecrated through sound and intention. What if people sang Gregorian chants in underground parking garages? Or Buddhist sutras under free-ways? A friend of mine takes his Native American flute when he goes to work at Sandia Labs and plays in stairwells during his lunch break.

Sometimes our search for harmony leads us to seek out natural places. Paul Winter had a mission to play and record in reverberant places like the Gates of the River in Montana and the Grand Canyon. For thirty years the Grand Canyon has been a place of pilgrimage for him. On one expedition he went "in search of the song of the canyon and the acoustic Shangri-la that I knew must exist somewhere in the vast labyrinth of the side canyons." Once he found this magic canyon, he made his first solo album, *Canyon Lullaby*. "Here," he said, "I feel the earth is answering me."[8]

In Ouray, Colorado, below the Weisbaden Hotel, is a place with amazing acoustics—a natural granite cave with a pool of hot water in the center where vapors rise into the air. People sit alongside the edge and sweat. Sometimes they sing. I have sung there alone and with others many times. The space reverberates for over four seconds. Singing into the rock crevices in the cave concentrates and amplifies the sound even further, adding to the mystery. Once the architect and photographer Georgemarc Schevené, with his lower range, sounded the keynote of the cave, making the entire cave vibrate. One time, I sang there with a woman who had sung at many sacred sites throughout the world, including sites in Egypt, and she said the vapor cave was one of the most powerful sonic experiences she had ever had. She felt the rock devas came out to listen and said they were grateful. One woman who heard us sing said, "That was like being in church, only better!" She was too shy to join in but sought me out later, and we sounded together in the dark of the cave.

Brooke Medicine Eagle believes that we need to renew the temple and sing it into being. Sound creates the pattern that is then sent out into the world. She believes groups need to gather at sacred sites to sing for the healing of our world. "Feeling is what creates reality. Emotional vibratory resonance magnetizes energy into reality. At sacred sites we can do very powerful magic when we gather and sing with a specific intent. The magnification of the intention is received by the space. Our sacred duty is to remember to sing."[9]

You can seek out the sacred wherever you are—in nature, inside your home, or in the city where you live. For instance, when I lived in Kansas City, Missouri, from my house I could walk to the Nelson Atkins Museum. There, in the Oriental section, Kuan Yin, the Boddhisattva of Compassion, sat in a place of honor, ready to spring to life to those who seek her. I developed a ritual of approach, pausing before crossing the threshold, then silently walking toward this larger-than-life embodiment of loving kindness. Her eyes seemed to see into me but also beyond me, into the crying hearts of the world. After I had soaked up her presence, I would sit on the museum bench and meditate. Then I would thank her for listening to my prayers. I bought a poster of Kuan

Yin at the gift shop and set up an altar at home where I lit candles, sang the names of people I love, and widened my own heart.

## SOUND ARCHITECTURE

The impulse to create holy places is a fundamental human need. Places do not need to be ancient to be sacred. All over the earth, in fact, people are building new sacred sites. Joseph Rael, of the Ute and Picuris Pueblo heritage, has built twenty-five sound chambers around the world. His inspiration for them sprang from a vision in which he saw a man standing before him who was made of singing light. "The man became an oval chamber, and I saw men and women singing in it. I was told they chant for peace. The vision lasted three seconds, yet I saw years of world peace."[10]

Visionary artist Vijali Hamilton dreamed she saw herself creating monumental sculptures and performing ceremonies with the people who live on the thirty-fifth latitudinal parallel of the globe. She enacted her vision by traveling along this line and cocreating sculptures and rituals with the people she met. Vijali called the work "The World Wheel Theatre." She built "The Mandala House," a ritual art piece, in West Bengal for the Bauls, wandering minstrels who go from village to village to sing whenever the spirit moves them.

"I was enchanted by them." Vijali told me. She had first met a group of Baul musicians on a train going to West Bengal in 1990. She kept giving them coins so they would stay in her compartment. They invited her to their village, where, she said, they "spread a mat under a tree and the children of the village came and danced and sang and put garlands around me."

Vijali went on, "What I do in every country is wait until I fall in love with something, just like I fell in love with the Bauls." When she has such an experience in a place, she stays and asks each community the same three questions:

> What is our essence?
> What is it that ails us?
> What is it that can heal us?

Vijali wasn't looking for answers that applied just to individuals; she also wanted to know what ails us as a global community. From the answers she received, she created ritual art for entire communities.

To Vijali's questions, the Bauls answered, "We come from the womb of our mother. We really come from our mother who is the Earth. We are part of the Great Goddess. Our essence is the Great Kali." They felt the strain of traveling far from their homes, sometimes to return with little money to feed their families. Sometimes the strain took them away from their search for God. They thought the healing would be really to "love our singing and not worry about the future.... We want to be God conscious every moment of our day."

Vijali meditated on their answers. "I became aware that the tribal village was made up of mixed castes, some of whom look down on the Bauls because they beg by singing. I kept imaging them all sitting down in a circle. Finally I saw what was needed: a communal house, a commons, a lodge where they could come together. Here they could practice and perform their music, have their own *pujas* (ceremonies), and it could serve as a schoolroom for their children."

One of the Bauls and his wife had some land. There Vijali drew a circle on the ground and hired two village men from a low caste who needed money to work alongside her. They had built the same kind of huts in the village before. With three hundred dollars and donated materials, they built a round mud hut with a thatched roof, similar to others in the village which blended into their environment. Some of the Bauls, who had never done manual labor, came to help when they saw their honored guest working so hard on their behalf.

"On the day of the consecration of the building everyone came," Vijali said. "The Bauls sang their responses to the three questions." They sat in a circle and offered mantras, incense, flowers, and butter into a sacred fire.

Vijali has been back to the village twice, first in 1992 at the first anniversary of the Mandala House. Over four hundred people from all over West Bengal came and celebrated with song. She said that "the Bauls were teaching music, five days a week, something they had never done before." Her original vision had been realized. Children were going to school, religious ceremonies were taking place, and wandering Bauls were given a place to sleep. The hut had become a circle of healing.[11]

## SANDSTONE SHRINE

Some people building new temples have no blueprints to follow. Artist Ra Paulette carved a shrine out of sandstone called Windows to the Earth. I saw an article about Ra in *New Mexico Magazine* in 1996. On the cover was a picture of a throne carved from the living earth. Inside were more pictures of this wonder, including a picture of Ra in a Panama hat with a pickax in his hand. Images of the miners of the Old West came to mind. But this was the 1990s, not the 1890s, and this was no ordinary miner. When we eventually spoke, Ra said, "People usually dig for coal and oil, gold and silver, and precious stones. The holes they leave are scars of wanting. Why not dig for beauty instead?"[12]

Ra approached the owners of the Rancho de San Juan Country Inn about digging a shrine out of the sandstone on their property. He showed them pictures of a sandstone cave—called the Heart Chamber—that he had carved on public land. Eventually he had had to close it when thousands of visitors had threatened the fragile chamber and its surrounding environment. Now he wanted to carve a similar shrine in a protected place. In time, the owners said yes. The shrine was started in late 1994 and completed in 1996.

As *New Mexico Magazine* relates, Ra had no preconceived plan. Instead, he believed that "the earth would tell him where to go." He listened to the sandstone and "developed a sense of where he was, where to proceed and how far to go. He called it intuitive engineering." Over the months he "fashioned vaulted ceilings, massive supporting pillars, doorways in the shape of a bishop's miter. He opened windows and a second exit. Shafts of light streamed into the cave. Cloud shadows danced across the sinuous trace of ancient sedimentation. The night wind whirled through hollows in the stone."[13]

Several months after I saw the magazine article, on a hot day in May 1996 I went alone to visit the Sandstone Shrine near Ojo Caliente, New Mexico. Along the trail I passed fossiled rocks, rings of grass, scurrying lizards, and mushroom-shaped rock formations called "hoodoos." The trail took me to carved steps that proceeded to a door leading into the sandstone, into the earth.

There was a marked contrast between the hot, dry trail—a trail of drought—and the cool interior of the shrine. Spirals and scallops were carved into the wall. Near the entrance was what looked like a baptismal font full of water. As I looked closer, I saw my face reflected there, and my own delighted expression. A mirror had been set in the sand to give the impression of liquid. Windows offered views looking out onto the landscape. Everything was smoothed and rounded, revealing the grain of the stone, swirled in amazing patterns, touched with such love. A variety of colored rocks were inlaid throughout the shrine, creating the effect of a jeweled mosaic. The hidden face of the earth seemed revealed. As I sang, my sound followed a labyrinthine path through the many chambers. I felt as if I were singing in a temple of the earth's ear.

That day stayed with me for a long time. Afterward, I asked the late seer Kip Davidson, who lived in Ojo Caliente, about this shrine near his home. He said it is a beacon of light, a place where the natural and the human kingdoms can meet and interact in harmony.

I knew then that I needed to meet Ra, so I called him and asked if we could go to the shrine together. Hearing of my interest of singing at sacred sites, he said he often sang while he worked. "Singing takes us directly to the Source of who we are," he told me. "I breathe in and take in columns of air to massage the sides of Earth Mama's body."[14]

Ra was comfortable and easy to be around. As we walked the trail, I remembered being here six months earlier during dry weather. Now there was snow on the sand. This time it was warmer inside the shrine than outside, but we still needed our coats. While Ra attended to a few details, I soaked up the stillness within the earth. An egg-shaped chamber that was being constructed the last time I was here was now finished. A small niche in the wall was filled with pictures of Mary, the Virgin of Guadalupe, Sai Baba, Miss Piggy, Santa Claus, coins, rings, and other gifts that people had offered.

Before we began talking, I suggested we tone together as an offering. Ra loved the idea. We walked through the shrine singing. His voice was rich. I traced the scalloped walls with my voice, allowing the space to inform my sounds, singing into all the grooves and curves. Our sounds opened but also became more detailed with overtones as we sang into the delicate shapes. The sand took in the sound and made it a part of its crystalline structure. It was as if the sandstone cave was singing itself, hearing itself reflected in the hollow of our mouths. It seemed to soak up our sounds like a sponge. Then Ra spoke at length of his work:

> The process of digging these caves encompasses everything of who I am. I work from a place of dance and song. I am at the service of how the earth is dancing with me. In the cave, I'm within the body of the earth. I can feel her here; I feel her in the blue sky that comes in through the skylights and feel the ocean a thousand miles away in the sand. I sense Mother Nature all around me, beneath the floor in the magma of her core.
>
> This space is a depository for feelings. The people who visit have all kinds of perspectives. I wanted to create a place where we can leave our baggage behind and enter into a suspended awareness. Here, the concerns of the ego get arrested. I don't see that happening in cities. The people calling the shots in our society are doing it from little boxes of buildings, in mental settings that amplify the ego. A place like this, on the other hand, helps people let go. People come here to listen, to be, to sing, to dance, to write. Some have their weddings here. Filled with these experiences, the space becomes happy.
>
> What makes a place sacred is our sense of wonder and thanksgiving. Our deepest and highest emotional states send off energy that turns the galaxies. In that sense we are magical beings. At the same time, we're nothing but a grain of sand.

The archetypal sense of connection to nature that occurs from being underground goes back to the Paleolithic. I think we were made to last. We've been here for a very long time knowing how to live in the cold, in the tropics, through catastrophes. If we continue to live only through a small state of ego consciousness, maybe we won't be here much longer and some other life form will emerge. There's enough time for that to happen—the life of the sun has three billion years left. But I feel nature is cheering us on. When I reach out in awareness to the soil, plants, and stones, I feel they are excited by my presence. I feel part of whatever they are part of. We energize each other. Nature wants us humans to be a living connection with its many forms. This is our identity.[15]

*Molly Neiman's labyrinth, Taos, New Mexico*

~ *Chapter 21* ~

# CONSECRATION

*The world is but a robe for the mystery within.*
*The mystery sees through these eyes,*
*Hears through these ears,*
*Expresses through this movement.*
*The body is its instrument.*
*The world is the sacred temple of the living spirit.*
                    —Georgemarc Schevené

Greeley, Colorado is where the Rocky Mountains meet the plains. It looks like many midwestern cities, with a town square surrounded by Victorian buildings and kids riding by on bikes. But there is another Greeley I'm about to enter—the greater Greeley underground, or "Greality," as artist Lydia Ruyle calls it. Lydia has lived here all her life. She married her kindergarten sweetheart and lives on the same land her grandparents did. Since 1987, she has been creating goddess banners and hanging them at sacred sites all over the world, including Machu Picchu and Ephesus.

I met Lydia after my trip to France. She too had been to Chartres on a pilgrimage to the Black Madonna. Now she has invited me to conduct a song workshop as part of a weekend gathering of women from all over the country. Linda Sewright, the director of the Northwest Labyrinth Project, is joining us from Seattle to lead a labyrinth workshop. Both events are to be held on the Monfort Concert Hall stage at the Union Colony Civic Center right in the middle of town.

The stage has been consecrated, and the auditorium has become a temple. A canvas replica of the Chartres labyrinth has become the temple floor. Candles form a boundary. Lydia's banners are the temple walls. To the participants, Linda describes the labyrinth as the path of a snake, the dance of cranes, the flow of water, the spiraling stars of the galaxy. She explains that at Chartres, before approaching the altar, one had to traverse the labyrinth, walking it four times on one's knees while saying the rosary. This ritual was analogous to making the pilgrimage to Jerusalem.

Under the banner of Mary Magdalene, I sit on the south side of the temple watching women walk this unicursal path—defined as one passage leading to the center and back to the beginning. In this way a labyrinth is different from a maze, where there are many paths. In the corner across from me, a banner of Notre-Dame du Pilier glows like a stained glass window. When it is my turn to walk the labyrinth, the journey becomes a joy, a dance, a song. I feel happy to be here with many women, walking together in prayer. At one moment, I feel I am back at Findhorn, singing with three hundred people; at another, in the crypt at Chartres singing to the Black Madonna; at another, in the forest by the Grandmother tree.

The Goddess lives in this auditorium cathedral in Greeley. We have become the cells of her living body, the blood coursing through her veins. We are her many faces.


## VERIDITAS: THE WORLDWIDE LABYRINTH PROJECT

The mission of Veriditas, located at Grace Cathedral in San Francisco, aims to have people all over the world walk labyrinths. The project is led by the Reverend Dr. Lauren Artress, honorary canon of Grace Cathedral and author of *Walking a Sacred Path* and *The Companion Guide: Using the Labyrinth to Heal and Transform*. Her mission became clear after months of wrestling with a question of what to do with the labyrinth. Her restlessness led her to walk in a circle around her living room asking, "What is it?" The third time she asked she heard a voice say, "Put the labyrinth in the cathedral." Following this guidance, she went to Chartres Cathedral to do research and found chairs covering the labyrinth. She and a few others took it upon themselves to move the chairs. As they then walked the labyrinth, the air became golden, and the rather dark and moody cathedral seemed to be smiling. Upon her return to San Francisco in 1992, she painted the Chartres-style design on a large piece of canvas and opened it to the public. By 1995 Grace Cathedral had two labyrinths, one indoors and one outside.

Several months after my experience in Colorado, I took a workshop with Lauren in Santa Fe. She said the labyrinth is a three-fold path. The walk inward to the center is the time to purge, cleanse, release, and surrender. At the center, having emptied oneself, one may receive guidance. On the return, one takes what has been received back out into the world. The labyrinth can be walked as an oracle to receive an answer to a question, or to have a heart-to-heart conversation between body, mind, and spirit. A blueprint where psyche meets spirit, it creates order out of confusion. It also, as Lauren puts it in her book, "captures the mystical union between heaven and earth, an understanding of death and rebirth. It is the path between faith and doubt, the complexities of the brain, the turns of the intestines, the birth canal and the Celestial City."[1] From Lauren's vision, hundreds of labyrinths have sprouted all over the world; people are consecrating the earth with this walking meditation.

## GLOBAL VILLAGE

On a high desert mesa north of Taos, a labyrinth of blue-white stones is traced on the ground. Eleven people helped designer Molly Nieman place them with prayer and intention when she led a workshop on her land in the spring of 2000. Molly said she had bowled down the rocks from the sides of a nearby arroyo. "They are locally harvested, revealed by the rains, a layer of geological history in my backyard." On the new moon of each month, this labyrinth is now available to be walked. It was initiated for public use on September 18, 2001, the first new moon after September 11. Fortunately, I had just returned from England and could be there. In the wake of September 11, my role as an American in the effort to help heal the heart of the global village suddenly took on new meaning.

At that initiation of the labyrinth, sixteen Taos women walked the meander of white stones on the mesa—a Chartres labyrinth here on home ground in the center of a circle of mountains and sky. We smudged ourselves with sage and washed our hands with water from a blue bowl. As we walked, we prayed for peace—for the peace of the people of Afghanistan and for the strength to face our shadows and fight the terrorist within. We prayed for guidance and courage, for children, for families we have never met, and for the thousands cremated in the twin towers. We chanted *Mitakuye Oyasin*, a Lakota phrase meaning that we are all related. We prayed for protection, for all those who live in fear. We prayed to understand voices different from our own. We walked together and sang for the peace of our world. After we had paused at the labyrinth's center to listen and then walked outward on the same spiraling path, we were no longer the same people; we were different, changed. As American women, we have been privileged, independent, and free to follow our own calling. Now we heard a call to be part of the world community. Together we sang and then stood in silence, watching the New Mexico sunset and the distant rain. Storm clouds overhead turned pink, gold, and then faded into night. Stars emerged as we broke bread, tore tortillas, and shared grapes and guacamole in the heart of our village, our home.

## A Cretan Labyrinth

From Chartres to an auditorium in Greeley, Colorado to a mesa in New Mexico, the labyrinth has been a touchstone on my journey. Years ago in a workshop, I learned how to build a seven-circuit "Cretan" labyrinth, named after those found in ancient Crete.

Incredibly, this form has also been found in Peru, India, Britain, and Northern Europe and among the Hopi people in my native Southwest.

On the summer solstice 2003, I started building a Cretan labyrinth in a field with a view of Taos Mountain in the background. It had been a year since my father's death, when I had received the message from Stonehenge that an old template of the masculine had been shattered and a new one was being received. I wanted to make this process tangible. It seemed important to find rocks and carry them one by one, feel their weight and shape, and place them on the earth with song.

Slowly, one rock at a time, my labyrinth has come into being. I have circled the sacred landscape of Taos and brought back rocks from hikes and weekend trips. On the Rio Grande Gorge trail I found black volcanic rocks forged deep within the earth; near the stupa in Questa, New Mexico, I found a white stone. There is a lichen-covered pink rock from Amma's Santa Fe ashram, a cream-colored rock from the Christ in the Desert Monastery, and a red and white stone from Molly's labyrinth that links them all together. Rocks from further away include a heart-shaped stone from Findhorn, a piece of speckled blue diorite from Egypt, and red sandstone from the Rosslyn Chapel, in a link with the Roseline. I have placed rocks from friends—purple Zuni sandstone from my friend Alison's labyrinth near the Albuquerque Bosque, a red rock from the Rosebud Mountains in Montana from Cecily, and white sandstone from a mosque in Abiquiu, New Mexico, given by Nancy in my writing group. Each stone is like a bead on my mala.

From the blooming of hollyhocks in June to that of sunflowers and chamisa in October, I have watched my labyrinth come into form. Standing in the center, I have seen shadows traced by gramma grass on each stone, heard meadow larks and magpies, witnessed aspens turn golden, and viewed the first snow fall on Lobo Peak. Chanting my mantra, I have seen a spotted horse in a neighbor's field, listened to sheep bleat, and watched a prairie dog emerge from his hole. I have circled the labyrinth with song through wild roses blooming in summer to their hipping in the fall; I have prayed to be an architect of Love and build my own cathedral of song here in the sage-covered field where I live.

Since our arrival as the species Homo sapiens, we have been singers and creators of sacred spaces where all the arts have been integrated. We have danced and sung incantations in painted caves, moved giant stones to form pyramids where sacred vowels were intoned in inner chambers, and built cathedrals where Gregorian chant could soar. In every time period, in every corner of the world, this universal impulse to create sacred space and music reflects an essential human hunger for spiritual sustenance. Perhaps this is intrinsic to our survival as a species. Why else would it be so ingrained in our nature? What is it that makes us compose hymns to Mary and chants to Isis, or to go on a quest to follow the Lady of Roses? Like the chimpanzees calling out in unison to the dark, we need to know we are not alone. We send a voice and are comforted when we hear its return.

Though the science of acoustics tells us that it is only the sound of our own enhanced voice that greets us when we sing in a holy place, a deeper part of us feels something more, as if an inexplicable magic has been awakened within us. I believe that our intention, and our unique spiritual essence, resonates to let us know that our bodies are sacred architecture that contains the Music of the Spheres in their design. We can set an intention to breathe into the temple of our bodies and make them holy.

And I believe that this intention is central to our role in creating the sense of the sacred outside ourselves as well. You don't have to wait to go to a place like the Taj Mahal to sing in a sacred site. The sacred is all around us. The golden mean is dancing in the opening of every flower, in the leaves unfurling every spring. To the setting sun or the rising moon, we can express our awe and gratitude for the beauty of whatever part of the world we experience.

With the joyful noise of a gospel choir, a circus tent becomes a revival church. Dances at southwestern pueblos transform a dusty courtyard into a giant prayer. Stones arranged on the ground in a certain formation become a path for contemplation and renewal. Wherever we are, what matters is that we become part of the dance, that we bring our attention, ecstasy, despair, and receptivity to a greater reality. Let us, then, make our own joyful noise, whether at Chaco Canyon or in our own backyard. As the great poet Walt Whitman says,

*Now I have heard you.*
*Now in a moment I know what I am for. I awake*
*And already a thousand singers, a thousand songs, clearer*
*louder and more sorrowful than yours,*
*A thousand warbling echoes have started to life within me,*
*never to die.*[2]

# NOTES AND
# SUGGESTED LISTENING

*Biblical references in the text are from the King James version.*
*All music cited is available in compact disc format.*

## INTRODUCTION

*Epigraph.* Joan Halifax, *The Fruitful Darkness: Reconnecting with the Body of the Earth* (San Francisco: HarperSanFrancisco, 1993), xv.

1. Iegor Reznikoff, lecture at Voices of Heaven and Earth Conference, Findhorn, Scotland, 1996.

2. Ibid.

3. Caroline Humphrey and Piers Vitebsky, *Sacred Architecture: Models of the Cosmos* (Boston: Little, Brown, 1977), 75.

4. Matthew Fox, *Illuminations of Hildegard of Bingen* (Santa Fe, NM: Bear and Company, 1985), 16.

SUGGESTED LISTENING

Robert Gass, *Chant: Spirit in Sound; The Best of World Chant*, Spring Hill Music, 1999.

## CHAPTER ONE: BLUEPRINT

*Epigraph.* Iegor Reznikoff, lecture at Voices of Heaven and Earth Conference, Findhorn, Scotland, 1996.

1. Branford Weeks, M.D., "The Physician, the Ear and Sacred Music," in *Music: Physician for Times to Come*, ed. Don Campbell (Wheaton, IL: Theosophical Publishing House, Quest Books, 1991), 45.

2. Alfred Tomatis, as quoted by Tim Wilson, "Chant," in *Music: Physician for Times to Come*, 11.

3. Alfred Tomatis and Billie M. Thompson, *The Ear and Language* (Norval, ON: Moulin Publishing, 1996), 58.

4. Ibid., 165.

5. William Anderson, *Green Man: The Archetype of our Oneness with the Earth* (San Francisco: HarperSanFrancisco, 1990), 23.

6. Jack Kornfield, "Song of the Spirit," *Utne Reader*, May–June 1996, 120.

7. Robert Lawlor, *Voices of the First Day: Awakening in Aboriginal Dreamtime* (Rochester, VT: Inner Traditions, 1991), 156.

8. Penelope Washbourn, ed., *Seasons of Woman: Song, Poetry, Ritual, Prayer, Myth, Story* (New York: Harper & Row, 1979), 104–5.

9. Weeks, "The Physician, the Ear and Sacred Music," 41.

10. Sophia Adams, as recorded by Cass Adams.

11. Don Campbell, *The Mozart Effect®: Tapping the Power of Music to Heal the Body, Strengthen the Mind, and Unlock the Spirit* (New York: Avon Books, 1997), 134.

12. Paul Shepard, *Coming Home to the Pleistocene* (Washington, D.C.: Island Press, 1998), 19.

SUGGESTED LISTENING

Pamela Ballington, *A Treasury of Earth Mother Lullabies*, Earth Mother Productions, 1996.

Tom Wasinger, producer and compiler, *The World Sings Goodnight* (1993) and *The World Sings Goodnight 2* (1995), Silver Wave Records.

CHAPTER TWO: FOUNDATION

*Epigraph.* Normandi Ellis, *Awakening Osiris: The Egyptian Book of the Dead* (Grand Rapids, MI: Phanes Press, 1988), 78.

1. John Reid, CymaScopy Brochure, 2003.

2. John Reid, "In the Beginning Was the Word," workshop, 2003.

3. Ibid.

4. Ibid.

5. See http://en.wikipedia.org/wiki/Golden_ratio#history.

6. William Harris, "The Golden Mean," www.middlebury.edu/~harris/Humanities/TheGoldenMean.html.

7. As cited in Kay Gardner, *Sounding the Inner Landscape: Music as Medicine* (Stonington, ME: Caduceus Publications, 1990), 222.

8. In my research I had hoped to find a correlation among the golden mean, architecture, and music, but it escaped me. The problem, according to mathematician Dr. Dan Kunz, is that "we are using today's musicology to determine universal proportions; we are trying to force the mathematics to fit the language with which we are comfortable. Each 'encultured' sound system has slightly different harmonics that its musicians think 'sound' good. Even the Western system changes its assessment of 'good' over time." Personal communication with Dr. Dan Kunz, July, 2002.

9. Michael S. Schneider, *A Beginner's Guide to Constructing the Universe: The Mathematical Archetypes of Nature, Art, and Science* (New York: Harper Perennial, 1995), 152.

10. Silvia Nakkach, personal interview, May, 2004.

11. Frank Waters, *The Book of the Hopi* (New York: Penguin Books, 1977), 4.

12. John Reid, *Egyptian Sonics* (Cumbria, England: Sonic Age Ltd., 2001), 41.

13. Jonathan Goldman, *Healing Sounds: The Power of Harmonics* (Rochester, VT: Inner Traditions, 2002), 13.

14. David Hykes, liner notes to the CD, *Earth to the Unknown Power*, BMG Music, 1996, 7.

15. David Hykes, "Harmonic Chant–Global Sacred Music," in *Music: Physician for Times to Come*, 62 (see chap. 1, n. 1).

16. Aryeh Kaplan, ed. *Sefer Yetzirah: The Book of Creation* (York Beach, ME: Weiser, 1997), 90.

17. Ibid., 193.

18. Ibid.

19. Daniel Abdal-Hayy Moore, *The Ramadan Sonnets* (San Francisco: City Lights, 1996), 59.

20. Campbell, *The Mozart Effect*, 40 (see chap. 1, n. 11).

21. Robert Bly, ed., *The Soul Is Here for Its Own Joy: Sacred Poems from Many Cultures* (Hopewell, NJ: Ecco Press, 1995), 88.

SUGGESTED LISTENING

David Hykes and the Harmonic Choir, *Breath of the Heart, Earth to the Unknown Power,*

*Harmonic Meetings, Hearing Solar Winds,* and *Rainbow Dances,* all available through www.harmonicworld.com.

## CHAPTER THREE: CAVES

*Epigraph.* Iegor Reznikoff, "On the Sound Dimensions of Prehistoric Painted Caves and Rocks," in *Musical Signification*, ed. Eero Tarasti (Berlin: Mouton de Gruyter, 1995), 544.

1. David Bjerklie, Andrea Dorfman, Bruce Crumley, and Tala Skari, "Behold the Stone Age," *Time Magazine*, February 13, 1995, 62.

2. Ibid., 60.

3. Reznikoff, "On the Sound Dimensions of Prehistoric Painted Caves and Rocks," 542.

4. Monica Sjöö and Barbara Mor, *The Great Cosmic Mother: Rediscovering the Religion of the Earth* (San Francisco: HarperSanFrancisco, 1987), 82.

5. Reznikoff, "On the Sound Dimensions of Prehistoric Painted Caves and Rocks," 547.

6. William Allman, "The Dawn of Creativity," *US News and World Report*, May 20, 1996.

7. *New York Times*, June 30, 1995.

8. Steven Waller, personal interview, March, 2002.

SUGGESTED LISTENING

*The Kilmartin Sessions*, available through Kilmartin House, www.kilmartin.org. Music played through swan-bone, eagle-bone, and cow-bone flutes, natural rock percussion and stone whistles, pottery drums, and other early instruments allow us to hear the sounds as people thousands of years ago would have heard them.

## CHAPTER FOUR: EARTH'S BODY

*Epigraph.* Shepard, *Coming Home to the Pleistocene*, 41 (see chap. 1, n. 12).

1. Ernest G. McClain, "Musical Theory and Ancient Cosmology," *The World and I* (February, 1994): 371–91.

2. Merlin Donald, *Origins of the Modern Mind: Three Stages in the Evolution of Culture and Cognition* (Cambridge, MA: Harvard University Press, 2005).

3. Dudley Young, *Origins of the Sacred* (New York: St. Martins Press, 1991), 97.

4. Ibid.

5. Catherine J. Ellis and Linda Barwick, "Artikirinja: Women's Song Knowledge," *Women: Rites and Sites*, ed. Peggy Brock (Sydney and Boston: Allen and Unwin, 1989).

6. James Shreeve, *The Neandertal Enigma: Solving the Mystery of Modern Human Origins* (New York: Avon Books, 1995), 3–4.

7. Robert Maynard reviewing the article, "Music and Voices of Disappearing Native Peoples: Amazonian Indians," *Shaman's Drum*, no. 17 (1989): 57.

8. David Abram, *The Spell of the Sensuous: Perception and Language in a More-Than-Human World* (New York: Pantheon, 1996), 146.

9. Shepard, *Coming Home to the Pleistocene*, 41.

10. Martin Prectel, *Secrets of the Talking Jaguar: A Mayan Shaman's Journey to the Heart of the Indigenous Soul* (New York: Tarcher, 1998).

11. Brooke Medicine Eagle, personal interview, July, 2001.

12. W. Y. Evans-Wentz, *The Fairy Faith in the Celtic Countries* (1911; repr., Atlantic Highlands, NJ: Humanities Press, 1978), 18.

13. Alvaro Estrada, *Maria Sabina: Her Life and Chants* (Santa Barbara, CA: Ross-Ericson, Inc., 1981), 108.

14. T. C. McLuhan, *Cathedrals of the Spirit: The Message of Sacred Places* (New York: Harper Perennial, 1996), 73.

15. R. Murray Schafer, *The Soundscape: Our Sonic Environment and the Tuning of the World* (Rochester, VT: Destiny Books, 1993), 23.

16. Anderson, *Green Man*, 31–32 (see chap. 1, n. 5).

17. Silvia Nakkach, personal interview, May 2004.

SUGGESTED LISTENING

Paul Winter, three CDs produced by Living Music: *Canyon* (2004), *Prayer for the Wild Things* (1994), and *Whales Alive* (1991).

Paul Horn and R. Carlos Nakai, *Inside Canyon de Chelly*, Canyon Records, 1997.

CHAPTER FIVE: MOUNTAINS

*Epigraph.* Zen Master Dogen, quoted in Richard Harris, "The Sacred Mountain of the East," *Four Corners Magazine* (1999).

1. Ani Williams, "Her Song Changes Everything," *Earthwalking Sky Dancers: Women's Pilgrimages to Sacred Places*, ed. Leila Castle (Berkeley, CA: Frog, Ltd., 1996), 178.

2. Andrew Schelling, "Thigh Bone Trumpets and Attendant Spirits," in *The India Book: Essays and Translations from Indian Asia* (Berkeley, CA: O Books, 1993), 59.

3. Halifax, *The Fruitful Darkness*, 77 (see introduction, *epigraph*).

4. Ibid., 82.

5. Reznikoff, "On the Sound Dimensions of Prehistoric Painted Caves and Rocks," 555 (see chap. 3, *epigraph*).

6. Wallace Black Elk, in William S. Lyon, *Black Elk: The Sacred Ways of a Lakota* (San Francisco: HarperSanFrancisco, 1991), 35.

7. John Anthony West, *The Traveler's Key to Ancient Egypt: A Guide to the Sacred Places of Ancient Egypt* (Wheaton, IL: Theosophical Publishing House, Quest Books, 1995), 252.

8. Ibid.

9. Mary Leakey, quoted in Sjöö and Mor, *The Great Cosmic Mother*, 118 (see chap. 3, n. 4).

10. Reznikoff, "On the Sound Dimensions of Prehistoric Painted Caves and Rocks," 554.

11. Steven J. Waller, "Psychoacoustic Influences of the Echoing Environments of Prehistoric Art," paper for the Acoustical Society of America (ASA), First Pan-American/Iberian Meeting of Acoustics in Cancun, December 2002, 4.

12. Steven J. Waller, "Sounds of the Spirit World," from a talk presented at The American Rock Art Research Association (ARARA) Conference, Pendleton, Oregon, May 2001, abstract, 12 (see www.arara.org/pdf_standard/LP-27-4.pdf).

13. Gertrude Jobes, *Dictionary of Mythology, Folklore, and Symbols* (New York: Scarecrow Press, 1961), 490; quoted in Steven J. Waller, "Spatial Correlation of Acoustics and Rock Art Exemplified in Horseshoe Canyon," 1997, 10 (see ARARA online publication, www.geocities.com/capecanaveral/9461/2000arara.pdf).

14. Steven J. Waller, "Conservation of Rock Art Acoustics: 'Unexpected' Echoes at Petroglyph National Monument," Rock Art Papers, ed. Ken Hedges, 16 (San Diego Museum Papers n. 41), 2003, 31–38. Also see www.geocities.com/CapeCanaveral/9461/Waller_Conserv_Unexpected_PNM_RA1631.

15. William F. Weahkee, Pueblo elder quoted in Petroglyph National Monument pamphlet, 6001 Unser Blvd. NW, Albuquerque, New Mexico, 87129, 2003.

SUGGESTED LISTENING

The section called Stone and Bones on *The Kilmartin Sessions*, available through Kilmartin House, www.kilmartin.org.

CHAPTER SIX: SINGING TOMBS

*Epigraph.* Miriam Arguelles and José A. Arguelles, *The Feminine: Spacious as the Sky* (Boulder, CO: Shambhala, 1977), 64.

1. Sjöö and Mor, *The Great Cosmic Mother*, 46 (see chap. 3, n. 4).

2. Frank MacEowen, *The Mist-Filled Path* (Novato, CA: New World Library, 2002), 136.

3. Ibid.

4. Michael Dames, *Mythic Ireland* (London: Thames and Hudson, 1992), 81.

5. Paul Devereux, *Stone Age Soundtracks: The Acoustic Archaeology of Ancient Sites* (London: Vega, 2001), 86.

6. Aaron Watson, "The Sounds of Transformation: Acoustics, Monuments and Ritual in the British Neolithic," in *The Archaeology of Shamanism*, ed. Neil S. Price (London: Routledge, 2001), 187.

7. Aaron Watson, *Monumental*, CD, available through www.monumental.uk.com.

8. Ibid.

## SUGGESTED LISTENING

Dr. Aaron Watson, *Monumental*, available through www.monumental.uk.com.

## CHAPTER SEVEN: STONE CIRCLES

*Epigraph.* Tim Wallace-Murphy and Marilyn Hopkins, *Rosslyn: Guardians of the Secret of the Holy Grail* (Shaftesbury, Dorset, UK: Element Books, 1999), 48.

1. Caroline Malone, *The Prehistoric Monuments of Avebury* (London: English Heritage, 1994), 6.

2. Sjöö and Mor, *The Great Cosmic Mother*, 133 (see chap. 3, n. 4).

3. Michael Dames, *The Avebury Cycle* (London: Thames and Hudson, 1996), 135.

4. Terence Meaden, *The Secrets of the Avebury Stones: Britain's Greatest Megalithic Temple* (London: Souvenir Press, 1999), 75.

5. Paul Devereux, *Places of Power: Measuring the Secret Energy of Ancient Sites* (London: Blandford Press, 1999), 12.

6. Louis Charpentier, *The Mysteries of Chartres Cathedral* (New York: Avon Books, 1975), 23.

7. Don Robins, *Circles of Silence* (London: Souvenir Press, Ltd, 1985).

8. Sjöö and Mor, *The Great Cosmic Mother*, 137.

9. M. Judge, "Stone Structures and Sound," online article at http://easyweb.easynet.co.uk/~m.judge/stones.htm.

10. Jean-Pierre Mohen, *Megaliths: Stones of Memory* (New York: Harry N. Abrams, 1998), 148.

11. As quoted in Devereux, *Stone Age Soundtracks*, 103 (see chap. 6, n. 5).

12. Ibid., 104.

13. Alan Richardson, *Spirits of the Stones: Visions of Sacred Britain* (London: Virgin Publishing, 2001), 234.

14. As quoted in Mohen, *Megaliths,* 142.

SUGGESTED LISTENING

Sing into a rock crevice.

CHAPTER EIGHT: EGYPTIAN SONIC TEMPLES

*Epigraph.* Ellis, *Awakening Osiris,* 108 (see chap. 2, *epigraph*).

1. Joachim-Ernst Berendt, *Nada Brahma: The World Is Sound; Music and the Landscape of Consciousness* (Rochester, VT: Destiny Books, 1987), 174.

2. West, *Traveler's Key to Ancient Egypt,* 448–49 (see chap. 5, n. 7).

3. Ibid., 85.

4. Christopher Dunn, *The Giza Power Plant: Technologies of Ancient Egypt* (Santa Fe, NM: Bear and Company, 1998), back cover.

5. R .A. Schwaller de Lubicz, *The Temple in Man: Sacred Architecture and the Perfect Man* (Rochester, VT: Inner Traditions, 1977), 35.

6. Richard H. Wilkinson, *The Complete Temples of Ancient Egypt* (London: Thames and Hudson, 2000), 89.

7. John Anthony West, *The Serpent in the Sky: The High Wisdom of Ancient Egypt* (New York: Julian Press, 1987), 124.

8. Antoine Seronde, *Myth and Music in Ancient Egyptian Temples,* self-published manuscript, 19.

9. Ibid., 20.

10. West, *The Traveler's Key to Ancient Egypt,* 402.

11. Ibid., 126.

12. Ibid., 129.

13. R. O. Faulkner, *The Ancient Egyptian Book of the Dead* (Austin: University of Texas Press, 1966), 121.

14. Robert Bauval and Adrian Gilbert, *The Orion Mystery: Unlocking the Secrets of the Pyramids* (New York: Three Rivers Press, 1994), 174.

15. Demetrius, ca 200 BC, quoted in Reid, *Egyptian Sonics,* 11 (see chap. 2, n. 12).

SUGGESTED LISTENING

Ani Williams, *Homage to Hathor*, Songaia Sound Productions, 2003, available through www.aniwilliams.com.

Paul Horn, *Inside the Great Pyramid*, Kluck Kluck Records, 1992.

CHAPTER NINE: INDIA'S SOUNDS OF CREATION

*Epigraph.* The Upanishads.

1. Vyass Houston, *The Gayatri Mantra*, American Sanskrit Institute, liner notes for audio tape.

2. Karunamayi Sri Vijayeswari Devi, "The Greatness of the Gayatri Mantra," *Hinduism Today*, September/October 2000. See www.hinduismtoday.com/2000/9-10/2000-9-30.html.

3. Alain Danielou, *The Hindu Temple: Deification of Eroticism* (Rochester, VT: Inner Traditions, 2001), 46.

4. Ibid., 15.

5. Ibid., 10.

6. Kabir, in Bly, trans., *The Soul Is Here For Its Own Joy*, 84 (see chap. 2, n. 21).

7. Thomas Ashley-Farrand, *Healing Mantras: Using Sound Affirmations for Personal Power, Creativity, and Healing* (New York: Wellspring/Ballantine, 1999), 48.

8. Elizabeth Harding, *Kali: The Black Goddess of Dakshineswar* (York Beach, ME: Nicolas-Hays, 1993), 22–23.

9. Ibid.

10. bid., 79.

11. Ibid.

SUGGESTED LISTENING

Sri Lalitha Sahasranamam, *1000 Names of the Divine Mother*, available through www.amma.org.

Purna Das Baul and Bapi, *Songs of Love and Ecstasy*, Womad Select, available through Real World Records, PO Box 35, Corsham, Wiltshire, SN13 8SZ, UK, 1996.

Ravi Shankar, *Chants of India*, Angel Records, 1997.

Thomas Ashey-Farrand, *Healing Mantras: Learn Sound Affirmations for Spiritual Growth, Creativity, and Healing*, Sounds True, 2000.

CHAPTER TEN: CIRCLING THE STUPA

*Epigraph.* Peter Gold, *Tibetan Pilgrimage* (Ithaca, NY: Snow Lion Books, 1988), 147.

1. Humphrey and Vitebsky, *Sacred Architecture*, 105 (see introduction, n. 3).
2. Gold, *Tibetan Pilgrimage*, 145.
3. Ibid., 157.
4. Ibid., 35.
5. Ibid., 36.
6. China Galland, *Longing for Darkness: Tara and the Black Madonna* (New York: Penguin Books, 1990), 106.
7. A. T. Mann, *Sacred Architecture* (Rockport, MA: Element, 1993), 54.

SUGGESTED LISTENING

*Chants and Music from Buddhist Temples*, available through www.amazon.com.

The Gyoto Monks, *Tibetan Tantric Choir*, available through www.amazon.com.

CHAPTER ELEVEN: THE TABLE AS TEMPLE

*Epigraph.* From CD by Anthony Coleman, *With Every Breath, The Music of Shabbat at BJ*, Knitting Factory Works, 1999.

1. Rabbi Leah Novick, personal interview, January, 2007.
2. Rabbi Noah Weinberg, "Shabbat: Heaven on Earth," online article at www.aish.com.
3. Ibid.
4. Amnon Shiloah, *Jewish Musical Traditions* (Detroit: Wayne State University Press, 1992), 147.
5. Rabbi Lynn Gottleib, *She Who Dwells Within: A Feminist Vision of a Renewed Judaism* (San Francisco: HarperSanFrancisco, 1995), 59–60.
6. Marjorie Agosin, ed., *Miriam's Daughters: Jewish Latin American Women Poets* (Santa Fe: Sherman Asher Press, 2001), 13.
7. Marjorie Agosin, personal interview, March, 2002.
8. John Michell and Christine Rhone, *The Twelve Tribe Nation and the Science of Enchanting the Landscape* (Grand Rapids, MI: Phanes Press, 1991), 91.
9. Suzanne Haik-Vantoura, *The Music of the Bible Revealed* (Berkeley: Bibal Press and San Francisco: King David's Harp, Inc., 1991), 23.
10. Gottleib, *She Who Dwells Within*, 6.
11. Rabbi Shefa Gold, "That This Song May Be a Witness: The Power of Chant," online article at www.rabbishefagold.hyper-mart.net/OnChant.html, 2.

12. Ibid., 4.

13. Robert Gass, *Chanting: Discovering Spirit in Sound* (New York: Broadway Books, 1999), 94.

14. Shava Segal, liner notes from CD by Ruth Wieder Magan, *Songs to the Invisible God*, Sounds True, 1999.

15. Bernie Glassman, *Bearing Witness: A Zen Master's Lessons in Making Peace* (New York: Bell Tower, 1998), 31.

Suggested Listening

Ruth Wieder Magan, *Songs to the Invisible God*, Sounds True, 1999.

Rabbi Shefa Gold's CDs available through www.rabbishefagold.com.

Rabbi Shlomo Carlbach's CDs available through www.rebshlomo.org.

Richard Kaplan and Michael Ziegler, *Tuning the Soul: The Worlds of Jewish Sacred Music*, Four Gates Music, 1999.

*La Musicique de la Bible Revelee* (The Music of the Bible Revealed), a thousand-year-old notation deciphered by Suzanne Haik-Ventura, available through www.harmoniamundi.com.

Ira Fein and Simme Bobrosky, *Come Beloved*, available through www.movingtoshalom.com.

## CHAPTER TWELVE: FIRST PEOPLE

*Epigraph.* Traditional Navajo song quoted in Jamake Highwater, *Ritual of the Wind: North American Indian Ceremonies, Music, and Dance* (New York: Alfred Van der Marck Editions, 1984), 44.

1. Donald Sandner, *Navajo Symbols of Healing* (New York: Harcourt Brace Jovanovich, 1979), 120–21.

2. Ibid., 43.

3. Ibid.

4. Peter Gold, *Navajo and Tibetan Sacred Wisdom: The Circle of the Spirit* (Rochester, VT: Inner Traditions, 1994), 204.

5. "The Song of the Wild Rose," traditional Lakota song translated by A. McBeede and quoted in Kelly Kindscher, *Edible Wild Plants of the Prairie: An Ethnobotanical Guide* (Lawrence: University of Kansas Press, 1987), 202.

6. Howard P. Bad Hand, *Native American Healing* (Chicago: Keats Publishing, 2002), 27–28.

7. Ibid., 32.

8. Ibid., 134.

9. Ibid., 135.

10. Ibid., 13.

11. Ibid., 17.

12. Marcia Keegan, *Taos Pueblo and Its Sacred Blue Lake* (Santa Fe, NM: Clear Light Publishers, 1991), 13.

13. Ibid.

Suggested Listening

Howard P. Bad Hand, *Lakota Sacred Songs of Native American Healing: Sung as in Ceremony*, available through www.highstarproductions.com.

*Pueblo Songs from San Juan Pueblo*, Canyon Records, 1997.

## CHAPTER 13: THE SONG AT THE WELL

*Epigraph.* Nicholas Mann, *The Isle of Avalon: Sacred Mysteries of Arthur and Glastonbury Tor* (St. Paul, MN: Llewellyn, 1996), 192.

1. Kathy Jones, *In the Nature of Avalon: Goddess Pilgrimages in Glastonbury's Sacred Landscape* (Glastonbury, Somerset, England: Ariadne Publications, 2000), 9.

2. John Matthews, *The Grail: Quest for the Eternal* (New York: Crossroads, 1981).

3. *Guidebook to The Chalice Well: Glastonbury* (Glastonbury, Somerset, England: The Chalice Well Trust), 9.

4. Charla Devereux, "Sensing Sacred Space," in *Earthwalking Sky Dancers*, 9 (see chap. 5, n. 1).

5. Nicholas Mann, lecture, Chalice Well Gardens, Glastonbury, Somerset, England, April 2002.

6. John Matthews, *Taliesin: Shamanism and the Bardic Mysteries in Britain and Ireland* (London: Aquarian Press, 1991), 55.

7. Ian Macdonald, ed., *Saint Bride* (Edinburgh, Scotland: Floris Books, 1992), 61.

8. Devereux, "Sensing Sacred Space," 9.

9. Erich Neumann, *The Great Mother: An Analysis of an Archetype* (Princeton, NJ: Princeton University Press, 1963), 296.

10. Sadly, I have recently learned from Nicholas Mann that the White Springs Café has been closed.

11. Linda Sussman, *The Speech of the Grail: A Journey toward Speaking that Heals and Transforms* (Hudson, NY: Lindisfarne, 1995), 33.

Suggested Listening

Go to a river or stream, close your eyes. Listen.

## CHAPTER FOURTEEN: GREGORIAN CHANT

*Epigraph.* St. Benedict, from *The Rule of St. Benedict: A Guide to Christian Living.* Full text of the Rule in Latin and English with commentary by George Holzherr, Abbot of Einsiedeln, translated by the monks of Glenstal Abbey (Ireland: Four Courts Press, 1994).

1. Gardner, *Sounding the Inner Landscape,* 109 (see chap. 2, n. 7).

2. Wilson, "The Healing Powers of Voice and Ear," in *Music: Physician for Times to Come,* 25 (see chap. 1, n. 1).

3. Ibid., 24.

4. David Hykes, personal interview, May 2002.

5. Ibid.

6. Katharine Le Mée, *Chant* (New York: Random House, 1996).

7. Nóirín Ní Riain, personal interview, September 2004.

8. Michael Deason-Barrow, personal interview, August 2001.

9. Campbell, *The Mozart Effect,* 104 (see chap. 1, n. 11).

10. Devereux, *Stone Age Soundtracks,* 91 (see chap. 6, n. 5).

SUGGESTED LISTENING

Nóirín Ní Riain and the Monks of Genstal Abbey, *Caoineadh na Maighdine (The Virgin's Lament),* Sounds True, 1998.

*The Monks of Christ in the Desert Monastery,* available through www.christdesert.org.

## CHAPTER FIFTEEN: ENGLISH EVENSONG

*Epigraph.* St. Augustine of Hippo, *Sermons 336, 1* PL 38, 1472.

1. "My Soul, There Is a Country," lyrics by Henry Vaughan (1622–95); composed by Sir Hubert Parry (1848–1918).

2. Michael Deason-Barrow, personal interview, August 2001.

3. T. S. Eliot, excerpt from "Little Gidding," no. 4 of the *Four Quartets.*

4. Frank Colquhoun, "Music," from David Silk, *Prayers for Use at the Alternative Services* (London: Mowbray, 1980), 87.

SUGGESTED LISTENING

Vivien Brett, *Cathedral Music: A Pitkin Guide* (Norwich, England: Jarrold Publishing, 2003) contains a CD of various composers performed at different cathedrals.

## CHAPTER SIXTEEN: THE VOICE OF THE CATHEDRAL

*Epigraph.* Johannes Kepler, quoted in Joachim-Ernst Berendt, *The Third Ear: On Listening to the World* (Shaftesbury, Dorset, UK: Element Books, 1988), 126.

1. Michael Deason-Barrow, personal interview, August, 2001.

2. Charpentier, *The Mysteries of Chartres Cathedral* (see chap. 7, n. 6).

3. Ibid., 19.

4. Marion Woodman, *The Pregnant Virgin: A Process of Psychological Transformation* (Toronto: Inner City Books, 1985), 122.

5. Ean Begg, *The Cult of the Black Virgin* (London: Arkana, 1985), 144.

6. Charpentier, *The Mysteries of Chartres Cathedral*, 19.

7. Ibid., 131.

8. Ibid., 93.

9. Michael Deason-Barrow, personal interview, August, 2001.

10. Gardner, *Sounding the Inner Landscape*, 135 (see chap. 2, n. 7).

11. Michael Deason-Barrow, personal interview, August 2001.

12. C. W. Leadbeater, *The Science and the Sacraments* (Adyar, India: Theosophical Publishing House, 1949), 12.

13. Ibid., 320.

SUGGESTED LISTENING

Theatre of Voices, *The Age of Cathedrals: Music from the Magnus Liber Organi*, available through www.harmoniamundi.com.

Gautier de Coincy, *Miracles of Notre Dame*, with Andrew Lawrence-King and The Harp Consort, 2003, available through www.harmonia-mundi.com.

Ensemble Unicorn, *The Black Madonna: Pilgrim Songs from the Monastery of Montserrat (1400–1420)*, available through Naxox, www.hnh.com.

## CHAPTER SEVENTEEN: ROSSLYN CHAPEL

*Epigraph.* Anderson, *Green Man*, 115 (see chap. 1, n. 5).

1. Wallace-Murphy and Hopkins, *Rosslyn*, 180 (see chap. 7, epigraph).

2. Ean Begg and Deike Begg, *In Search of the Holy Grail and the Precious Blood: A Travelers Guide* (San Francisco: Thorsons, 1995), 23.

3. Anderson, *Green Man*, 100.

4. Wallace-Murphy and Hopkins, *Rosslyn*, 107.

5. Ibid., 132.

6. Ibid., 135.

7. Ibid., 136.

8. Ibid., 97.

9. Begg, *The Cult of the Black Virgin*, 129 (see chap. 16, n. 5).

10. Jim Shaw and Tom McKenney, "The Legend of Hiram Abiff—the Egyptian Connection," online article at http://www.watch.pair.com/symbol.html, 12.

11. Stuart Mitchell, personal interview, January, 2007.

12. Ashley Cowie, personal interview, January, 2007.

13. Christopher Knight and Robert Lomas, *The Hiram Key: Pharaohs, Freemasonry, and the Discovery of the Secret Scrolls of Jesus* (Gloucester, MA: Fair Winds Press, 2001).

SUGGESTED LISTENING

Sutherland and Son (John and Isaac) featuring Mark Naples, *The Rose-Line Connection*, recorded live at Rosslyn Chapel, available through www.rosslynmatrix.com.

Thomas J. Mitchell, *The Rosslyn Motet*, available through www.tjmitchell.com/rosslyn.html.

CHAPTER EIGHTEEN: DESECRATION

*Epigraph.* György Doczi, *The Power of Limits: Proportional Harmonies in Nature, Art, and Architecture* (Boulder, CO: Shambhala, 1981), 28.

1. Michael Deason-Barrow, personal interview, August 2001.

2. Abram, *The Spell of the Sensuous*, (see chap. 4, n. 8).

3. Schafer, *The Soundscape*, 10 (see chap. 4, n. 15).

4. Sjöö and Mor, *The Great Cosmic Mother*, 357 (see chap. 3, n. 4).

5. Morris Berman, *Coming to Our Senses; Body and Spirit in the Hidden History of the West* (New York: Bantam Books, 1989), 240.

6. Michael Deason-Barrow, personal interview, August 2001.

7. Joseph Campbell with Bill Moyers, *The Power of Myth* (New York: Doubleday, 1988), 94.

8. Schafer, *The Soundscape*, 219.

9. Keith Critchlow, "The Golden Proportion: A Conversation Between Richard Temple and Keith Critchlow," *Parabola: The Magazine of Myth and Tradition* 16, no. 4 (November 1991): 32.

SUGGESTED LISTENING

*Montségur: la tragédie cathare*, written and performed by the French Canadian early music ensemble La Nef, available through www.dorian.com.

## CHAPTER 19: DISSONANCE

*Epigraph.* Schafer, *The Soundscape*, 78 (see chap. 4, n. 15).

1. Associated Press, "Population Boom Makes for a Noisy Planet," *The New Mexican*, Sunday, June 27, 1999.
2. John Diamond, as quoted in Steven Halpern with Louis M. Savary, *Sound Health: The Music and Sounds That Make Us Whole* (San Francisco: Harper and Row, 1985), 12–13.
3. Ibid., 25.
4. Ibid., 138.
5. Schafer, *The Soundscape*, 63.
6. Abram, *The Spell of the Sensuous*, 265–66 (see chap. 4, n. 8).
7. Christopher Day, *Places of the Soul: Architecture and Environmental Design as a Healing Art* (San Francisco: Aquarium Press, 1990), 60.
8. Black Elk as quoted in T. C. McLuhan, *Touch the Earth: A Self-Portrait of Indian Existence* (New York: Touchstone, 1971), 152.
9. "Earthweek," *The Albuquerque Journal*, Saturday, July 22, 1995.
10. Nara Schoenberg, "Can You Hear Me?" *The Albuquerque Journal*, August 4, 2002.
11. Shonda Novak, *The New Mexican*, Sunday, September 12, 1999.
12. Abram, *The Spell of the Sensuous*, 86.
13. René Dubos, "Environmental Determinants of Human Life," in *Environmental Influences,* ed. David C. Glass (New York: Random House, 1968), 149–50.

SUGGESTED LISTENING

Walk down a busy city street.

Listen to the refrigerator in your home.

## CHAPTER TWENTY: RETURN TO THE TEMPLE

*Epigraph.* Naomi Littlebear Morena, "Can't Kill the Spirit," in *Rise Up Singing: The Group Singing Songbook,* ed. Peter Blood and Annie Patterson (Bethlehem, PA: Sing Out Publications, 2004), 115.

1. Micheal Deason-Barrow, personal interview, August 2001.

2. Shannon Frediani, personal interview, March, 1998.

3. Michael Deason-Barrow, personal interview, August 2001.

4. Jean Shinoda Bolen, *Crossing to Avalon: A Woman's Midlife Pilgrimage* (San Francisco: HarperSanFrancisco, 1994), 5.

5. Ani Williams, personal interview, June, 2000.

6. Jenny Bird, personal interview, April, 1999.

7. Jonathan Goldman, personal interview, August 2003.

8. Paul Winter, CD, *Paul Winter's Greatest Hits*, Living Music, 1998.

9. Brooke Medicine Eagle, personal interview, July 2001.

10. Joseph Rael, quoted in Susan Elizabeth Hale, *Song and Silence: Voicing the Soul* (Albuquerque, NM: La Alameda Press, 1995), 166.

11. Vijali Hamilton, "World Wheel: Theatre of the Living Earth," Newsletter 1, no. 1, 1994, 4.

12. Ra Paulette, personal interview, June, 1998.

13. Marcus Wilson, "Windows to the Earth: Artist Carves Niche in Sandstone," *New Mexico Magazine*, April, 1996, 39.

14. Ra Paulette, personal interview, June, 1998.

15. Ibid.

Suggested Listening

Jennifer Berezan, *Returning*, recorded in the Oracle Chamber in the Hypogeum at Hal Saflieni, Malta, available at www.edgeofwonder.com.

## CHAPTER TWENTY-ONE: CONSECRATION

*Epigraph.* Georgemarc Schevené, "The Heart of True Love," self-published booklet, Paonia, Colorado, 1997, available through www.theheartoftruelove.com.

1. Lauren Artress, *Walking a Sacred Path: Rediscovering the Labyrinth as a Spiritual Practice* (New York: Riverhead Books, 2006), 96.

2. Walt Whitman, "Out of the Cradle Endlessly Rocking," *Leaves of Grass* (New York: Pocket Books, 2006), 285.

Suggested Listening

Ani Williams's CDs available through www.aniwilliams.com.

Jenny Bird's CDs available through www.jennybird.com.

Jonathan Goldman's CDs available through www.healingsounds.com.

# SELECTED BIBLIOGRAPHY

## BOOKS ON SOUND, SPEECH, AND SONG

Abram, David. *The Spell of the Sensuous: Perception and Language in a More-Than-Human World*. New York: Pantheon, 1996.

Amiga, John and Steven Cornelius. *The Music of Santeria: Traditional Rhythms of the Bata Drums*. Crown Point, MN: White Cliffs Media Co., 1992.

Anderson, William. *Green Man: The Archetype of our Oneness with the Earth*. San Francisco: HarperSanFrancisco, 1990.

Andrews, Ted. *Sacred Sounds: Transformation through Music and Word*. Stipule, MN: Llewellyn, 1993.

Ashley-Farrand, Thomas. *Healing Mantras: Using Sound Affirmations for Personal Power, Creativity, and Healing*. New York: Wellspring/Ballantine, 1999.

Barks, Coleman, trans. and ed. *The Essential Rumi*. San Francisco: HarperSanFrancisco, 1995.

————, trans. *Naked Song: Lela*. Athens, GA: Maypop Books, 1992.

Berendt, Joachim-Ernst. *Nada Brahma: The World Is Sound; Music and the Landscape of Consciousness*. Rochester, VT: Destiny Books, 1987.

————. *The Third Ear: On Listening to the World*. Shaftesbury, Dorset, UK: Element Books, 1988.

Bhattacharyya, Bhaskar, Nik Douglas, and Penny Slinger. *The Path of the Mystic Lover: Baul Songs of Passion and Ecstasy*. Rochester, VT: Destiny Books, 1993.

Bierhorst, John. *A Cry from the Earth: Music of North American Indians*. Santa Fe, NM: Ancient City Press, 1979.

Blacking, John and Reginald Byron. *Music, Culture, and Experience: Selected Papers of John Blacking*. Chicago: University of Chicago Press, 1995.

Blood, Peter and Annie Patterson, eds. *Rise Up Singing: The Group Singing Songbook*. Bethlehem, PA: Sing Out Publications, 2004.

Bly, Robert, ed. *The Soul Is Here for Its Own Joy: Sacred Poems from Many Cultures*. Hopewell, NJ: Ecco Press, 1995.

Bowra, C. M. *Primitive Song*. New York: New American Library, 1962.

Campbell, Don. *The Mozart Effect®: Tapping the Power of Music to Heal the Body, Strengthen the Mind, and Unlock the Spirit*. New York: Avon Books, 1997.

_____, ed. *Music: Physician for Times to Come*. Wheaton, IL: Theosophical Publishing House, Quest Books, 1991.

Draper, Maureen McCarthy. *The Nature of Music: Beauty, Sound, and Healing*. New York: Riverhead Books, 2001.

Estrada, Alvaro. *Maria Sabina: Her Life and Chants*. Santa Barbara, CA: Ross-Ericson, Inc., 1981.

Feld, Steven. *Sound and Sentiment: Birds, Weeping, Poetics, and Song in Kaluli Expression*. Philadelphia: University of Pennsylvania Press, 1982.

Fox, Matthew. *Illuminations of Hildegard of Bingen*. Santa Fe, NM: Bear and Company, 1985.

Gardner, Kay. *Sounding the Inner Landscape: Music as Medicine*. Stonington, ME: Caduceus, 1990.

Gass, Robert. *Chanting: Discovering Spirit in Sound*. New York: Broadway Books, 1999.

Glazerson, Rabbi M. *Music and Kabbalah*. Northvale, NJ: Jason Aronson, Inc., 1997.

Godwin, Joscelyn. *Harmonies of Heaven and Earth: The Spiritual Dimensions of Music*. Rochester, VT: Inner Traditions, 1987.

_____. *The Mystery of the Seven Vowels: In Theory and Practice*. Grand Rapids, MI: Phanes Press, 1991.

Goldman, Jonathan, *Healing Sounds: The Power of Harmonics*. Rochester, VT: Inner Traditions, 2002.

_____. *Shifting Frequencies*. Sedona, AZ: Light Technology Publishing, 1998.

Haik-Vantoura, Suzanne. *The Music of the Bible Revealed*. Berkeley: Bibal Press and San Francisco: King David's Harp, Inc., 1991.

Hale, Susan Elizabeth. *Song and Silence: Voicing the Soul*. Albuquerque, NM: La Alameda Press, 1995.

Halpern, Steven with Louis M. Savary. *Sound Health: The Music and Sounds That Make Us Whole*. San Francisco: Harper and Row, 1985.

Hamel, Peter Michael. *Through Music to the Self.* Boulder, CO: Shambhala, 1979.

Hayes, Michael. *The Infinite Harmony: Musical Structures in Science and Theology.* London: Weidenfeld and Nicolson, 1994.

Highwater, Jamake. *Ritual of the Wind: North American Indian Ceremonies, Music, and Dance.* New York: Alfred Van der Marck Editions, 1984.

Hirshfield, Jane, ed. *Women in Praise of the Sacred: 43 Centuries of Spiritual Poetry by Women.* New York: HarperPerennial, 1995.

James, Jamie. *The Music of the Spheres: Music, Science, and the Natural Order of the Universe.* New York: Grove Press, 1993.

Jenny, Hans. *Cymatics: A Study of Wave Phenomena.* Newmarket, NH: MACROmedia, 2001.

Jourdain, Robert. *Music, the Brain, and Ecstasy: How Music Captures Our Imagination.* New York: William Morrow, 1997.

Lewis, Robert C. *The Sacred Word and Its Creative Overtones: Relating Religion, Science, and Music.* Oceanside, CA: Rosicrucian Fellowship, 1986.

Manniche, Lisa. *Music and Musicians in Ancient Egypt.* London: British Museum Press, 1991.

McClellan, Randall. *The Healing Forces of Music: History, Theory, and Practice.* Amity, NY: Amity House, 1988.

Newham, Paul. *The Healing Voice: How to Use the Power of Your Voice to Bring Harmony into Your Life.* Shaftesbury, Dorset, UK: Element Books, 1999.

———. *The Singing Cure: An Introduction to Voice Movement Therapy.* Boulder, CO: Shambhala, 1993.

Ortiz, John M. *The Tao of Music: Sound Psychology and Using Music to Change Your Life.* New York: Samuel Weiser, 1997.

Rael, Joseph. *Being and Vibration.* Tulsa, OK: Council Oak Books, 1993.

Ralls-MacLeod, Karen. *Music and the Celtic Otherworld: From Ireland to Iona.* New York: St. Martin's Press, 2000.

Rayborn, Timothy. "Sacred Sound, Sacred Song: Chant in Five Religious Traditions." In Huston Smith, ed. *Gregorian Chant: Songs of the Spirit.* San Francisco: KQED Books, 1996.

Redmond, Layne. *When the Drummers Were Women.* New York: Three Rivers Press, 1997.

Reid, John. *Egyptian Sonics.* Cumbria, England: Sonic Age, Ltd., 2001.

Rudhyar, Dane. *The Magic of Tone and the Art of Music.* Boulder, CO: Shambhala, 1982.

Ruland, Heiner. *Expanding Tonal Awareness: A Musical Exploration of the Evolution of Consciousness.* London: Rudolf Steiner Press, 1992.

Ruthstein, Edward. *Emblems of the Mind: The Inner Life of Music and Mathematics.* New York: Random House, 1995.

Schafer, R. Murray. *The Soundscape: Our Sonic Environment and the Tuning of the World.* Rochester, VT: Destiny Books, 1993.

Seronde, Antoine. "Myth and Music in Ancient Egyptian Temples." Unpublished manuscript, 1995.

Steindl-Rast, David and Sharon Lebell. *The Music of Silence: Entering the Sacred Space of Monastic Experience.* San Francisco: HarperSanFrancisco, 1995.

Sussman, Linda. *The Speech of the Grail: A Journey toward Speaking that Heals and Transforms.* Hudson, NY: Lindisfarne, 1995.

Thurman, Dr. F. Leon and Anna Peter Langness. *Heartsongs: A Guide to Active Pre-birth and Infant Parenting through Language and Singing.* Englewood, CO: Music Study Services, 1986.

Tomatis, Alfred and Billie M. Thompson. *The Ear and Language.* Norval, ON: Moulin Publishing, 1996.

Von Lange, Anny. *Man, Music, and Cosmos: A Goethean Study of Music.* Sussex, England: Rudolf Steiner Press, 1992.

Wigman, Tony. "The Psychological and Physiological Effects of Low Frequency Sound and Music." *Music Therapy Perspectives* 13, 1995.

_____, B. Saperson, and R. West, eds., *The Art and Science of Music Therapy: A Handbook.* London: Harwood Academic Publishing, 1996.

## BOOKS ON SACRED SITES, ARCHITECTURE, WORLD RELIGIONS, AND CONSCIOUSNESS

Adams, Henry. *Mont-Saint Michel and Chartres.* Garden City, NY: Doubleday, 1959.

Afterman, Allen. *Kabbalah and Consciousness.* River-on-Hudson, NY: Sheep Meadow Press, 1998.

Alexander, Christopher. *The Timeless Way of Building.* New York: Oxford University Press, 1979.

Anderson, Lorraine, ed. *Sisters of the Earth: Women's Prose and Poetry about Nature.* New York: Vintage Books, 1991.

Anderson, Sherry Ruth and Pamela Hopkins. *The Feminine Face of God: The Unfolding of the Sacred in Women.* New York: Bantam, 1991.

Anderton, Bill. *Guide to Ancient Britain.* London: Foulsham, 1991.

Arguelles, Miriam and José A. Arguelles. *The Feminine: Spacious as the Sky.* Boulder, CO: Shambhala, 1977.

Artress, Lauren. *Walking a Sacred Path: Rediscovering the Labyrinth as a Spiritual Practice.* New York: Riverhead Books, 2006.

Bachelard, Gaston. *The Poetics of Space.* Boston: Beacon Press, 1969.

Bad Hand, Howard P. *Native American Healing.* Chicago: Keats Publishing, 2002.

Baignet, Michael and Richard Leigh. *The Temple and the Lodge.* New York: Arcade Publishing, 1989.

Balfour, Michael. *Stonehenge and Its Mysteries.* New York: Charles Scribner's Sons, 1980.

Bamford, Christopher, ed. *Homage to Pythagoras: Discovering Sacred Science*, New York: Lindisfarne, 1982.

Barlow, Bernyce. *Sacred Sites of the West.* St. Paul, MN: Llewellyn, 1997.

Barrie, Thomas. *Spiritual Path, Sacred Place: Myth, Ritual, and Meaning in Architecture.* Boston: Shambhala, 1996.

Bauval, Robert and Adrian Gilbert. *The Orion Mystery: Unlocking the Secrets of the Pyramids.* New York: Three Rivers Press, 1994.

Beck, Peggy V. and Anna L. Walters. *The Sacred Ways of Knowledge: Sources of Life.* Tsaile, AZ: Navajo Community College Press, 1977.

Begg, Ean. *The Cult of the Black Virgin.* London: Arkana, 1985.

Begg, Ean and Deike Begg. *In Search of the Holy Grail and the Precious Blood: A Travelers Guide.* San Francisco: Thorsons, 1995.

Bender, Tom. *Building with the Breath of Life.* Manzanita, OR: Fire River Press, 2000.

_____. *Silence, Song, and Shadows: Our Need for the Sacred in Our Surroundings.* Manzanita, OR: Fire River Press, 2000.

Berman, Morris. *Coming to Our Senses: Body and Spirit in the Hidden History of the West.* New York: Bantam Books, 1989.

Berry, Thomas. *The Dream of the Earth.* San Francisco: Sierra Club Books, 1990.

Bolen, Jean Shinoda. *Crossing to Avalon: A Woman's Midlife Pilgrimage.* San Francisco: HarperSanFrancisco, 1994.

Brabbs, Derry. *Abbeys and Monasteries.* London: Weidenfeld and Nicolson, 1999.

Broadhurst, Paul. *In Search of the Old Holy Wells.* Launceston, Cornwall: PendragonPress, 2000.

Brock, Peggy, ed. *Women: Rites and Sites.* Sydney: Allen and Unwin, 1989.

Burl, Aubrey. *A Guide to Stone Circles of Britain, Ireland, and Brittany.* New Haven: Yale University Press, 1995.

_____. *Prehistoric Avebury.* New Haven: Yale University Press, 1979.

Cahill, Sedonia and Joshua Halpern. *The Ceremonial Cycle.* San Francisco: HarperSanFrancisco, 1990.

Carmi, T., ed. and trans. *The Penguin Book of Hebrew Verse.* New York: Penguin Books, 1981.

Cash, Marie Romero. *Built of Earth and Song: Churches of Northern New Mexico*, Albuquerque, NM: Red Crane Press, 1993.

Castle, Leila, ed. *Earthwalking Sky Dancers: Women's Pilgrimages to Sacred Place*s. Berkeley, CA: Frog, Ltd., 1996.

Charpentier, Louis. *The Mysteries of Chartres Cathedral.* New York: Avon Books, 1975.

Chester, Laura. *Holy Personal: Looking for Small Private Places of Worship.* Bloomington: Indiana University Press, 2000.

Conway, Timothy. *Women of Power and Grace: Nine Astonishing, Inspiring Luminaries of Our Time.* Santa Barbara, CA: Wake Up Press, 1994.

Cooke, Ian. *Mermaid to Merrymaid: Journey to the Stones.* Penzance, Cornwall, UK: Men-an-Tol Studio, 1987.

Cooper, J. C. *An Illustrated Encyclopedia of Traditional Symbols.* London: Thames and Hudson, 1978.

Cowan, Painton. *Rose Windows.* San Francisco: Chronicle Books, 1979.

Cowan, Tom. *Fire in the Head: Shamanism and the Celtic Spirit.* San Francisco: HarperSanFrancisco, 1993.

Cummings, Joe. *Buddhist Stupas in Asia: The Shape of Perfection.* Melbourne: Lonely Planet, 2001.

Dames, Michael. *The Avebury Cycle.* London: Thames and Hudson, 1996.

_____. *Mythic Ireland.* London: Thames and Hudson, 1992.

Danielou, Alain. *The Hindu Temple: Deification of Eroticism.* Rochester, VT: Inner Traditions, 2001.

Day, Christopher. *Places of the Soul: Architecture and Environmental Design as a Healing Art.* San Francisco: Aquarium Press, 1990.

Devereux, Paul. *Earth Memory: Sacred Sites; Doorways into Earth's Mysteries.* St. Paul, MN: Llewellyn, 1992.

_____. *The Illustrated Encyclopedia of Ancient Earth Mysteries.* London: Cassel, 2000.

_____. *Places of Power: Measuring the Secret Energy of Ancient Sites.* London: Blandford Press, 1999.

_____. *Re-Visioning the Earth: A Guide to Opening Healing Channels between Mind and Nature.* New York: Simon and Schuster, 1996.

_____. *The Sacred Place: The Ancient Origin of Holy and Mystical Sites.* London: Cassel, 2000.

_____. *Stone Age Sound Tracks: The Acoustic Archaeology of Ancient Sites.* London: Vega, 2001.

Doczi, György. *The Power of Limits: Proportional Harmonies in Nature, Art, and Architecture.* Boulder, CO: Shambhala, 1981.

Eaton, Robert. *The Lightning Field: Travels in and around New Mexico.* Boulder, CO: Johnson, 1995.

Ellis, Normandi. *Awakening Osiris: The Egyptian Book of the Dead.* Grand Rapids, MI: Phanes Press, 1988.

Ernst, Carl W. *The Shambhala Guide to Sufism: An Essential Introduction to the Philosophy and Practice of the Mystical Tradition of Islam.* Boulder, CO: Shambhala, 1997.

Evans Wentz, W. Y. *The Fairy Faith in the Celtic Country.* Atlantic Highlands, NJ: Humanities Press, 1911.

Fagan, Brian. *From Black Land to Fifth Sun: The Science of Sacred Sites.* Reading, MA: Perseus Books, 1998.

Fairman, H. W., ed. and trans. *The Triumph of Horus: The Oldest Play in the World.* Berkeley: University of California Press, 1974.

Fergusson, Erna. *Dancing Gods: Indian Ceremonials of New Mexico and Arizona.* Albuquerque: University of New Mexico Press, 1931.

Frazier, Sir James George. *The Golden Bough: A Study in Magic and Religion.* New York: Macmillan, 1951.

French, R. M., trans. *The Way of the Pilgrim and the Pilgrim Continues His Way.* New York: Quality Paperback Books, 1998.

Gadon, Elinor W. *The Once and Future Goddess.* San Francisco: HarperSanFrancisco, 1989.

Gardner, Laurence. *The Bloodline of the Holy Grail: The Hidden Lineage of Jesus Revealed.* Shaftesbury, Dorset, UK: Element Books, 1996.

Gimbutas, Marija. *The Language of the Goddess.* New York: Thames and Hudson, 1989.

_____. *The Living Goddesses.* Berkeley: University of California Press, 1999.

Glassman, Bernie. *Bearing Witness: A Zen Master's Lessons in Making Peace.* New York: Bell Tower, 1998.

Gold, Peter. *Navajo and Tibetan Sacred Wisdom: The Circle of the Spirit.* Rochester, VT: Inner Traditions, 1994.

_____. *Tibetan Pilgrimage.* Ithaca, NY: Snow Lion Books, 1988.

Gottlieb, Lynn. *She Who Dwells Within: A Feminist Vision of a Renewed Judaism.* San Francisco: HarperSanFrancisco, 1995.

Gray, Martin. *Places of Peace and Power: Teachings from a Pilgrim's Journey.* Prepublication manuscript. Sedona, AZ, 1997.

Green, Arthur and Barry Holtz, eds. *Your World Is Fire: The Hasidic Masters of Contemplative Prayer.* New York: Schocken Books, 1987.

Green, Hannah. *Little Saint.* New York: Random House, 2000.

Gustafson, Fred. *The Black Madonna.* Boston: Sigo Press, 1991.

Halifax, Joan. *The Fruitful Darkness: Reconnecting with the Body of the Earth.* San Francisco: HarperSanFrancisco, 1993.

Hall, Nor. *The Moon and the Virgin: Reflections of the Archetypal Feminine.* New York: Harper and Row, 1980.

Hancock, Graham and Santha Faiia. *Heaven's Mirror: Quest for Lost Civilization.* New York: Three Rivers Press, 1998.

Harding, Elizabeth. *Kali: The Black Goddess of Dakshineswar.* York Beach, ME: Nicolas-Hays, 1993.

Harding, Mike. *A Little Book of the Green Man.* London: Aurum Press,, 1998.

Hawkins, Gerald S. *Stonehenge Decoded.* New York: Dell, 1965.

Hersey, G.L. *Pythagorean Palaces: Magic and Architecture in the Italian Renaissance.* Ithaca, NY: Cornell University Press, 1976.

Heselton, Paul. *Earth Mysteries.* Shaftesbury, Dorset, UK: Element Books, 1995.

Highwater, Jamake. *Native Land: Sagas of the Indian Americas.* Boston: Little, Brown, 1986.

Howell, Alice. *The Dove in the Stone: Finding the Sacred in the Commonplace.* Wheaton, IL: Theosophical Publishing House, Quest Books, 1988.

Humphrey, Caroline and Piers Vitebsky. *Sacred Architecture: Models of the Cosmos.* Boston: Little, Brown, 1997.

Husemann, Armin J. *The Harmony of the Human Body: Musical Principles in Human Physiology.* Edinburgh: Floris Books, 1994.

Jackson, John Brinckerhoff. *A Sense of Place, A Sense of Time.* New Haven: Yale University Press, 1994.

James, John. *Chartres: The Mason Who Built a Legend.* London: Routledge and Kegan Paul, 1982.

Johnson, Buffie. *Lady of the Beasts: Ancient Images of the Goddess and Her Animals.* San Francisco: Harper and Row, 1988.

Jones, Kathy. *In the Nature of Avalon: Goddess Pilgrimages in Glastonbury's Sacred Landscape.* Glastonbury, Somerset, England: Ariadne Publications, 2000.

Kaplan, Aryeh, ed. *Sefer Yetzirah: The Book of Creation*. York Beach, ME: Weiser, 1997.

Knight, Christopher and Robert Lomas. *The Hiram Key: Pharaohs, Freemasonry, and the Discovery of the Secret Scrolls of Jesus*. Gloucester, MA: Four Winds Press, 2001.

Laidler, Keith. *The Head of God: The Lost Treasure of the Templars*. London: Orion, 1998.

Lamott, Anne. *Traveling Mercies: Some Thoughts on Faith*. New York: Pantheon Books, 1999.

Lawlor, Anthony. *The Temple in the House: Finding the Sacred in Everyday Architecture*. New York: G. P. Putnam and Sons, 1994.

Lawlor, Robert. *Sacred Geometry: Philosophy and Practice*. London: Thames and Hudson, 1982.

————. *Voices of the First Day: Awakening in Aboriginal Dreamtime*. Rochester, VT: Inner Traditions, 1991.

Leadbeater, C. W. *The Science of the Sacraments*. Adyar, India: Theosophical Publishing House, 1949.

Lippman, Thomas W. *Understanding Islam: An Introduction to the Muslim World*. New York: Penguin Books, 1990.

Lundquist, John, M. *The Temple: Meeting Place of Heaven and Earth*. London: Thames and Hudson, 1993.

Luxton, Richard with Pablo Balam. *The Mystery of the Mayan Hieroglyphs: The Vision of an Ancient Tradition*. San Francisco: Harper and Row, 1981.

Lyon, William S. *Black Elk: The Sacred Ways of a Lakota*. San Francisco: HarperSanFrancisco, 1991.

MacEowen, Frank. *The Mist-Filled Path*. Novato, CA: New World Library, 2002.

MacNulty, W. Kirk. *Freemasonry: A Journey through Ritual and Symbol*. London: Thames and Hudson, 1991.

Malone, Caroline. *The Prehistoric Monuments of Avebury*. London: English Heritage, 1994.

Mann, A. T. *Sacred Architecture*. Rockport, MA: Element Books, 1993.

Mann, Nicholas. *The Isle of Avalon: Sacred Mysteries of Arthur and Glastonbury Tor*. St. Paul, MN: Llewellyn, 1996.

Marshall-Stoneking, Billy. *Singing the Snake: Poems from the Western Desert*. Australia: Angus and Pymble, 1990.

Matt, Daniel C. *The Essential Kabbalah*. New York: Quality Paperback Books, 1995.

Matthews, John. *The Grail: Quest for the Eternal.* New York: Crossroads, 1981.

_____. *Taliesin: Shamanism and the Bardic Mysteries in Britain and Ireland.* London: Aquarian Press, 1991.

McClain, Ernest. "Musical Theory and Ancient Cosmology." *The World and I* (February 1994): 371–91.

McLuhan, T. C. *Cathedrals of the Spirit: The Message of Sacred Places.* New York, Harper Perennial, 1996.

_____. *Touch the Earth: A Self-Portrait of Indian Existence.* New York: Touchstone, 1971.

McNeeley, James Kale. *Holy Wind in Navajo Philosophy.* Tucson: University of Arizona Press, 1981.

McPherson, Robert S. *Sacred Land Sacred View: Navajo Perceptions of the Four Corners Region.* Salt Lake City: Brigham Young University Press, 1993.

Meaden, Terence. *The Secrets of the Avebury Stones: Britain's Greatest Megalithic Temple.* London: Souvenir Press, 1999.

_____. *Stonehenge: The Secret of the Solstice.* London: Souvenir Press, 1992.

Meehan, Gary. *The Traveler's Guide to Sacred Ireland.* Glastonbury, Somerset, England: Gothic Image Publications, 2002.

Merz, Blanche. *Points of Cosmic Energy.* Essex, England: C. W. Daniel, 1983.

Meyer, Carolyn and Charles Gallenkamp. *The Mystery of the Ancient Maya.* New York: Atheneum, 1985.

Michell, John. *The Dimensions of Paradise: The Proportions and Symbolic Numbers of Ancient Cosmology.* London: Thames and Hudson, 1988.

_____. *New Light on the Ancient Mystery of Glastonbury.* Glastonbury, Somerset, England: Gothic Image Publications, 1990.

_____. *The Temple of Jerusalem: A Revelation.* York Beach, ME: Samuel Weiser, 1990.

_____. *The Traveler's Key to Sacred England.* New York: Alfred A. Knopf, 1988.

Michell, John, and Christine Rhone. *The Twelve Tribe Nation and the Science of Enchanting the Landscape.* Grand Rapids, MI: Phanes Press, 1991.

Miller, Hamish and Paul Broadhurst. *The Sun and the Serpent: An Investigation into Earth Energies.* Cornwall, England: Pendragon Press, 1989.

Milne, Courtney. *Sacred Places in North America: A Journey into the Medicine Wheel.* New York: Stewart, Tabori, and Chang, 1994.

Moore, Daniel Abdal-Hayy. *The Blind Beekeeper*. Syracuse, NY: Syracuse University Press, 2002.

————. *The Ramadan Sonnets*. San Francisco: City Lights, 1996.

Moura, Ann. *Dancing Shadows: The Roots of Western Religious Beliefs*. St. Paul, MN: Llewellyn, 1995.

Moyers, Bill. *Fooling with Words: A Celebration of Poets and their Craft*. New York: William Morrow, 1999.

Naydler, Jeremy. *Temple of the Cosmos: The Ancient Egyptian Experience of the Sacred*. Rochester, VT: Inner Traditions, 1996.

Neumann, Erich. *The Great Mother: An Analysis of the Archetype*. Princeton, NJ: Princeton University Press, 1963.

Newcomb, Franc J. and Gladys A. Reichard. *Sandpaintings of the Navajo Shooting Chant*. New York: Dover, 1975.

Norwich, John Julius, ed. *Great Architecture of the World: An Illustrated History from Stonehenge to the Twentieth Century*. New York: Random House, 1975.

O'Kelly, Michael J. *Newgrange: Archaeology, Art, and Legend*. London: Thames and Hudson, 1982.

Olsen, Brad. *Sacred Places North America: 108 Destinations*. Santa Cruz, CA: Consortium of Collective Consciousness, 2003.

Osmen, Sarah Ann. *Sacred Places: A Journey into the Holiest Lands*. New York: St. Martins Press, 1990.

Palmer, Martin and Nigel Palmer. *The Spiritual Traveler: The Guide to Sacred Sites and Pilgrim Routes in Britain*. London: Hidden Spring, 2000.

Patterson-Rudolf, Carol. *On the Trail of Spider Woman: Petroglyphs, Pictographs, and Myths of the Southwest*. Santa Fe, NM: Ancient City Press, 1997.

Pepper, Elizabeth and John Wilcock. *Magical and Mystical Sites: Europe and the British Isles*. Grand Rapids, MI: Phanes Press, 1993.

Picknett, Lynn and Clive Prince. *The Templar Revelation: Secret Guardians of the True Identity of Christ*. London: Corgi Books, 1998.

Potter, Jean and Marcus Braybrooke, eds. *All in Good Faith: A Resource Book for Multi-Faith Prayer*. Oxford: The World Congress of Faiths, 1997.

Prectel, Martin. *Secrets of the Talking Jaguar: A Mayan Shaman's Journey to the Heart of the Indigenous Soul*. New York: Tarcher, 1998.

Ramdas, Swami. *In Quest of God: The Saga of an Extraordinary Pilgrimage*. San Diego: Blue Dove Press, 1994.

Reznikoff, Iegor. "On the Sound Dimensions of Prehistoric Painted Caves and Rocks." In Eero Tarasti, ed. *Musical Signification*. Berlin: Mouton de Gruyter, 1995.

Richardson, Alan. *Spirits of the Stones: Visions of Sacred Britain.* London: Virgin Publishing, 2001.

Roberts, Alison. *Hathor Rising: The Power of the Goddess in Ancient Egypt.* Rochester, VT: Inner Traditions, 1997.

Roberts, Elizabeth and Elias Amidon. *Earth Prayers from around the World: 365 Prayers, Poems, and Invocations for Honoring the Earth.* New York: Harper Collins, 1991.

Ruyle, Lydia. *Goddess Icons: Spirit Banners of the Divine Feminine.* Boulder, CO: Woven Word Press, 2002.

Sandner, Donald. *Navajo Symbols of Healing.* New York: Harcourt Brace Jovanovich, 1979.

Schelling, Andrew. "Thigh Bones and Attendant Spirits." In *The India Book: Essays and Translations from Indian Asia.* Berkeley, CA: O Books, 1993.

Schneider, Michael S. *A Beginner's Guide to Constructing the Universe: The Mathematical Archetypes of Nature, Art, and Science.* New York: Harper Perennial, 1995.

Schwaller de Lubicz, R. A. *The Temple in Man: Sacred Architecture and the Perfect Man.* Rochester, VT: Inner Traditions, 1949.

Schwenk, Theodor. *Sensitive Chaos: The Creation of Flowing Forms in Water and Air.* New York: Schocken Books, 1978.

Shreeve, James, *The Neandertal Enigma: Solving the Mystery of Modern Human Origins.* New York: Avon Books, 1995.

Silva, Freddy. *Secrets in the Fields: The Science and Mysticism of Crop Circles.* Charlottesville, VA: Hampton Roads, 2002.

Simmons, Marc, Donna Price, and Joan Myers. *Santiago: Saint of Two Worlds.* Albuquerque: University of New Mexico Press, 1991.

Sjöö, Monica and Barbara Mor. *The Great Cosmic Mother: Rediscovering the Religion of the Earth.* San Francisco: HarperSanFrancisco, 1987.

Slifer, Dennis and James Duffield. *Kokopelli: Flute Player Images in Rock Art.* Santa Fe, NM: Ancient City Press, 1994.

_____. *Signs of Life: Rock Art of the Upper Rio Grande.* Santa Fe, NM: Ancient City Press, 1998.

Snodgrass, Adrian. *The Symbolism of the Stupa.* Ithaca, NY: Cornell University Press, 1985.

Soesman, Albert. *Our Twelve Senses: Wellsprings of the Soul.* Stroud, England: Hawthorn Press, 1990.

Stewart, Desmond Stirling. *The Pyramids and the Sphinx.* New York: W. W. Norton, 1979.

Strassfeld, Michael. *The Jewish Holidays: A Guide and Commentary*. New York: Harper and Row, 1985.

Swan, James A., ed. *The Power of Place: Sacred Ground in Natural and Human Environments*. Wheaton, IL: Theosophical Publishing House, Quest Books, 1991.

_____. *Sacred Places: How the Living Earth Seeks Our Friendship*. Santa Fe, NM: Bear and Company, 1990.

Thompson, William Irwin. *Coming into Being: Artifacts and Texts in the Evolution of Consciousness*. New York: St. Martins Press, 1998.

Thurman, Robert and Tad Wise. *Circling the Sacred Mountain: A Spiritual Pilgrimage through the Himalayas*. New York: Bantam Books, 1999.

Tobias, Michael, Jane Morrison, and Bettina Gray, eds. *A Parliament of Souls: In Search of Global Spirituality*. San Francisco: KQED Books, 1995.

Tompkins, Peter. *Secrets of the Great Pyramid*. New York: Harper Colophon, 1971.

Tucci, Giuseppe. *The Theory and Practice of the Mandala*. New York: Samuel Weiser, 1969.

Vaughan-Thomas, Wynford and Michael Hales. *Secret landscapes: Mysterious sites, deserted villages, and forgotten places of Great Britain and Ireland*. Exeter, England: Webb and Bower, 1980.

Versluis, Arthur. *Sacred Earth: The Spiritual Landscape of Native America*. Rochester, VT: Inner Traditions, 1992.

Vidler, Mark. *The Star Mirror: The Cosmic Symmetry of Heaven and Earth*. London: Thorsons, 1999.

Wallace-Murphy, Tim, and Marilyn Hopkins. *Rosslyn: Guardian of the Secrets of the Holy Grail*. Shaftesbury, Dorset, UK: Element Books, 1999.

Washbourne, Penelope, ed. *Seasons of Woman: Song, Poetry, Ritual, Prayer, Myth, Story*. New York: Harper and Row, 1979.

West, John Anthony. *The Serpent in the Sky: The High Wisdom of Ancient Egypt*. New York: Julian Press, 1987.

_____. *The Traveler's Key to Ancient Egypt: A Guide to the Sacred Places of Ancient Egypt*. Wheaton, IL: Theosophical Publishing House, Quest Books, 1995.

Westwood, Jennifer. *Sacred Journeys: Paths for the New Pilgrim*. Stroud, England: Gaia Books, 1997.

Wilkinson, Richard H. *The Complete Temples of Ancient Egypt*. London: Thames and Hudson, 2000.

Witherspoon, Gary. *Language and Art in the Navajo Universe*. Ann Arbor: University of Michigan Press, 1977.

Young, Dudley. *Origins of the Sacred*. New York: St. Martins Press, 1991.

Young, Stanley. *Paradise Found: The Beautiful Retreats and Sanctuaries of California and the Southwest*. San Francisco: Chronicle Books, 1995.

# Annotated Discography

*Unless otherwise noted, all listings are available in compact disc format.*

Altramar. *Saint Francis and the Minstrels of God.* Dorian Discovery, 1996.

Ashey-Farrand, Thomas. *Healing Mantras: Learn Sound Affirmations for Spiritual Growth, Creativity, and Healing.* Sounds True, 1999.

Ballington, Pamela. *Earth Mother Lullabies from Around the World, vol.2.* Earth Mother Productions, 1987. Contains the "Hymn to a Moon Goddess-A Hurrian" song from Ancient Urgarit.

Barks, Coleman. *There is Some Kiss We Want With Our Whole Lives: Rumi Poems Translated and Read by Coleman Barks.* Viking Press, 1999.

The Benedictine Monks of Santo Domingo de Silos. *Chant* (1994) and *Chant II* (1995). Angel Recordings. Both recorded at the Benedictine Monastery of Santo Domingo de Silos in Spain.

Berezan, Jennifer. *Returning.* Edge of Wonder Records, 2000. Recorded in the Oracle Chamber in the Hypogeum at Hal Saflieni, Malta.

B'nai Jeshurun Congregation. *With Every Breath: The Music of Shabbat at BJ.* Knitting Factory Works, 1999.

Dala, Yair. *Shacharut: Live in the Desert.* Najema Music, 2000. Yair Dalal is a leading figure in the Israeli music scene. Recorded in a tent on the Shacharut Mountain in the Avara. From the liner notes: "The sound of the desert has its own individual character, weight, space, shade, power, emotion and beauty, particularly when love of the desert, its landscapes and people is the driving force behind the music."

Dufay, Gautier de Coincy. *Miracles of Notre-Dame.* The Harp Consort, Andrew Lawrence-King, dir. Harmonia Mundi, 2003.

Ensemble Giles Binchois. *Le Manuscript du Puy.* Dominique Vellard, dir. Virgin Classics, 1992. Recorded in Eglise de Saint-Seine l'Abbaye in France.

Ensemble Unicorn. *The Black Madonna: Pilgrim Songs from the Monastery of Montserrat (1400–1420).* Michael Posch, cond. Naxos, 1998.

Gasparya, Djivan. *The Moon Shines at Night.* All Saints Records, 1993.

Gass, Robert. *Chant: Spirit in Sound; The Best of World Chant.* Spring Hill Music, 1999.

Goldman, Jonathan. *Ultimate Om.* Etherean, 2002. See www.healingsounds.com.

Goodchild, Chloe. *Devi.* Raven, 1996. Sacred chants from different traditions.

Harvey, Andrew. *The Feather in Your Heart: Tales of Wonder from India and from the Sufi Masters of Old Persia.* 2 audio cassettes. Sounds True/Windhorse Productions, 2000.

Hillier, Paul and the Theater of Voices. *The Age of Cathedrals: Music from the Magnus Liber Organi.* Harmonia Mundi, 1996.

_____. *Arvo Pärt: I Am the True Vine.* Harmonia Mundi, 1999. Recorded in part in Ely Cathedral, Ely, Cambridgeshire, England.

Hirschfield, Rabbi Aryeh. *Let the Healing Begin.* Recorded live in Freiburg, Germany, August, 1992. Available through Aryeh Hirschfield, www.rebaryeh.com.

Horn, Paul and Carlos Nakai. *Inside Canyon de Chelly.* Canyon Records, 1997.

_____. *Inside the Great Pyramid.* Celestial Harmonies, 1976.

_____. *Inside the Taj Mahal I and II.* Transparent Music, 2001.

Hykes, David and the Harmonic Choir. *Earth to the Unknown Power.* BMG, 1996. From the liner notes: "This recording from The Kitchen in New York City presents the world premiere of the 'Virtual Abbey,' developed by John Hobbs, Luc Martinez, and David Hykes. The live sound of the concert was digitally encoded and sent into Le Thoronet Abbey in France over ISDN telephone lines, played back live through a sound system in the extraordinary abbey acoustics, then encoded and sent back to The Kitchen, placing us 'here' within the 'Virtual Abbey.'"

_____. *Harmonic Meetings.* Celestial Harmonies, 1992. 2 disc set recorded at Le Thoronet Abbey in France.

Kaplan, Richard and Michael Ziegler. *Tuning the Soul: The Worlds of Jewish Sacred Music.* Four Gates Music, 1999.

La Nef. *Montsegur: La Tragedie Cathare.* Dorian Recordings, 1996. Troubadour songs from the medieval era of the Cathars.

Madrigal Ensemble of Moscow. *Celestial Litanies: The Ultimate Journey to Mystical Russian Soundscapes.* BMG, 1996. Provides a history of Russia's sacred music in sound.

Magan, Ruth Wieder. *Songs to the Invisible God.* Sounds True, 1999. Recorded on location at Ein Karem in Jerusalem.

Paniagua, Eduardo and El Arabi Trio, Música Andalusi. *El Agua de la Alhambra (The Water of the Alhambra)*. Pneuma, 2001. Eduardo Paniagua is a musician and architect and specialist in Spanish medieval music. He produces and records under his own record label, Pneuma. See www.ctv.cs/USERS/pneuma.

Pickett, Philip, cond., with the New London Consort. *Llibre Vermill: Pilgrim Songs and Dances*. Decca Records, 1992. Pilgrim songs and dances associated with the Shrine of the Virgin at Montserrat, Spain, where there is a famous Black Madonna.

Purna Das Baul and Bapi. *Songs of Love and Ecstasy*. Real World Records, 1996.

Riain, Nóirín Ní. *Caoineadh na Maighdine (The Virgins Lament)*. Sounds True, 1998. Recorded in Glenstal Abbey, Limerick, Ireland.

_____. *Stor Amhran: A Wealth of Songs*. Sounds True, 1988.

Sedov, Alexander, dir., with the Chorovaya Akademia. *Ancient Echoes*. BMG Music, 1995.

Sequentia. *Shining Light: Music from Aquitanian Monasteries* (12th Century). BMG Classics, 1996.

_____. *Vox Iberica I: Donnersöhne (Sons of Thunder): Music for St. James the Apostle*. Codex Calixtinus, Santiago de Compestella, 12th Century. Harmonia Mundi, 1992.

Shankar, Ravi. *Chants of India*. Angel Records, 1997.

Southern Journey. *Georgia Sea Islands: Biblical Songs and Spirituals, Vol. 12*. Rounder Records, 1998. From the liner notes: "In his studies of Gullah, the path-breaking linguist Lorenzo D. Turner found that the term 'shout' comes from the Arabic *saut*, meaning to dance around the Kaaba, as Sea Islanders used to dance around the pulpit. Shouting usually took place after a prayer meeting, or at other times. Older shouts contained stylized dramatizations of actions referenced in song texts. The dancers flapped their arms to imitate angels' wings, or held out their hands as if reading from Bibles, like John the Revelator." liner notes. See www.rounder.com.

*Sri Lalitha Sahasranamam: 1000 Names of the Divine Mother*, Mata Amritanandamayi Mission Trust, 2001. Available through www.Mothersbooks.org.

*Tibetan Buddhism, Tantras of Gyütò, Vols. 1 and 2*. Electra/Asylum/Nonesuch Records, 1988. Recorded at Gyuto Tantric College Dalhousie, Himachal Pradesh.

Vantoura, Suzanne Haik. *La Musique de la Bible Révélée*, Harmonia Mundi, 2000.

Williams, Ani. *Homage to Hathor*. Songaia Sound Productions, 2003. This music with harp and voice is based on the sacred harmonic proportions of actual Egyptian temple architecture, the result of years of on-site research. Available through www.aniwilliams.com.

Winter, Paul. *Canyon*. Living Music, 1985.

_____. *Missa Gaia (Earth Mass)*. Living Music, 1982, A mass in celebration of Mother Earth recorded live in the Cathedral of Saint John the Divine in New York City and at the Grand Canyon.

_____. *Prayer for the Wild Things: An Earth Music Celebration of the Northern Rockies*. Living Music, 1994.

Winter, Paul and Paul Halley. *Whales Alive*. Living Music, 1987. Narrated by Leonard Nimoy with the voices of humpback whales.

# ADDITIONAL RESOURCES

Marjorie Agosin
www.wellesley.edu

Ammachi
www.amma.org

Jenny Bird
www.jennybird.com

Brooke Medicine Eagle
www.medicine-eagle.com

Don Campbell
www.mozarteffect.com

Rabbi Shlomo Carlbach
www.rebshlomo.org

Ashley Cowie
www.rosslynmatrix.com

Christopher Dunn
www.gizapower.com

Robin Easton
www.nakedineden.com

Ira Fein
www.movingtoshalom.com

Shannon Frediani,
aka Shannon White Eagle
www.thevoicesofangels.com

Rabbi Shefa Gold
www.rabbishefagold.com

Jonathan Goldman
www.healingsounds.com

Susan Elizabeth Hale
www.songkeeper.net

Vijali Hamilton
www.vijali.net

David Hykes
www.harmonicworld.com

Consuelo Luz
www.consueloluz.com

Stuart Mitchell
www.stuart-mitchell.com

Monastery of Christ in the Desert
www.christdesert.org

Daniel Abdal-Hayy Moore
www.danielmoorepoetry.com

Silvia Nakkach
www.voxmundiproject.com

Cindy Pavlinac
www.sacred-land-photography.com

Petroglyph National Monument
www.nps.gov/petr/

John Reid
www.soundhealingresources.com

Nóirín Ní Riain
www.noirinniriain.wtcsites.com

Lydia Ruyle
www.lydiaruyle.com

R. Murray Schafer
www.patria.org

Georgemarc Schevené
www.theheartoftruelove.com

Linda Sewright
Northwest Labyrinth Project
Brigid272@aol.com

Sandstone Shrine
www.ranchodesanjuan.com

Freddy Silva
www.cropcirclesecrets.org

Tonalis: Centre for the
Development of Music
www.tonalismusic.co.uk

Veriditas: The Worldwide
Labyrinth Project
www.veriditas.net

Dr. Aaron Watson
www.monumental.uk.com

John Anthony West
www.jawest.net

Ani Williams
www.aniwilliams.com

# INDEX

# Quest Books

encourages open-minded inquiry into
world religions, philosophy, science, and the arts
in order to understand the wisdom of the ages,
respect the unity of all life, and help people explore
individual spiritual self-transformation.

Its publications are generously supported by
The Kern Foundation,
a trust committed to Theosophical education.

Quest Books is the imprint of
the Theosophical Publishing House,
a division of the Theosophical Society in America.
For information about programs, literature,
on-line study, membership benefits, and international centers,
see www.theosophical.org
or call 800-669-1571 or (outside the U.S.) 630-668-1571.

## RELATED QUEST TITLES

*Essential Musical Intelligence,* by Louise Montello

*The Healing Energies of Music,* by Hal Lingerman

*Healing Powers of Tone and Chant* (CD), by Don Campbell,
with Tim Wilson

*Music: Physician for Times to Come,* by Don Campbell

*Pilgrimage,* by David Souden

*The Roar of Silence,* by Don Campbell

*Self-Transformation through Music,* by Joanne Crandall

*The Traveler's Key to Ancient Egypt,* by John Anthony West

*The Wisdom and Power of Music* (CD set), by Don Campbell

To order books or a complete Quest catalog,
call 800-669-9425 or (outside the U.S.) 630-665-0130.

296

# SACRED SPACE, SACRED SOUND

In *Sacred Space, Sacred Sound* Susan Hale describes her awakening and enlivening experiences of listening to and singing with songs perceptible in places and spaces made holy by hundreds of years of prayer and sacred rite and intention. In this perceptive, beautifully and poetically written account, she also encourages us to listen to and dialogue with the unique vibrations of all of creation immediately surrounding us, thus creating a holy and respect-filled relationship.
—Katharine Le Mée, author of *Chant: The Origins, Form, Practice, and Healing Power of Gregorian Chant* and *The Benedictine Gift to Music*

Susan Elizabeth Hale's exploration of sound in the context of the world's sacred places leads inexorably to the conclusion that what we commonly think of as consciousness must be more expansive. It is, in fact, the ground state of the universe, and through resonance and harmony we can experience a genuine unity. My own experience of meditation and sound in the King's Chamber of the Great Pyramid at Giza confirms Hale's revelatory message in this remarkable book.
—Richard Geldard, author of *The Traveler's Key to Ancient Greece* and the forthcoming *Parmenides and the Way of Truth*